Se...   ...tudents

Third Edition

ENGLISH for BUSINESS and SECRETARIAL STUDENTS

Third Edition

John F. Scott

Gill & Macmillan

Gill & Macmillan Ltd
Goldenbridge
Dublin 8
with associated companies throughout the world
© John F. Scott 1996
0 7171 2368 5
Print origination in Ireland by Graham Thew Design

All rights reserved.
No part of this publication may be reproduced, copied or transmitted in any form or by any means without written permission of the publishers or else under the terms of any licence permitting limited copying issued by the Irish Copyright Licensing Agency, The Writers' Centre, Parnell Square, Dublin 1.

Acknowledgments
For permission to reproduce copyright material grateful acknowledgment is made to Hamish Hamilton Ltd for an extract from *The Great Jest* by Jennifer Johnston, *The Sunday Tribune*, *The Irish Times* and *The Independent on Sunday* and John Hennessy. Photos are reproduced by permission of Pacemaker (Belfast) and Alan O'Connor.

Do mo bhean chéile,
Bernadette agus mo pháiste Enda,
Conor agus Iseult

CONTENTS

Part 1 Introduction to Communication

    Chapter 1 Introduction to Communication   2

Part 2 Verbal Communication Skills

    Chapter 2 Speaking   15
    Chapter 3 Meetings   31
    Chapter 4 Documents for Meetings   44
    Chapter 5 Listening   58
    Chapter 6 Reading 1: Finding Information – The Books You Need   62
    Chapter 7 Reading 2: Finding Information – Basic Research   74
    Chapter 8 Reading 3: Reading Critically   92
    Chapter 9 Writing 1: In Words There Is Power   123
    Chapter 10 Writing 2: . . . And Yet More Power   133
    Chapter 11 Writing 3: You Must Know the Basics   145
    Chapter 12 Writing 4: Punctuation Gives Meaning   153
    Chapter 13 Writing 5: Starting a Letter   171
    Chapter 14 Writing 6: Collecting Money   185
    Chapter 15 Writing 7: Letters of Complaint   199
    Chapter 16 Writing 8: Memo, Notice, Press Release   209
    Chapter 17 Writing 9: Reports, Reports, Reports   219

Part 3 Non-verbal Skills

    Chapter 18 Interactive Skills   233
    Chapter 19 Media Analysis   242
    Chapter 20 Visual Presentation   258

Part 4 New Information Technology

    Chapter 21 New Technology   277
    Chapter 22 Computer Literacy   287

Part 5 Finding Employment

    Chapter 23 Get That Job   304

PART I

INTRODUCTION TO COMMUNICATION

INTRODUCTION to COMMUNICATION

Introduction

Communication is the life-blood of any organisation. People are constantly transmitting information. An organisation's need for an effective communication system increases as the firm gets bigger.

But we, as individuals, communicate constantly every day. Most of the time we are not even aware of it. From the time you got out of bed this morning, and perhaps even before that, you have engaged in communicating several times.

Definition of communication: *communication is the passing on of feelings, ideas, opinions and information from one person or group to another person or group and the eliciting of a discriminating response.*

A few elements of this definition are important.

1) Communication is not just passing on of information. When you transmit information you also transmit, to some extent, your feelings about the information.

2) Communication is a two-way process. You must get a response to your message. So you transmit a communication to another person, but the other must respond in some way. Our definition says it must be a discriminating response. That means that the response must be a reaction to the specific communication.

Fig. 1 – A model of one-way communication

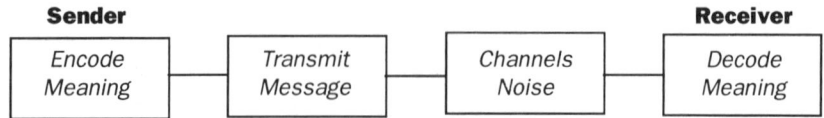

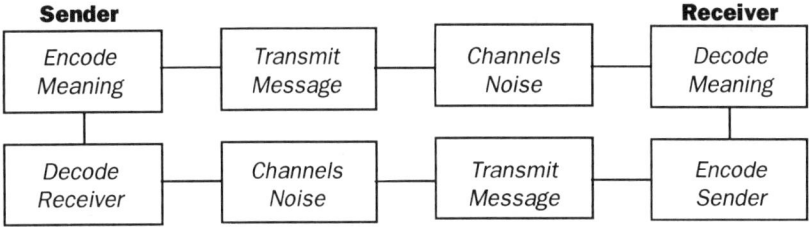

Fig. 2 – A model of two-way communication

The *sender* is the person or group who wishes to transmit a meaning to another person or group.

To *encode* is to put the message in a form understood by the receiver. The usual form used is words. Other ways of transmitting meaning would be sign language, smoke symbols, flags and silence.

Channel is the medium by which you transmit a communication. You could send a memo, hold a meeting, use the telephone or send the message by e-mail.

All channels contain *noise*, which is any interference that may hinder the communication. A meeting held before dinner when people are hungry would be an example of noise.

To *transmit* a message is to send it across to the receiver. Timing can be very important here as transmitting a message at an inappropriate time could result in it being misunderstood.

The *receiver* is the person or group which perceives the sender's message. If there is no receiver, there is no communication.

To *decode* a message is to translate the symbols in the message into meaning for the receiver. If you are told to do something 'as soon as you can', does that mean you are to do it immediately, or when you have your present task completed?

Feedback is the reaction to a communication.

There are three types of feedback:

1) *Informational feedback* is when the receiver simply provides the sender with non-evaluative information. For example, the sender asks how many students study at Carlow RTC and the receiver provides the information.

2) *Corrective feedback* is when the receiver responds by challenging or correcting the original message. For instance, the receiver may point out that it is not his responsibility to monitor student numbers.

3) *Reinforcing feedback* is when the receiver acknowledges clear receipt

of the intended message. An example of this would be the grade a student receives in an examination. It is important to note that reinforcing feedback can be either positive or negative.

GROUP ACTIVITY

One-way communication

Form the class into groups of five. One person is appointed as the sender of the communication, three are the receivers and the fifth person is the timekeeper. The sender of the communication can use only words to transmit the message. The receivers, who must have a pen and blank page, cannot ask questions. The timekeeper simply records the time it took to complete the exercise. The sender must transmit the following message to the receivers:

When the receivers have the message recorded on paper to their satisfaction the exercise is complete. Do not show the message to the receivers before going on to the second part of the exercise.

Two-way communication

Again form the class into groups of five. One person is appointed as the sender of the communication, three are the receivers and the fifth person is the timekeeper. The sender of the communication can use all the techniques available to transmit the message. However the message must not be shown to the receivers. The receivers, who must have a pen and blank page, may ask as many questions as they wish and the sender may answer all questions. The timekeeper again simply records the time it took to complete the exercise. The sender must transmit the following message to the receivers:

Normally, two-way communication will take longer but the message will be transmitted more accurately. Discuss the difficulties which the senders and the receivers experienced during the exercise. What mistakes did the senders make? How did the receivers misinterpret the message?

ACTIVITY I

1. List five communications you engaged in today in which you were the sender of the communication.
2. List five communications you engaged in today in which you were the receiver of the communication.
3. In what way were the five messages encoded? For example, did you write, speak or give signs?
4. What feedback did you get to the five messages you sent?
5. What was the purpose of each of the five communications you sent?
6. What problems did you have in decoding the five messages you received?
7. What feedback did you give to the five messages you received?
8. In what way were the five messages you received encoded?
9. What channels were used in each of the five messages you sent?
10. What channels were used in each of the five messages you received?
11. Give examples of any noise which occurred in the messages you sent.
12. Give examples of any noise which occurred in the messages you received.

Organisational communication

Communication can be formal or informal.

- *Formal communication* flows up, down and across the lines of the organisation. It follows the hierarchy as depicted in the organisation chart.
- *Informal communication* flows up, down and across the organisation independent of the organisation chart. All organisations have informal communication networks. It is sometimes known as the grapevine. Good managers are aware of the importance of informal communication and use it as part of the communication process.

Formal communication is of three types:

- *Upward* – goes from a person or group to a higher level of the organisation.
- *Downward* – goes from a person or group to a lower level in the organisation.
- *Horizontal (lateral)* – goes from a person or group on one level of the organisation to a person or group on the same level of the organisation.

Upward communication tends to be the least successful as it flows against the authority structure of the organisation. Downward communication tends to be the most successful from the point of view of getting things done as it carries authority with it. Horizontal or lateral communication is the most successful from the point of view of understanding between the communicators.

ACTIVITY 2

1. Give three examples of formal communication which you engaged in during the past week.
2. Give three examples of informal communication which you engaged in during the past week.
3. Give an example of upward communication.
4. Give an example of downward communication.
5. Give an example of horizontal communication.
6. The teacher asks you a question in class. What type of communication is this?
7. You respond to the teacher's question. What type of communication is taking place?
8. You have a discussion with your friend during lunch hour. What type of communication is taking place?
9. Draw an organisation chart of your school and show how upward, downward, and horizontal communication take place.
10. Give one example of a communication you are aware of that is both formal and downward.

Barriers to communication

Barriers to communication are any elements which may hinder or prevent communication from taking place. It is possible to generate a lengthy list of such barriers. The most important ones are:

- *Language*: using too many words or words with which people are not familiar can be a barrier to communication. For example, Samuel Johnson is said to have defined a window as 'an orifice in an edifice for the admission of luminary particles'.
- *Jargon*: jargon is technical language belonging to a profession. Economists use such terms as 'GDP' and 'GNP'. You should be careful of using jargon with people who do not understand it.
- *Status*: people at different levels of an organisation may have difficulty in communicating with each other. What the managing director may express as merely a desire may be taken as a command by someone further down the line.
- *Education*: this can be a barrier as educated people tend to see matters, not as black and white, but as various shades of grey.
- *Timing*: if a communication is badly timed it can be misunderstood.
- *Placing*: if a communication is placed or posted in an incorrect position it may not be noticed by the people for whom it is intended. This can happen frequently at work when notices are placed on the wrong notice board.
- *Noise*: noise can be physical or psychological. If people cannot hear a speaker clearly they may not understand the message. If a room is too hot it can interfere with communication. When a person is tired communication will be somewhat unsuccessful.
- *Observation/inference confusion*: this barrier arises when you observe something and based on that evidence you infer or arrive at some conclusion. For example, when you are driving up the street and the traffic lights are green, you infer that the other lights are red. That is a reasonable inference to arrive at. However, you may sometimes make the incorrect inference. For instance, if you see a person with a tattoo, you may come to certain conclusions about the person which may not be accurate.
- *Information overload*: this occurs when so much information is available to a person that he cannot process or understand all of it. It is becoming more and more of a problem as computers generate so much information.

Some examples of barriers to communication

The Black Hole of Calcutta

In 1756 the Nawab (governor) of Calcutta led a successful rising against the British East India Company. The British surrendered and the Nawab ordered the 146 captives to be put in prison for the night. He then went to bed. There was only one cell available and this was just 20 feet by 20 feet. All 146 captives were placed in the cell. Without air, panic broke out among the captives. In the morning 123 of the prisoners were dead.

'Get me coffee'

The former president of the US, Mr Richard Nixon, was working late one night in his hotel room while on a trip. He opened the door and asked his aide to 'Get me coffee.' It was late and the hotel kitchen was closed. Some hotel personnel were contacted and a fresh pot of coffee was brewed. On a number of occasions while this was being done the president kept asking for coffee. Finally, a tray arrived with the coffee. It was only then that it was discovered that the president did not want coffee to drink, but wanted to talk to his assistant whose name was Coffee.

(Recounted in D. Rather and G. Gates, *The Palace Guard*, New York: Harper and Row, 1974, p. 109.)

The Duggan case

Mr Harry Whelehan, the attorney general, was nominated president of the High Court by the government on Friday, 11 November 1994. Before his appointment, the Labour members of the government withdrew from the Cabinet meeting because of the delay in executing an extradition warrant for Fr Brendan Smith. Within a few hours, Mr Whelehan was sworn in as High Court president at Áras an Uachtaráin by President Robinson. Mr Eoghan Fitzsimons was appointed as the new attorney general. On Monday, 14 November the Fianna Fáil ministers were meeting to discuss and work on the Taoiseach, Mr Reynolds's speech to be delivered in the Dáil on the following day. The new attorney general was called to the meeting and he told those present that he had discovered a new case similar to the Smith case. Mr Fitzsimons later said he made it clear that the Duggan case should be referred to in the Taoiseach's speech next day. Others present said his information was not clear. Fianna Fáil ministers and advisers spent all day and late into the night drafting the speech. Some of them admitted to being very tired. For example, Mr McCreevy was just back from a trip to India and had had very little sleep. When the Taoiseach spoke in the Dáil on Tuesday, 15 November he did not mention the Duggan case. He was accused of misleading the Dáil and the future of the government was threatened. The question was asked later did the Fianna Fáil ministers deliberately mislead the Dáil, did they not understand the significance of the Duggan case because of tiredness and confusion, or was the attorney general's advice unclear.

This was the beginning of an episode that ended in the fall of a government which was very popular as it had just helped to negotiate a ceasefire in Northern Ireland.

ACTIVITY 3

1. 'Be back as soon as you can.' How might a person misinterpret that message?
2. 'Move it over a little.' What barrier to communication might be present in this sentence?
3. Give two examples of jargon which you have experienced.
4. A manager in a company calls an important meeting for 3.00 p.m. on 23 December. Comment on this.
5. Give two examples of notices which you think were posted in the wrong place.
6. A company puts a memo about threatened redundancies in with the monthly cheques. Comment on the barriers to communication which might arise.
7. Give two examples of observation/inference confusion from your own experience.
8. Judges in court wear wigs. Comment on this as a barrier to communication.
9. Give examples of other clothes which may be a barrier to communication.
10. 'All I expect of you is that you do your best in the exam.' What different interpretations might a student put on this sentence?

Perception

Definition of perception: *perception is the process by which a person selects, organises and interprets stimuli to give them meaning*. Stimulus or stimuli (the plural) are anything we see, feel, hear, etc. We get stimuli through our senses. The senses are seeing, hearing, smelling, tasting and touching. An old philosopher said that there is nothing in the mind that was not first in the senses. We learn through our senses. Perception is a very individual aspect of behaviour. We all perceive in our own way. Perception is the interpretation of a message by the receiver.

There are a multitude of objects and stimuli that vie for our attention. We select the ones that are important to us. This is called *perceptual selectivity*. In driving a car we perceive what is important such as traffic lights, people crossing the road and road signs. We tend to perceive what we are motivated to perceive.

Many things compete for our attention. Why do we pay attention to some and not to others? The following are the factors which influence our attention:

- *Size*: we will perceive a big object before a small object.
- *Intensity*: we will pay attention to a loud sound rather than a whisper.
- *Contrast*: if three people are sitting down and one person is standing we will pay attention to the person standing. Directors of plays make use of this technique frequently.
- *Novelty*: something we have not seen before will engage our attention.
- *Movement*: most advertisements make use of this fact and have plenty of movement. They also tend to use intensity in speech and music. Guinness had an advertisement in contrast to this which had no sound at all. A quiet voice said at the end of the ad: 'This 20 seconds of darkness was brought to you by Guinness.'
- *Repetition*: if something is repeated often enough you will pay attention to it.

Social perception

Social perception is concerned with the processes by which we perceive people. Social perception is far more complex than perception of inanimate objects such as chairs, tables and signs. This is true for two reasons: (i) people are more complex than things, and (ii) an accurate perception of people is far more important to us personally than perception of inanimate objects. The consequences of misperceiving people are great. Failure to perceive a desk in a room may mean that we will bump into it. Failure to perceive accurately a social situation may have serious consequences at work.

Factors which influence social perception include physical appearance, verbal and non-verbal communication and ascribed attributes.

Fig. 3 – Major influences on social perception in organisations

	Characteristics of the situation 1. Organisational role 2. Location of event
Characteristics of the person perceived 1. Physical appearance 2. Verbal communication 3. Non-verbal communication 4. Ascribed attributes	
	Characteristics of the perceiver 1. Self-concept 2. Previous experience with individual

Characteristics of the person perceived: we partly perceive people on the basis of how they look. Clothing, which is part of the physical, also influences our perception. Our use of words (verbal) and such elements as tone of voice and accent (non-verbal) also help to determine our perception of others.

We often ascribe or give certain attributes to a person before or at the beginning of an encounter. These attributes can influence how we perceive the person. Status, occupation and personal characteristics are three ascribed attributes. If we are told the person we are about to meet is the managing director we will have certain perceptions of the person before she arrives. Likewise, if you are told that the medical consultant will see you now, you will begin to behave towards the person who arrives with a certain amount of deference. An example of a personal characteristic would be intelligence. If you are told by someone whose view you respect that a person is very intelligent, you will conjure up a picture of what you think an intelligent person is like.

Characteristics of the situation: a person's place in the organisation can influence her perceptions. Production workers in a firm will see production as the most important department; members of the sales force will tend to put sales and marketing at the top. Also, where an event takes place may influence perception. To walk about in your bare feet in your home may be acceptable, but a different view of it would be taken at work.

Characteristics of the perceiver: people with a positive self-concept tend to see favourable characteristics in others. Also, our previous experience with others will often influence how we view their current behaviour.

ACTIVITY 4

1. List the items that gain your attention when coming to college each morning.
2. What techniques does your teacher use to attract your attention?
3. Explain how the organisation of your classroom helps your teacher to gain the attention of the class.
4. Explain why social perception is more complicated than perception of inanimate objects.
5. Why is it important to understand the process of perception?
6. Give three examples of when you and your friend had different perceptions of the same event.
7. What is meant by saying that 'perception is a very individual aspect of behaviour'?
8. What attributes would you ascribe to a person with red hair?
9. What attributes would you ascribe to a person with a tattoo on his arm?
10. What attributes would you ascribe (a) to a man who dyes his hair? (b) to a woman who dyes her hair?

Review

1. Explain why communication is not just 'sending information from one person to another'.
2. In a good dictionary look up the origin of the word communication.
3. Why is an understanding of perception important in communication?
4. Find two other meanings for the word communication.
5. A lecturer once went into his classroom when no students were present and locked the door. He then proceeded to deliver his lecture. He explained afterwards that his contract obliged him to teach ten hours a week but it made no mention of students having to be present. Did communication take place in this instance?
6. What is meant by self-concept?
7. What is meant by organisational role?

Pitfalls

prostrate prostate

The two words *prostrate* and *prostate* are very similar. The word 'prostrate' means lying with face to the ground. The word 'prostate' refers to a gland near the neck of the bladder.

Confusing words

commissar	commissariat	commonable	commonage
commonality	commoner	commutable	commutate
countervail	countervalue	covey	covin

Quiz

The following words all have their origins in languages other than English. Can you find which languages they spring from?

apartheid, blitz, ersatz, slogan, coup d'état.

Spellings

The words most commonly misspelled are highlighted.

abolition	admittance	anonymous
absence	advertisement	**anxiety**
accelerate	**aerial**	**appearance**
accessible	**agreeable**	appreciate
accidental	agriculture	architecture
accommodation	already	**argument**
accomplished	alteration	**arrangement**
ache	alternate	**ascend**
achieved	although	assassin
acknowledge	altogether	**athletic**
acquainted	amiable	atmosphere
acquiesce	**among**	auctioneer
address	**analysis**	**awful**
admirable	anniversary	awkward

PART 2

VERBAL COMMUNICATION SKILLS

SPEAKING

Introduction

(a) 'Fourscore and seven years ago our fathers brought forth on this continent a new nation conceived in liberty and dedicated to the proposition that all men are created equal. Now we are engaged in a great civil war testing whether that nation, or any nation so conceived and so dedicated, can long endure. We are met on a great battlefield of that war.'
(Abraham Lincoln, 'Gettysburg Address')

(b) 'The title I have chosen for my talk, as most of you know, is "The Camel's Nose is Under the Tent". The expression comes from an old Arabian fable, and to an Arab it spells trouble and disaster. The fable of the Arab and his camel goes something like this:

One cold night, as an Arab sat in his tent, a camel gently thrust his nose under the flap and looked in.

"Master," he said, "let me put my nose in your tent, for it is cold and stormy out here."

"By all means, and welcome", said the Arab, and turned over and went to sleep. A little later he awoke and found that the camel had not only put his nose in the tent but his head and neck, as well.

The camel, who had been turning his head from side to side, said, "I will take but little more room if I place my forelegs within the tent. It is difficult standing without."

"You may also plant your forelegs within", said the Arab, moving a little to make room, for the tent was small.

Finally the camel said: "May I not stand wholly within? I keep the tent open by standing as I do."

"Yes, yes", said the Arab. "Come wholly inside. Perhaps it will be better for both of us." So the camel crowded in.

The Arab with difficulty in the crowded quarters again went to sleep. The next time he woke up he was outside in the cold and the camel had the tent to himself.

Independent of how he got there, the important point is that the camel of government control now has his nose under the tent of free competitive industry and is crowding in. We will all have to watch him or he will take over the tent . . .'

(W. R. Gondin, E. W. Mammen and J. Dodding, *The Art of Speaking Made Simple*, London: W. H. Allen, 1967)

(c) 'It's not often I get a chance to do this. I know when I was getting married there was no presentation made to me. It says something about the great esteem in which I was held! However, Michael is held in great esteem, not only by his colleagues as evidenced by the great number of you who came to this presentation but also by me. I found that I could always depend on Michael. It is good to have highly organised people like Michael on the staff. Enough of us are disorganised – such as myself – so we need people like Michael who are constant as the Northern Star. I'm becoming poetical now. Was it Shakespeare said that?' (Manager making presentation to staff member who is getting married)

These are three quite different speeches: the first very formal and dignified; the second making a serious point in a somewhat lighthearted fashion; and the third very informal and simple as befits the occasion.

As there are different types of writing for different occasions, so the same holds for speeches. Speech is, after all, the most normal method of expression. Speech comes before writing. The business of life depends on speech. No business organisation could function without it. The higher you climb in the business world the more you will use speech to communicate.

Speaking

Speaking differs from writing in:

(i) use of language

(ii) importance of non-verbal elements

(iii) speed

(iv) immediate feedback

(v) flexibility

(i) *Use of language*
The type of language used in speeches tends to be less formal than that used in writing. Some speeches can use formal language as in Lincoln's

'Gettysburg Address' but, in general, there is a tendency towards informal constructions and simple vocabulary. The degree of formality used will depend on the situation and the more important the situation the more formal will the language be.

(ii) *Non-verbal elements*

'You look terrible, what happened?'

'I knew by the look in his eyes that he was telling a cock-and-bull story.'

'With that sort of voice sure you couldn't believe anything he says!'

'You can't go dressed in that rig-out!'

'When he walked away he looked a beaten man.'

We have all heard some if not all of the previous statements. They refer to non-verbal aspects of communication. This is one of the most important aspects of speech. The speaker can use a variety of non-verbal elements to support his message. These may include (a) gesture, (b) appearance, (c) dress, (d) posture, (e) facial expression, (f) eye contact, (g) orientation.

(a) *Gestures.* It is difficult to speak without using gestures. We tend to use our hands to make emphasis. Some cultures use gesture more than others. When a person is speaking watch his gestures to see what sort of emphasis it adds to the speech.

(b) *Appearance.* How you look will have a bearing on how seriously you will be taken. A middle-aged man wearing the hairstyle of a teenager will have difficulty in holding attention when he gets up to speak.

(c) *Dress.* People make judgments on us according to how we dress. Your dress is determined by your age, position, sex, personality and the occasion.

(d) *Posture.* When giving a speech much communication has taken place before you begin to use words. Do you sit or stand? Do you stand up straight or slouch? Do you lean on the table or stand free with no props?

(e) *Facial expressions.* The face is very expressive. Some people have very interesting faces; others have faces that are blank. We look pale when sick, blush when embarrassed, and perspire when angry. We only have to look at people's faces to see if they are happy, sad, depressed, anxious or annoyed.

(f) *Eye contact.* The eyes are very powerful communicators. Teachers keep attention through eye contact. We look at people in different ways. Do you stare, glance, gaze or 'stick someone to the floor' with a look? Our culture determines how long you may look at a person. Children are told not to stare. Staring makes people uncomfortable.

(g) *Orientation*. This refers to how close or how far away we place ourselves in relation to others. You place yourself close to your friends. You can use space in this way to strengthen your position. Speakers sometimes stand on a raised platform to enhance their position. The spotlight on stage performs a similar function. In the work situation a person may use a big, heavy desk to add to her power and importance.

(iii) *Speed*

Oral communication is quick. If the person is available to you there is no need to find pen, paper, typewriter or computer. Since with speech you can use many non-verbal elements also it is likely to be more successful.

(iv) *Immediate feedback*

In oral communication the response from your listener is immediate. No need to wait for a letter or memo.

(v) *Flexibility*

When communicating orally you can alter the presentation of your message as you proceed depending on the feedback you are getting from your listener. This feedback need not be verbal. Watch the person's eyes and facial expressions.

ACTIVITY I

1. What do the following gestures mean: (a) clapping hands, (b) scratching head, (c) hand over mouth, (d) putting hand up in the air, (e) folding arms, (f) drumming fingers on table?

2. What gestures do people use to express the following types of behaviour: (a) happiness, (b) tiredness, (c) annoyance, (d) self-consciousness?

3. What type of dress do the following people adopt: (a) solicitors, (b) doctors, (c) nurses, (d) teenagers, (e) artists?

4. What type of clothes do the following males wear: (a) aged 9-12, (b) aged 16-18, (c) aged 20-30, (d) aged 35-50, (e) aged 50-70?

5. What type of clothes do the following females wear: (a) aged 9-12, (b) aged 16-18, (c) aged 20-30, (d) aged 35-50, (e) aged 50-70?

6. Choose five different hairstyles for women and indicate what type of person would wear each one.

7. What is the significance of wearing a tie?

8. *Study the following drawings of people and indicate what emotional state each position suggests.*

9. *Find ten pictures from newspapers or magazines and write a few sentences on each, indicating which emotion each person is feeling and which elements of the picture tell you the person's emotional state.*
10. *Draw a manager's office with the furniture arranged in various ways (desk, chair, visitor's chair, etc.) and say how communication is affected by the various arrangements.*
11. *Find ten pictures from newspapers or magazines showing groups in conversation. Study the composition of the groups and indicate whether they are friendly, uncivil, aggressive, etc.*
12. *Describe four types of bodily contact (e.g. shaking hands, backslapping) and indicate what each type says about the relationships between the individuals.*

What makes an effective speaker?

An effective speaker:
- can be *heard*
- has something *interesting* to say
- is *clear*
- is *logical*
- uses *variety* of expression, tone, pace and language.

The aim of speech is to communicate ideas, opinions and feelings. It will be effective if the speaker:
- considers his audience
- knows what he wants to say
- is sincere
- takes steps to retain interest
- is well prepared.

Types of talks

There are basically three types of talks:

(i) talks that compliment
(ii) talks that explain
(iii) talks that persuade.

(i) *Talks that compliment*
The occasion may be that you are a special guest at a function, representing the firm at a prize-giving or thanking a speaker at a local function. On such occasions:
- be brief
- congratulate, do not criticise
- be polite and diplomatic
- be sincere.

(ii) *Talks that explain*
An expository talk may be called for when describing your firm's product to a group of visitors, representing your firm at a conference, or explaining the financial affairs of the company to shareholders. On such occasions:
- know your audience
- be certain of the facts
- be aware of time limit
- be clear about objectives
- ensure time for questions.

(iii) *Talks that persuade*
This type of talk may be given to an audience of potential customers, or to staff on certain occasions. On such occasions:
- be frank
- be positive
- be sincere
- answer objections honestly
- be enthusiastic.

Preparing your speech

Advance preparation
(1) As early as possible find out all you can about the circumstances in which the speech is to be delivered such as:

- audience
- time of day
- time allowed for speech
- situation – will others speak before you, after you?

(2) Allow the topic to germinate in your mind for a while. Have some small cards with you always so that when a good idea strikes you it can be noted.

(3) If the opportunity presents itself discuss the topic with friends and colleagues.

A speech has an introduction, body and conclusion. Begin the preparation with the body of the speech as the introduction and conclusion will depend on the main contents.

Main part of speech

Spread out before you the cards with notes on them. Eliminate the ones which do not advance the aim of your speech.

If your speech is on 'Absenteeism' and the aim is to encourage staff in your firm to be absent less often, cards might contain notes such as the following:

(1)	Extent of absenteeism in firms in local town.
(2)	Extent of absenteeism in similar firms.
(3)	Extent of absenteeism in own firm.
(4)	Effects of absenteeism.
(5)	Absenteeism in your firm according to age, skills, sex, etc.
(6)	Days when absenteeism is highest.
(7)	Days when absenteeism is lowest.
(8)	Periods of year when absenteeism is highest.
(9)	Periods of year when absenteeism is lowest.
(10)	Suggestions for improvement.
(11)	Causes of absenteeism.

These cards should now be arranged in a logical sequence. Some may be eliminated. Points should now be developed, e.g. card 4.

Effects of absenteeism:

(1)   more work for colleagues,

(2)   leads to inefficiency in firm,

(3)   affects motivation,

(4)   causes firm to be less competitive.

Introduction

The introduction must:

(1) catch attention of audience immediately

(2) lead logically into subject.

The attention of the audience can be caught by using:

- Rhetorical questions – 'Do you realise that one out of every three people does not have enough to eat?'
- Personal incidents – 'Last week I was talking to a man from London . . .'
- Stories – 'When George B. Shaw was asked . . .'
- Humour – should not be used for its own sake. If you think it will divert the audience, omit it.

Conclusion

Conclusions of speeches should be brief, crisp and delivered with spirit. *Do not allow your speech to die painfully.* A conclusion usually consists of:

(1) summary of main points

(2) urging audience to action.

How will you give your speech?

Types of delivery

There are several methods of delivery. The speaker must choose the method most appropriate for the occasion and the audience.

(i) *Impromptu speech* (delivered without preparation):

Only fairly accomplished speakers can handle this situation. If called upon, say a few sentences appropriate to the situation such as, 'Mary Woods has been one of the most conscientious secretaries we've had and I am sorry to see her leave.'

(ii) *Memorised speech* (memorised completely and then delivered):

Stage fright affects the memory and part of the speech may be forgotten. Memorisation also affects the delivery as one is so intent on delivering the speech word perfect that the audience tends to be forgotten.

(iii) *Written speech or prepared statement* (written out and then read to the audience):

This method is sometimes necessary for people in positions where their every word will be analysed. It is not recommended in most business situations. Written style is much more formal than oral style and a speech delivered like this can sound like an essay. Also, few people today have much experience of reading aloud. Eye contact, a very important aspect of public speaking, is lost.

(iv) *Speech delivered from notes* (prepared in content and structure but not in exact wording):

This is the most popular method. The speaker has jotted down the main points on cards but chooses the exact words while on her feet. Advantages include:

(a) less risk of forgetting

(b) allows for more spontaneity and flexibility

(c) allows eye contact

(d) enables speaker to have greater rapport with audience.

Helpful hints

- *Posture*: Take up a comfortable position. Avoid stiffness and exaggerations.
- *Hands*: Concentrate on what you are saying and the hands will move naturally.
- *Gestures*: Do not overuse.
- *Movement*: Avoid the extremes of standing stock-still and of pacing back and forth.
- *Mannerisms*: Can be extremely irritating. Ask your friends about yours.

- *Style*: Depends on topic and audience. Older people may not like too casual an approach.
- *Slang*: If it is the best word use it. However, remember some audiences may resent it.
- *Vulgarity*: Never!
- *Audience reaction*: Try to anticipate reactions and take them into account.
- *Diction*:

  Major – 'I do not'

  Minor – 'I don't'

  Always use the minor unless you want to be emphatic.
- *Dress*: Appropriate for the occasion. Anything which might take the audience's attention from your speech should be avoided.
- *Sitting or standing*: Depends on size of audience and atmosphere you want to create.
- *Rehearsal*: Rehearse speech the night before delivery and the following morning. Be rested and in good form.
- *Nerves*: It is natural to be nervous before giving a speech. Everyone is somewhat nervous though some may conceal it better than others. It is, in fact, good to be a little nervous. This shows you consider the occasion important. Your nervousness will mean that you will think faster and your body will be ready to react faster than usual. If you were not a little nervous it would be unusual. So, to be a little nervous is good. This will also mean that you will prepare well, and good preparation will give you confidence.

Fig. 1 – Self-evaluation sheet for speeches

(1) Name: _____

(2) Title of speech: _____

(3) Duration: _____

A. Content

(4) Was aim of speech clear? _____

(5) Was body of speech stimulating and interesting? _____

(6) Was it logical and coherent? _____

(7) Was the content suitable to this type of audience? _____

(8) Did the speaker know his/her subject? _____

Grade for content ABCDEF.

B. Introduction and conclusion

(9) Did the introduction get audience's attention? _____

(10) Did conclusion follow logically from body of speech? _____

(11) Was conclusion successful? _____

Grade introduction ABCDEF; grade conclusion ABCDEF.

C. Delivery

(12) Did speaker use enough variety in voice? _____

(13) Was speaker's voice pleasant to listen to? _____

(14) Were gestures and movements effective? _____

(15) Did speaker's conviction come across? _____

(16) Did speaker establish contact with audience? _____

Grade ABCDEF.

D. Language

(17) Was the speaker's language suitable to his/her audience? _____

(18) Was the speaker's language suitable to his/her subject? _____

(19) Did the speaker use rhetorical questions and were they successful?

_____

Grade ABCDEF.

E. Questions

(20) Did the speaker encourage questions? _____

(21) How well did speaker answer questions? _____

Grade ABCDEF.

F. Overall

(22) Did speaker use words effectively? _____

(23) What were the three most positive aspects of the speech?

(a) _____

(b) _____

(c) _____

(24) What were the three aspects of the speech which need to be improved?

(a) _____

(b) _____

(c) _____

Overall grade for speech ABCDEF.

GROUP ACTIVITY

Speakers' corner

Divide the class into groups of about five. Write three topics on some cards (one card for each group) and place the cards face down on the table. The first person in group 1 picks up a card and chooses one of the topics. He speaks on it for three minutes. The second person in the group takes a different aspect of the topic for the same length of time and so on until the whole group has spoken. Each speaker must disagree with the previous speaker. Thus continue with the other groups in the class. This is very good practice and forces students to 'think on their feet'.

To make it a little easier you may allow the first speaker of each group a minute to prepare.

Topics for speakers' corner

Emigration	Books	Work
Anger	Humour	Stupidity
Banks	Unions	Jails
Money	History	Courage
Love	Hate	Hair
Religion	Smoking	Hobbies
Sun	Fitness	Parties
Roads	Politics	Music
Holidays	Marriage	Teenagers

ACTIVITY 2

1. In the following oral exercise pay particular attention to the final consonants. For example, in (a) make sure you pronounce the 't' of get and the 't' of it.

    (a) Go and get it.

    (b) I did not do it.

    (c) I got it.

    (d) Get off the board.

    (e) Wait until I see a bit of it.

    (f) Around about that time I went.

    (g) The party was tip-top.

    (h) I kept it.

    (i) It is better but a little bitter.

    (j) I cannot meet him tonight.

(k) That is quite all right.

(l) Has Peter the strength to lift it?

(m) I doubt it.

(n) When did you send that letter?

(o) I sent it last Thursday.

(p) Is the criminal still at large?

(q) He is, according to the British news of this morning.

2. Some people have difficulty pronouncing 'th'. Practise the following words:

this, that, these, those, thigh, though, then, thoroughly, mother, father, thunder, thin, thick, path, author, myth, clothes, bath, depth, either, width, length, thistle, their.

Variety

An effective speaker varies the pitch, tone, pace, even the volume of her voice. All of this is done to attract and hold the audience's attention. Much will depend on the vitality and enthusiasm of the speaker.

3. (i) Recall a speaker who conveyed ideas effectively. Compare her techniques to a speaker who was ineffective.

   (ii) Show how it is possible to communicate different meanings in each of the following sentences depending upon the word stressed:

   (a) I saw you going there.

   (b) I want you to get the book.

   (c) I fixed the car yesterday.

   (iii) Watch a programme on television or listen to one on radio and decide which speaker involved was the most effective. What made him more effective than the other?

4. (i) Compose and deliver a one-minute talk for the following situations:

   (a) thanking visiting speaker;

   (b) complimenting committee who organised annual function;

   (c) praising work of local school on prize day;

   (d) complimenting retiring secretary of voluntary organisation for service;

   (e) wishing retiring employee a happy future.

   (ii) Compose and deliver a short talk on:

   (a) the most economical means of duplicating material;

   (b) how a particular piece of new equipment should be operated;

(c) how flexi-time operates;

(d) how your college or firm is organised.

(iii) Compose and deliver a short talk:

(a) on why your firm should introduce flexi-time;

(b) to a local consumer association on why it should purchase your products;

(c) to the local chamber of commerce on why it should promote cultural events;

(d) to a group of customers on why they should buy your product.

5. Arrange cards for a speech on punctuality in logical order.

6. Prepare an introduction and conclusion for the same speech.

7. Borrow a book from your local library containing the speeches of some well-known person and analyse the introductions to them under the headings:

(a) Does it arouse interest?

(b) What devices are used?

8. Analyse the conclusions of the speeches under the following headings:

(a) Are the conclusions successful? Why? Why not?

(b) What devices are used?

9. List four typical situations in which you might have to give a speech and in each situation:

(a) analyse the composition of the audience;

(b) write down the aim of your speech.

10. What is the topic on which you have to speak most frequently?

(a) Write down the main points of that topic.

(b) Arrange them in logical order.

11. Topics for speeches

Alcohol; The best film I ever saw; The best book I ever read; Why read newspapers?; Life is marvellous?; Teenage music; The songs of my parents; Equality; What is a fair wage?; Sport is a waste of time; Jails should be abolished; Capital punishment; Betting should be banned; Our politicians should be paid more; TV; Roads; Unleaded petrol; Big families; Small families; What I hate most; Made matches; Food; Grandparents; When I was sick; Businessmen; Women in business; Money; Retirement; Make-up; Strikes; Dole; House design; Prejudice; The army; Education; Teachers; Students; The Gardaí; Charity; Violence; College life; Pollution.

Review

1. In what way does speaking differ from writing?
2. Which type of communication is the more successful, oral or written?
3. 'The apparel doth oft proclaim the man.' How important is this quotation from the point of view of giving a speech?
4. What is meant by flexibility in oral communication?
5. What are the characteristics of an effective speaker?
6. How can you make the introduction to your speech interesting?
7. Discuss the use of humour in a speech.
8. What are the disadvantages of reading a speech?
9. What is the danger of memorising a speech?
10. What is a rhetorical question? Why are rhetorical questions useful in speeches?

Pitfalls

won't wont

Won't comes from the words *will not*, e.g. I *won't* do it.
Wont means accustomed to doing something, e.g. As he was *wont* to say.

Confusing words

calendar	calender	complacent	complaisant
candid	candied	concert	consort
cede	seed	confidant	confident
chance	chants	creak	creek
chord	cord	dam	damn

Quiz

colour color

In Europe we spell colour c-o-l-o-u-r, in the US c-o-l-o-r. Find five other words where the spelling in the US differs from that in Europe.

Spellings

The words most commonly misspelled are highlighted.

bachelor	barometer	benefit
bacteria	barren	**benefited**
baffle	barrister	beware
bagful	battalion	bewilderment
bail	beautiful	binary
bailiff	beauty	**breathe**
banal	bedevil	**breathing**
banana	**beginning**	budget
baneful	behaviour	**budgeted**
banquet	belief	bulletin
barbarous	**believed**	**bureau**
barbecue	belligerent	**bureaucracy**
bargain	**beneficial**	**business**

③

MEETINGS

Introduction

'I have to attend a meeting.'

'I'm off to a meeting now.'

'I have an important meeting.'

'Not another meeting and all the work I have to do.'

How often have we heard these phrases? People often consider meetings as an interruption to their normal work. They resent the enormous amount of time spent at them and are often irritated at how little seems to be achieved. They become frustrated with the procedures, the rambling discussions, high-handed chairpersons and internal disputes. Some people get so frustrated that they try to avoid meetings altogether. But there is no way of avoiding meetings. For the smooth running of an organisation, people must meet and discuss issues and problems. Meetings should be useful and stimulating and should be seen to make progress. In order for this to happen it is important to understand how meetings should be conducted. The rules for the holding and conducting of meetings are there to ensure that they are efficient. It is impossible to participate effectively unless you understand procedures at meetings.

A meeting has been defined as 'an assembly of people for a lawful purpose'. The implication of this definition is that a meeting must have more than one person (case of Sharp and Dawes 1826). There are some exceptions in the context of company meetings where a single person may be treated as a meeting. The word 'assembly' implied that the people should be gathered in one place. However, with modern technology it is now possible to hold meetings without all being gathered in the same place.

Types of meetings

- Public meeting – anyone may attend, e.g. a political meeting in the

town square.
- Private meeting – membership is restricted. The Dáil is a private meeting. The public attend as observers but cannot participate.

The meetings we are concerned with are private meetings.
- Formal – conducted according to rules and regulations such as constitution, standing orders and articles of association.
- Informal – conducted according to no definite set of rules. This type of meeting is not all that common. A group meeting with any frequency will build up rules, regulations and customs over a period.
- Ordinary – the regular meeting held each week or month.
- Extraordinary (special) – a meeting held to deal with one specific important issue that must be decided before the next ordinary meeting. It may deal with a complex issue that demands the sort of time that cannot be devoted at an ordinary meeting because of routine business.
- General – all members may attend.
- Committee – a small group acting on behalf of the general membership of the organisation.
- Annual general meeting (AGM) – held once a year to review the work of the year and elect new officers.

Purpose of meetings

Meetings may also be classified according to the purpose they serve:

(a) to give information

(b) to receive information

(c) to solve a problem

(d) to boost morale

(e) to allow people to relieve their frustrations

(f) to reach decisions.

Many meetings might do a number of the above at the same time.

What is a valid meeting?

For a meeting to be valid a number of requirements must be fulfilled.

(a) It must be properly convened. It can be held on regular specified days, e.g. first Monday of every month. If this is not the case a notice must be issued. The notice must indicate where and when the meeting is to be held and give some indication as to the agenda to be covered.

(b) It must be properly constituted. This means that the proper person must take the chair. It may be also that a certain number of members may have to be present before the meeting can take place. This is called the quorum.

(c) It must be conducted according to the rules and regulations of the group. These are often referred to as the constitution or the standing orders.

(d) A proper record of the proceedings must be kept. These are known as the minutes.

Role of the chairperson

The success or otherwise of the meeting depends to a great extent on the chairperson. To carry out her role effectively, she must understand her duties and powers. But as well as understanding these she needs to know when to be flexible.

Duties of the chairperson

(1) ensure that the meeting is properly convened

(2) ensure it is properly constituted

(3) maintain order

(4) draw up agenda with secretary

(5) guide the meeting through its business

(6) permit an adequate amount of discussion

(7) deal with questions about procedure (points of order)

(8) ascertain the sense of the meeting by conducting a vote or summing up the discussion.

Powers of the chairperson

The chairperson's powers come from the general rules for conducting meetings and from the standing orders or constitution of the particular group of which she is the chairperson. If a group does not have standing orders or a constitution, then the chairperson derives her authority from custom and practice. The chairperson's powers allow her to:

- maintain order
- decide points of procedure
- decide order of speakers
- adjourn the meeting if it becomes impossible to maintain order.

But the chairperson's real power comes from her careful preparation for meetings, her knowledge of the rules, regulations and procedures, and especially her fair and impartial dealings with members. *The chairperson must deal impartially with all members.*

Role of the secretary

Before the meeting
(a) draw up agenda with chairperson
(b) send out notice and agenda to members
(c) prepare any necessary documents for the meeting
(d) prepare the room.

At the meeting
(a) take attendance
(b) read minutes of last meeting
(c) read correspondence
(d) give secretary's report
(e) take notes for minutes
(f) assist chairperson.

After the meeting
(a) write up minutes
(b) act on decisions taken.

Motions and amendments

Motions
'I want to propose a motion . . .' Those who attend meetings regularly will be familiar with that phrase. At meetings which are run on very formal lines the chairperson will not allow discussion unless there is a motion proposed and seconded.

A motion is a proposal to take some action or to decide some policy issue. For example: I propose 'that the annual subscription be raised from £5 to £7.50'.

All motions must:

(a) be proposed

(b) be seconded

(c) begin with the word 'that'

(d) be positive rather than negative

(e) be unambiguous

(f) be within the scope of the meeting as indicated in the agenda.

When a motion is passed or carried, it is called a *resolution*.

Amendments

An amendment is a proposal to alter a motion which has been put before the meeting but has not been voted upon.

All amendments must:

(a) be proposed

(b) be seconded

(c) begin with the word 'that'

(d) be relevant to the original motion

(e) be positive rather than negative

(f) be in character with the original motion. The chairperson will have to use her judgment here as to whether it is in character or not.

Amendments may:

(a) add words to a motion. For example (with reference to the motion: I propose 'that the annual subscription be raised from £5 to £7.50'): I propose 'that after £7.50 add "and no further increase take place for at least three years"'.

(b) delete words from the original motion. For example: I propose 'that the ".50" after £7 be deleted'.

(c) replace part of a motion with different words. For example: I propose 'that £7.50 be deleted and replaced by £10'.

Always vote on the amendments first. If some amendments are carried, then vote on the original motion as amended. If, for example, amendment (c) were carried, the original motion would then read 'that the annual subscription be raised from £5 to £10'. You must then vote on that amended motion. An amended motion is called a substantive motion.

Procedural motions

Procedural motions may be put forward in order to facilitate or regulate the business of a meeting. They are sometimes referred to as formal motions. A procedural motion cannot be amended.

The meeting may decide that it has heard enough discussion on a particular topic. A procedural motion can be put forward to cut short the debate.

The following are the types of procedural motions:

(a) The closure – 'I propose that the question be now put.' or 'I propose that a vote be now taken.' If carried, the vote on the original motion is taken immediately. If lost, the debate continues.

(b) The previous question – 'I propose that the question be not now put.' or 'I propose that the vote be not now taken.' If carried, the debate on the original motion is ended without a vote. If lost, the original motion is immediately put to a vote.

(c) Next business – 'I propose that the meeting proceed to the next business.' If carried, the meeting drops the matter under discussion without a vote and moves on to the next item.

(d) Adjourn debate – 'I propose that the debate be adjourned.' If a debate is getting very heated this can be a good idea, or if sufficient information is not available to make a decision.

(e) Adjourn meeting – 'I propose that the meeting be adjourned.' The meeting may adjourn simply because people must leave. When a meeting is resumed after an adjournment, it is treated as a continuation of the earlier session.

Other terms used at meetings

(a) Quorum

A quorum is the smallest number of people who must be present at a meeting in order for business to be transacted. The number to make up a quorum is usually written into the constitution or standing orders of an organisation. The quorum should be big enough to represent a range of viewpoints but not so large that it would be difficult to have enough persons present to hold a meeting.

(b) Point of order

When a member questions the chairperson as to whether proper procedures are being followed, it is called a point of order. The chairperson must always answer a point of order.

(c) Casting vote

The chairperson, as well as having a vote just like every other member of the organisation (called the deliberative vote), usually has a casting vote which can be used in the event of a tie. The chairperson should avoid using her ordinary or deliberative vote to retain her impartiality. How she should use her casting vote depends on the circumstances.

(d) Voting

It is not necessary to vote on every matter. The chairperson may say 'Are we all agreed?' and members may nod assent. At meetings voting is usually by show of hands or by secret ballot.

(e) *Sine die*

If a meeting adjourns without setting a date to meet again, it is said to have adjourned *sine die*.

(f) *Nem. con.*

If a motion or amendment is passed unanimously, it is said to have been carried *nem. con.*

Business meetings

Many meetings which take place daily in businesses do not necessarily have all the formality described in the previous pages. The meeting may be called to allow people to air their views, to give their reactions to a plan or to discuss a problem. An element of formality, however, is necessary at all meetings if they are to be productive. The chairperson of such a meeting must:

(a) decide who is to attend

(b) plan carefully

(c) control the discussion

(d) cope with difficult members.

Who is to attend?
Sociologists who have studied the efficiency of groups recommend that the most effective group contains about seven members. Meetings should, then, be confined to small groups if possible. Restricting the number has obvious advantages: the shy person is more likely to

contribute; the specialist has greater possibility of explaining difficult concepts; the leader is in a better position to lead and guide the discussion.

Plan

Effective meetings are the product of careful planning and sensitive leadership. A skilled chairperson devises a plan in advance of the meeting but she is prepared to modify, adjust or even change her plan if her 'feel' of the meeting so directs.

The meeting room should be clean, bright and comfortable. It should be arranged to promote maximum participation in the discussion. Classroom-style arrangement discourages this. A circular arrangement will encourage discussion and allow the leader to merge more with the group.

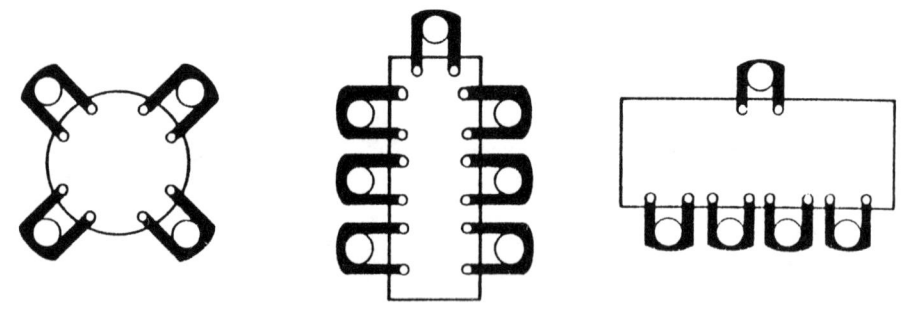

Chairpersons develop their own style, but the following formula may be a useful basis to work from:

(1) inform members of purpose of meeting
(2) state precise topic or problem to be dealt with
(3) indicate procedure you intend to adopt and proposed duration of meeting
(4) allow for, indeed encourage, free-flow participation from all
(5) sum up progress of discussion at suitable intervals
(6) summarise conclusions and decisions reached at close of meeting
(7) suggest for adoption future actions related to decisions taken.

Fig. 1 – Sample outline

Purpose of meeting: to deal with the problem of unpunctuality.

Aim: to reduce the problem of unpunctuality among employees at all levels.

Introductory remarks:

(a) gives bad image to company

(b) shows lack of interest in work

(c) problem must be eased if it is not to get completely out of hand.

Consequences of unpunctuality:

(a) lack of punctuality creeping in at all levels

(b) customers on telephone at 9.05 a.m. and no one to answer it

(c) machines being underutilised

(d) production falling off

(e) costs increasing

(f) losing goodwill.

Rules for discussion:

1. Consider the following points:

(a) lack of punctuality at morning

(b) lack of punctuality in returning from tea breaks

(c) lack of punctuality in returning from lunch.

2. Reasons for lack of punctuality:

(a) traffic problems

(b) buses late

(c) lack of interest in job.

3. Possible solutions to problems:

(a) introduce flexi-time

(b) circular to all employees emphasising the extent of problem

(c) supervisors and foremen to keep details of chronic offenders for future action.

Forward plan: further meeting two weeks hence to assess progress.

Controlling the discussion

The skilled group leader creates an atmosphere which encourages maximum participation. She will stimulate the discussion by injecting questions calculated to draw shy members into the discussion and to encourage members with needed specialist knowledge to contribute at appropriate points.

The types of questions used by the leader may be divided into five categories.

1. *The open-ended question*

This is a question which cannot be answered by a simple yes or no. For example: 'What do you think are the chief reasons for lack of punctuality in the mornings?' This will allow a member to give an expanded answer.

2. *The closed question*

This should be used sparingly as it allows only a yes or no answer. For example: 'Is lack of punctuality having a bad effect on morale?'

3. *The overhead question*

This can be usefully employed in stimulating the discussion and in getting everyone's attention. It is not directed at anybody in particular, e.g. 'Could I have your suggestions on how big the sample should be for this survey?' It is a mistake to put the question to one person first as it allows all other members to relax.

4. *The direct question*

This is directed at a specific individual. It is a useful means of drawing a quiet member into a discussion. However, it should be a simple question that he can answer, otherwise he may be reluctant to contribute in future. It is also used for eliciting knowledge from an expert member.

5. *The leading question*

For example: 'You will agree, I'm sure, that we should postpone action until next week?' This type of question encourages members to agree with the questioner. It is not useful when the leader is seeking an open exchange of views.

Coping with difficult members

1. *The chatterer*

This person knows all and scatters his wisdom indiscriminately. He can be arrested by a searching question which requires real and detailed knowledge or with a polite comment: 'We've just heard from you.

Perhaps we could hear the views of Mr Ryan who did not have an opportunity yet?'

2. *The rambler*
He wanders off the topic completely. Summarise the relevant part of his contribution to get back to the topic.

3. *The thunderer*
Do not invite him to the meeting if possible. If this is unavoidable, try to find merit in some of his contributions and then move on. Keep your temper.

4. *The mumbler*
Ask him to repeat contribution or summarise his points.

5. *The silent member*
Ask him a direct question.

6. *Member with persecution complex*
This member feels that some wrong was done to him at some time and he brings it up at every opportunity. Point out to him that the business of this particular meeting does not include his point. Indicate pressure of time.

7. *Member who engages in side conversation*
Ask him a direct question. A look of displeasure may suffice.

8. *The superior type*
This person acts as if he is above all of this and considers most of the other members beneath him. Challenge his contributions every now and then to bring him down to earth.

9. *Member who always quotes the rules*
This member constantly calls for points of order and highlights infringements of the rules. Answer each point of order with patience and always be familiar with the standing orders and rules for conducting meetings.

10. *Member with little to contribute but comes to hear himself talk*
When not speaking directly to the topic under discussion rule this type of person out of order.

ACTIVITY 1

1. Your organisation is electing a new treasurer at your AGM. How would you conduct the voting and why?

2. What is the difference between a motion and a resolution?
3. Give some suggestions for formulating motions.
4. Write down a sample motion.
5. Write three different types of amendments to the motion you wrote in no. 4.
6. If amendments no. 1 and 3 were carried and no. 2 was lost, how would the amended motion read?
7. Why should organisations have a quorum for meetings?
8. Why might a member at a meeting propose the closure?
9. What type of seating arrangement should be used at a meeting where the chairperson wishes to encourage discussion?

Review

1. Why do many people hate going to meetings?
2. What requirements must be fulfilled for a meeting to be valid?
3. What is the difference between an ordinary and an extraordinary meeting?
4. Should the chairperson just referee the debates at meetings or should she give leadership?
5. What is the role of the secretary:
   (a) before the meeting?
   (b) at the meeting?
   (c) after the meeting?
6. What power has a chairperson at a meeting?
7. Define:
   (a) motion
   (b) amendment.
8. Why are motions sometimes amended?
9. What are procedural motions and how should they be dealt with by the chairperson?
10. How should the chairperson use her casting vote?

Pitfalls

e.g. i.e.

e.g. means 'for example' from the Latin *exempli gratia*. It can be remembered in English as 'example given'. 'I will finish this chapter some day next week, e.g. Monday.'

i.e. means 'that is' from the Latin *id est*. 'I will finish the book in two weeks' time, i.e. the end of July.'

Confusing words

lean	lien	main	mane
lends	lens	maize	maze
lineament	liniment	mantel	mantle
loath	loathe	marshal	martial
lose	loose	mean	mien

Quiz

'The English', said Oscar Wilde, 'have really everything in common with the Americans, except, of course, language.'

What is the meaning of the following American terms: band aid; billfold; diaper; closet?

Spellings

The words most commonly misspelled are highlighted.

calendar	censure	colleague
campaign	census	commemorate
carpenter	**centre**	**committee**
casualties	**centred**	**competent**
catalogue	**centring**	concede
catastrophe	century	**conscientious**
categories	ceremony	**conscious**
category	changeable	consensus
cathedral	**chaos**	convalescent
cautious	character	**convenient**
ceiling	chasm	
cemetery	chemistry	

④

DOCUMENTS FOR MEETINGS

Notice and agenda

There are two main ways of calling a meeting:
- The meeting is held at pre-arranged times and always in the same place. So, for example, the meetings are held on the first Tuesday of every month in the staff common room. If this is the practice it is not necessary to issue a notice for each meeting. However, some bodies such as local authorities issue notices and agendas even though their meetings are held at regular times.
- Issue a notice of each meeting. Notice could be issued by telephone or word of mouth or could be put in a newspaper for an AGM. The notice should be issued by the proper authority, usually the secretary in consultation with the chairperson.

A notice should:

(i) be issued by the proper authority

(ii) observe minimum period of notice

(iii) state where and when meeting is to be held

(iv) be accompanied by agenda

(v) be sent to all individuals entitled to receive it.

The minimum period of notice is often taken as 'seven clear days'. For company meetings the period of notice is fixed by law. The 'clear days' begin when the notice is delivered at the correct address or after an interval specified in the standing orders, e.g. forty-eight hours after posting.

The agenda is drawn up by the secretary with the approval of the chairperson. The secretary should:

(a) consult the chairperson

(b) keep folder of items which colleagues want on the agenda

(c) refer to minutes of previous meetings to bring forward any items which were deferred.

The usual order for an agenda is:
(a) preliminary business such as:
- apologies for absence
- minutes of last meeting
- matters arising from minutes;

(b) ordinary business such as:
- treasurer's report;

(c) new business such as:
- proposal for new projects;

(d) closing items such as:
- any other business
- date of next meeting.

Fig. 1 – Notice of meeting incorporating the agenda

STAFF SOCIAL CLUB

5 August 199?

The next meeting of the Staff Social Club will be held on Wednesday, 13 August at 8.00 p.m. in the Staff Common Room.

Signed: Kate McGrane
(Secretary)

Agenda

The Agenda will include the following:

1. Apologies for Absence
2. Minutes of Last Meeting
3. Matters Arising from Minutes
4. Correspondence
5. Treasurer's Report
6. Snooker Tournament
7. Trip to All-Ireland Hurling Final
8. Any Other Business.

Secretary's agenda

At a meeting the secretary need not be writing furiously all the time trying to take down everything that is said. He should have a copy of the agenda and just make brief notes opposite the various items to help in writing the minutes. This will allow the secretary to assist the chairperson and participate at the meeting.

Fig. 2 – Secretary's agenda

STAFF SOCIAL CLUB

13/8/9? at 8.00 p.m.

Chair – K. Kenny   Secretary – Kate McGrane

Present: P. Ryan (Treasurer), O. Dunphy, G. Carr, T. Hearne, P. Meehan, M. Murray.

Agenda   *Notes*

1. Apologies for Absence
2. Minutes of Last Meeting
3. Matters Arising
4. Correspondence
5. Treasurer's Report
6. Snooker Tournament
7. Trip to All-Ireland Hurling Final
8. Any Other Business.

Chairperson's agenda

Before the meeting begins the chairperson needs to study the agenda and make notes on it to help him run the meeting. These will usually be very brief. He might put down times opposite items to indicate the rate at which the meeting should progress.

Fig. 3 – Chairperson's agenda

STAFF SOCIAL CLUB

13/8/9?   8.00 p.m.

Agenda   *Notes*

1. Apologies for Absence

2. Minutes of Last Meeting

3. Matters Arising

4. Correspondence » 8.15

5. Treasurer's Report

6. Snooker Tournament

7. Trip to All-Ireland Hurling Final » People who have not paid for last year's tickets cannot participate until debt cleared.

8. Any Other Business.

Minutes

The minutes are a brief, accurate record of the business transacted at a meeting. They should contain the following:

(1) name of organisation

(2) place, date and time of meeting

(3) names of chairperson and secretary

(4) names of other members present

(5) all motions and amendments no matter how they may have fared

(6) names of movers and seconders of all motions and amendments

(7) results of voting.

Minutes should be:

- concise but sufficiently detailed to make clear the sense of the meeting
- precise and unambiguous
- impersonal and impartial
- written in the past tense
- numbered in ascending order from one meeting to another. In our sample minutes (Fig. 4), the first minute is numbered 149. The last minute of the previous meeting was 148.

Fig. 4 – Sample minutes

STAFF SOCIAL CLUB

Minutes of the meeting of the Staff Social Club held on 13 August 199? at 8.00 p.m. in the Staff Common Room.

Chairperson: Kevin Kenny

Secretary: Kate McGrane

Present: P. Ryan, O. Dunphy, G. Carr, T. Hearne, P. Meehan, M. Murray

149 – Apologies for Absence

The Secretary reported that N. Doyle and P. Foran sent apologies for being unable to attend.

150 – Minutes of Meeting of 12 July 199?

The Minutes of the meeting of 12 July 199? were read, approved on the proposal of P. Ryan, seconded by G. Carr, and signed by the Chairperson.

151 – Decorating Staff Common Room

The Secretary read a letter from the Manager proposing redecoration of the Staff Common Room and requesting the Social Club's views.

Proposed P. Ryan, seconded O. Dunphy

'that a committee be appointed consisting of G. Carr, P. Meehan, and T. Hearne to make recommendations for redecorating of Common Room and to report to the next meeting.'

Result – Carried unanimously

152 – Treasurer's Report

The Treasurer reported that the Club is £200 in credit. However, some subscriptions are still outstanding. The Chairperson urged the Treasurer to attempt to collect outstanding subscriptions.

153 – Snooker Tournament

Proposed T. Hearne, seconded P. Meehan

'that the Secretary be assisted by O. Dunphy and M. Murray in making arrangements for the Autumn Snooker Tournament.'

Result – Carried: 6 for, 1 against, 1 abstention.

154 – Trip to All-Ireland Hurling Final

It was agreed that the Secretary should write to Croke Park immediately for ten tickets and book a minibus for the trip. To participate in draw for tickets all outstanding debts must be paid.

Next Meeting: 13 September 199?

Meeting concluded at 9.10 p.m.

Signed: _____ (Chairperson)   Signed: _____ (Secretary)

Date: _____   Date: _____

The minutes should be approved at the next meeting. The secretary should read the minutes and then the chairperson should ask if they are a fair and accurate record of the last meeting. If the meeting agrees, the chairperson should sign them. If the meeting approves an alteration to the minutes the secretary should make the alteration and the chairperson initial it. If the alteration is substantial, it may be necessary to rewrite the minutes.

When the minutes are being approved the chairperson should not allow questions that have been decided to be re-opened again.

Standing orders

Standing orders are the rules by which an organisation decides to run its affairs. They are sometimes called a constitution.

Fig. 5 – Standing orders

STAFF SOCIAL CLUB

Standing Orders for Meetings

1. At each meeting of the club the chair shall be taken at the time for which the meeting is convened and business immediately proceeded with. At all meetings the chairperson (or deputy chairperson) shall take the chair, or in his/her absence, the secretary or failing both a chairperson from the meeting shall be elected.

2. (a) The order of business for ordinary meetings shall be as follows:

    (i) Minutes of last meeting

    (ii) Matters arising from the minutes

    (iii) Correspondence

    (iv) Minutes of special meetings

    (v) Treasurer's Report

    (vi) Elections

    (vii) Motions

    (viii) Any other business.

    (b) The order of business for the Annual General Meeting shall be as follows:

    (i) Minutes of previous AGM

    (ii) Chairperson's Report

(iii) Secretary's Report

(iv) Elections of Chairperson, Secretary, Treasurer and committee members.

3. Speaking Rights:

    (a) No speech shall be permitted which is not strictly to a distinct and competent motion or amendment or to a point of order or information.

    (b) A motion or amendment shall not be discussed by anyone except the mover, put to the meeting, or entered on the minutes until the same shall have been seconded. On a motion being ruled out of order, no further discussion on it may take place at the meeting.

    (c) The proposer of any motion, or of an amendment to a motion, shall have the right to make a proposing speech on such motion or amendment and to reply before it is put to a vote. The seconder of such motion or amendment, and any other member called upon by the chairperson, shall be entitled to speak on the motion or amendment.

    (d) The proposer of an original motion shall have the right to speak immediately after the proposer of an amendment which has not been accepted by him/her. If an amendment which has not been accepted by the proposer of the original motion is carried, the proposer of such amendment shall be deemed, for all purposes, to be the proposer of the motion.

    (e) No ordinary member can speak more than once on the same motion.

4. Points of Order: Points of order must be strictly to questions relating to rules of debate. No member may speak until the chairperson has ruled on the point of order.

5. Points of Information:

    (a) A member when asking or giving information on matters referred to by any member may do so only with the consent of the chairperson.

    (b) No point of information shall be made in a speech of reply by the proposer of a motion or amendment.

6. Questions: Members may ask questions arising out of the business before the meeting. Any member who wishes to put a question to the chairperson of any committee as to the general work or procedure of that committee not included in a report submitted for approval, shall forward it in writing to the chairperson of the meeting. Such questions shall be answered by the chairperson of the committee at that meeting if possible. No other speech or discussions shall be allowed on any question so put.

7. Amendments: When a motion is under debate at any meeting of the branch, a further motion shall not be received, except the following:

(a) to amend the motion

(b) that the meeting be adjourned

(c) that the debate be adjourned

(d) that the question be now put

(e) that the meeting proceed to next business

(f) that the question be not now put.

When amendment (a) is on the floor, any of amendments (b) through (f) may be moved. Subject to this, there shall not be two amendments on the floor at the same time. A member shall not move an amendment without the permission of the chairperson if s/he has previously spoken to the motion, or move more than one amendment to the motion.

8. An amendment must be germane. It must not merely negate the motion, and it must not be inconsistent with anything already agreed upon at the same meeting.

   If an amendment be carried the motion as amended shall take the place of the original motion and shall become the question upon which any further amendment shall be moved.

9. Motion (f) must be seconded. The proposer of the motion must speak and the proposer of any substantive motion on the floor may oppose it. The motion will then be put.

10. Should disorder arise, the chairperson shall be entitled to adjourn the meeting and quit the chair and on doing so the meeting shall be held to be, *ipso facto*, immediately adjourned. The chairperson shall give his/her reasons at the following meeting of the club, and there shall be no discussion thereon.

11. The club by a two-thirds majority of those present at a meeting may suspend standing orders.

12. Suspension of Members:

    (a) In the event of any member at a meeting of the club disregarding the authority of the chairperson or being guilty of obstructive or offensive behaviour, the club may, on a motion duly moved and seconded by a resolution of at least two-thirds of the members present, suspend such a member for the remainder of the meeting, and may in addition order the suspension to continue until submission of apology by the offending member. The motion to suspend shall be put without discussion.

    (b) The motion to suspend may be put at any time during the meeting and it shall be put to a vote immediately on being proposed.

13. Voting Powers of Chairperson: At all meetings of the branch the chairperson shall have a deliberative vote. In cases of equality of votes, s/he may give the casting vote.

ACTIVITY I

1. Write a notice and agenda for a meeting of any organisation of which you are a member.
2. Prepare the chairperson's agenda for the conduct of the same meeting.
3. Also prepare the secretary's agenda and make the appropriate notes which would be made during the conduct of the meeting.
4. Write the minutes for the meeting from your notes on the secretary's agenda.
5. Draw up a chairperson's agenda for the canteen committee of the students' union. The meeting is to discuss (a) space, (b) seating, (c) slow service and (d) provision of health foods.
6. You are secretary of the students' union social committee. Write the minutes of the last meeting from the notes on the agenda below.

STUDENTS' UNION SOCIAL COMMITTEE

Meeting 28 January 199? at 7.00 at the Social Club.

Attendance: L. Ahearn, R. Foran, J. Fogarty, T. Delaney, T. Doyle (Chairperson), D. McDonough (Secretary).

Agenda		Notes
1. Apologies	»	Roisin Foran
2. Minutes of Last Meeting	»	ok
3. Matters Arising	»	none
4. Correspondence	»	none
5. Treasurer's Report	»	£400 in bank, some subs due (Liam Ahearn)
6. Rag Week Gigs	»	No gig to cost more than £5.00 – proposed, J. Fogarty seconded, T. Delaney
7. Cleanliness of Rooms		
8. Any Other Business	»	None. Next meeting 17 February.

7. Look up a good dictionary and find the original meaning of the word 'minute'.
8. Why is it a good idea not to include what people said in the minutes?
9. Minute the following items from the secretary's agenda:

Secretary's Agenda

Agenda	Notes
1. Apologies	None
2. Minutes	OK
3. Matters Arising	Every member expected to sell 20 tickets for £100 draw.
	Prop. B. Scully
	Sec. D. Finn

ACTIVITY 2

Preparing for that meeting

You are secretary of the Golden Dramatic Society and you have met the chairperson to discuss the agenda for the August meeting.

Chairperson: 'What do you think of having the next meeting on Tuesday? That night usually suits everyone. It's sort of traditional.'

Secretary: 'Well, we decided at the last meeting to have it on Monday as Costello and O'Rourke are going on a holiday on Tuesday 16th. The room is in a bit of a mess but it will do for the meeting.'

C: 'The Tidy Towns Committee want to know would we put on a bit of street theatre during the last week of August.'

S: 'It's a bad time to get people together. Anyway, the committee can discuss it and decide what to do. By the way, the rooms are in a terrible mess; they need to be cleaned up.'

C: 'Well, it might be possible to get a few volunteers, but if people were considerate it wouldn't need to be done at all.'

S: 'Oh, Louise and Ann are going to Australia for a year. We probably should have a bit of a do for them.'

C: 'Look, put it on the agenda and see what people think.'

S: 'I don't think there is anything else except the usual items.'

Based on the above conversation write the notice and agenda for the next meeting of the Golden Dramatic Society.

GROUP ACTIVITY

Now hold that meeting

This exercise can be carried out by groups of six. You are now members of Golden Dramatic Society and you have the agenda for the meeting from the previous exercise. Each person plays the role of one of the committee members based on the details below.

Chairperson: M. O'Neill

Secretary: S. McSweeney

Treasurer: J. Lonergan

Committee members: M. Costello

J. O'Rourke

P. Murphy

Chairperson: M. O'Neill

Open meeting.

Ask if any apologies.

Ask secretary to read minutes of last meeting.

Ask if you can sign them.

Ask if any matters arising.

Deal with objections to holding meetings on a Monday instead of Tuesday.

Speak strongly to members about the mess of the rooms and ask for volunteers to clean it up.

Guide discussion on Tidy Towns request for street theatre.

Suggest party for Louise and Ann in local pub. Ask for further suggestions.

Ask if there is any other business.

Close the meeting.

Secretary: S. McSweeney

Apologies for absence received from J. Branagan.

Letter from Naas Drama Club thanking us for our participation in their festival.

Matters arising – booked hotel for One Act Drama Festival in December.

The cleaning up of the rooms always left to the secretary. People have very little consideration. A group should be in charge of keeping rooms clean and tidy.

Street theatre very difficult at this time of year with so many on holidays.

'Do' for Louise and Ann would need to be very soon as they're leaving on Friday. Will check with pub about a room for private party. It will be difficult to notify all members.

Treasurer: J. Lonergan

Propose signing of minutes.

Some people missing too many meetings. Should they be on committee at all?

Will Tidy Towns Committee pay us for putting on street theatre? They have plenty of money and they should pay us something.

Funds are low. We should charge for party for Louise and Ann. £2 each wouldn't kill anybody. No 'do' for self when going to US three years ago.

Committee member: M. Costello

Second signing of minutes.

Personally cleaned up rooms several times. Fed up doing it. No point of cleaning them; all will be in a mess again.

No problem putting on a bit of street theatre. Leixlip did it last year. A bit of mime and dance is all you need.

Of course there should be a party for Louise and Ann – great members. Charging is ridiculous.

Committee member: J. O'Rourke

Tidying up should not be left to secretary. Member of committee should be in charge of rooms.

Why so low in money? Where is all the money we made last year?

Party for Louise and Ann should be paid for out of funds. They deserve it.

Has idea for street theatre. Would like chance to pursue it. Idea still at the gestation stage. Would committee allow him to try to pull something together?

Committee member: P. Murphy

Nothing wrong with rooms. It's the nature of theatre premises to be messy.

Street theatre is not our work. Theatre should be in a theatre. Waste of talent and energy. It is not art. Would most certainly not prostitute her own talents on such nonsense.

Parties now at the drop of a hat. In the old days remembers only one party and that to a member of very long standing and very exceptional talent. Did these girls ever act in a real play? Have they just played in what is now called 'pub theatre'? What have they contributed?

Review

1. What is the difference between a notice and an agenda?
2. What is meant by 'clear days'? How are clear days calculated?
3. If you cannot contact someone who is entitled to attend a meeting, what should you, as secretary, do?
4. What is the advantage of sending out an agenda to members before a meeting?
5. Why are the minutes of a meeting read at the following meeting?
6. How and by whom is the agenda drawn up?
7. What is the value of having a secretary's agenda?
8. What is the value of having a chairperson's agenda?
9. What should a chairperson do if a member disagrees with the minutes of the last meeting?
10. What are standing orders?

Pitfalls

to too two

Examples: 'I will go *to* Dublin.'

'I will go there *too*.'

'The *two* of us will go there tomorrow.'

Confusing words

miner	minor	nick	niche
moat	mote	oar	ore
naval	navel	oracle	auricle

nave	knave	packed	pact
neither	nether	pail	pale

Quiz

In some parts of the country the following words are used. Do you know their meanings?

(a) bairn, (b) lug, (c) oxter.

Spellings

The words most commonly misspelled are highlighted.

dearth	derive	discern
debris	descendent	**discipline**
debtor	design	**discrepancy**
deceit	designation	**dissatisfied**
deceive	**desirable**	dissent
decision	**desperate**	dissipate
defence	**deterrent**	**distributor**
deferred	development	**dossier**
deficient	disagree	draught
definite	disagreement	dubious
definition	**disappeared**	
delicious	**disappointed**	
derivation	**disastrous**	

⑤

LISTENING

In the 1970s the Sperry Corporation in the US brought in consultants to help to deliver a better service to their customers. The consultants found that the typical employee could remember no more than 20 per cent of what he or she had been told twenty-four hours earlier. Even when questioned about material they had just heard, they were likely to get facts mixed up. The management of Sperry decided that improving the listening skills of their customer service representatives was vital. They brought in a team of trainers to develop listening skills. Top management were so impressed with the improvement that they expanded the programme to the whole firm. Today, all Sperry employees attend training workshops to develop their listening skills and they must also attend refresher courses periodically. Sperry have even now entered the market as a provider of listening skills workshops.

Most people have never practised listening. But it is like any other skill in that if practised, it can be improved. Thomas J. Peters and Robert H. Waterman in their influential book on management, *In Search of Excellence* (New York: Harper and Row, 1982), identified the ability to listen as one of the keys to success.

In traditional organisations it was assumed that all expertise resided with the top management. Thus, managers issued directives and employees implemented them. In modern firms it is assumed that expertise can be found at all levels. It is not uncommon at present to find that new employees have higher educational qualifications than some top managers. Listening is, therefore, a very important skill. Listening means receiving messages in a thoughtful manner that leads to understanding of the meaning of the message. The receiver has a great responsibility in the communication process. Many people do not listen well. They have prejudices about the sender or about the message and they formulate their response while the sender is still transmitting the message.

Effective listening requires *active listening*, not passive tolerance of the sender. Active listening means becoming involved in the communication process by asking questions, and perhaps rewording what the sender has said. It is important that the receiver not prejudge the sender or the message.

In dealing with people, listening is a very important skill. It shows consideration and courtesy to listen attentively to what people say. Many people are great talkers but poor listeners. Listening is different from hearing. Hearing requires little effort. It is quite possible to hear sounds such as music while still concentrating on something different. But it is not possible to listen and concentrate on something else. You could, of course, listen while performing some mechanical task such as washing a car.

You cannot listen attentively for long periods. The mind will wander and try to take a rest. Your listening ability will depend on anxiety, tiredness and boredom. We can listen to a stimulating speaker for much longer than to a dull one. We listen attentively for short periods, less than half a minute, and then we process or try to make sense of what we have heard.

Certain factors will affect our listening:

a) distractions

b) preconceived negative ideas about the speaker

c) dull voice or message, or both

d) message we find disturbing and hence don't want to listen to it.

Improving listening

- *Remove as many distractions as possible.* These distractions may consist of music, radio, people talking or traffic. Some distractions perhaps cannot be moved, but even the noise of traffic can be softened by closing a window.

- *Listen actively.* Be alert. When people say their name, listen to it. It is often a good idea to repeat the name to help you remember it.

- *Ask questions.* Ask questions of the speaker every now and then. If the speaker in some formal situation is not taking questions until the end, form questions quickly in your mind as you listen.

- *Watch non-verbal elements.* People communicate by voice but they also communicate by posture, gesture and facial expressions. Listen to the tone of voice used. We should listen with our eyes as well as with our ears.

- *Listen objectively.* Try not to allow your personal feelings prevent you giving the speaker a chance. If you are not favourably disposed towards the speaker, you are then obliged to try harder to listen objectively. It is easy to listen to people we agree with. Good listeners are able to listen to those with whom they disagree.

- *Withhold judgment.* Hear the speaker out and do not make up your mind immediately. You have not heard the full story until the speaker is finished. First judgments are difficult to change so you should not jump to them too quickly.

GROUP ACTIVITY

1. Tell one member of the class the following message. 'The end-of-term test will be given on Thursday, unless the preceding Tuesday is a holiday, in that case the test will be on the following Monday. It will take place in the Seminar Room in the Barrow Centre at 9.30 and will cover the first seven chapters of the text.'

   Exercise: Now have each member of the class relay the message one at a time to each other so that the others cannot hear it. The last member of the class to hear the message should write it down. Then compare this with the original version to see how much of the message was lost.

2. Tell one member of the class the following message. 'The new prospectus is almost ready but there is a little difficulty with the cover. The colour separations have not worked out as well as hoped for and will have to be done again. It will have to be taken to Dublin but there will be no extra cost involved. One of the colour pictures, the one on page 3, is blurred and will not be used at all. The prospectuses will be ready on Wednesday but the first 1,000 will have a cover that is not as good as it should be. The rest of the run will have a perfect cover. They will be delivered on Tuesday night by courier. Printers will pay the courier. The error in the map on page 7 has been corrected. Posters to go with the prospectus will be ready on Thursday.'

   Exercise: Now have each member of the class relay the message one at a time to each other so that the others cannot hear it. The last member of the class to hear the message should write it down. Then compare this with the original version to see how much of the message was lost.

Review

1. Explain the importance of listening in an organisation.
2. What is active listening?
3. Explain the difference between hearing and listening.
4. Discuss the factors which affect listening.
5. How can listening be improved?

Pitfalls

prescribe proscribe

Prescribe means to lay down or impose authoritatively, for example, to prescribe a drug for a patient.

Proscribe comes from the Latin words *pro* meaning 'before' and *scribere* meaning 'to write'. It has now come to mean to ban something. The government might proscribe certain organisations.

Confusing words

mitten	mittimus	momentous	momentum
motto	mottle	mugger	muggins
nape	napery	mumps	munch
natter	natty	moil	moiety

Quiz

The ship, the *Titanic*, which was built in Belfast, sank in April 1912. How did it get its name?

Spellings

The words most commonly misspelled are highlighted.

eccentric	encyclopaedia	exceedingly
efficiency	endeavour	**excellent**
eight	enormous	exceptional
eighteenth	**enthusiasm**	excessive
eighty	epidemic	exchequer
elapse	**equipment**	excitable
electricity	**equipped**	exclamation
elegance	**erroneous**	**exercise**
eliminate	**especially**	**exhausted**
embarrass	**essential**	exhibit
emigrated	establishment	expedite
eminent	etiquette	**expense**
emphasise	eventually	**extremely**
encouragement	**exaggerated**	

READING 1:
FINDING INFORMATION – THE BOOKS YOU NEED

Introduction

As a person working in a business there are certain books you need to have available at all times. No one is capable of spelling all the words in the English language, so a dictionary is of vital importance. When you write business documents you must be accurate or your message will be affected. Sometimes you cannot think of the precise word you want to use so a thesaurus should be near you as you work. Or perhaps you want to find the address of the Department of Foreign Affairs. Where would you find it? The IPA *Yearbook & Diary* is the answer. How much does it cost to post a parcel to the USA? *An Post Services* provides all the information you would need in this area.

In this chapter we are going to look at the books you, as a business employee, need to have available at all times.

Dictionary

Always have a dictionary available to you at work. Read the introduction to your dictionary and it will tell you how to use it. Even the smallest dictionary will indicate the spelling, pronunciation, meaning and grammatical function of words. It also explains abbreviations, foreign words and phrases in common use, and some will also give synonyms and antonyms. The last two items mentioned will be explained later in this chapter.

ACTIVITY 1

1. Read the introduction to your dictionary and it will tell you, for example, how its entries are arranged, what type of pronunciation it is putting forward and the conventions it is following in spellings.

In the specimen from The Concise Oxford Dictionary *(8th edition,1990), it can be seen that the word **business** can be used in several senses. The pronunciation of the word is given as is its part of speech. The formal meanings of the word business are given as is its use as a colloquial term.*

business /'biznis/ *n.* **1** one's regular occupation, profession, or trade. **2** a thing that is one's concern. **3 a** a task or duty. **b** a reason for coming (*what is your business?*). **4** serious work or activity (*get down to business*). **5** *derog.* **a** an affair, a matter (*sick of the whole business*). **b** a structure (*a lath-and-plaster business*). **6** a thing or series of things needing to be dealt with (*the business of the day*). **7** buying and selling; trade (*good stroke of business*). **8** a commercial house or firm. **9** *Theatr.* action on stage. **10** a difficult matter (*what a business it is!; made a great business of it*).
□ **business card** a card printed with one's name and professional details. **the business end** *colloq.* the functional part of a tool or device. **business park** an area designed to accommodate businesses and light industry. **business person** a businessman or businesswoman. **business studies** training in economics, management, etc. **has no business to** has no right to. **in business 1** trading or dealing. **2** able to begin operations. **in the business of 1** engaged in. **2** intending to (*we are not in the business of surrendering*). **like nobody's business** *colloq.* extraordinarily. **make it one's business to** undertake to. **mind one's own business** not meddle. **on business** with a definite purpose, esp. one relating to one's regular occupation. **send a person about his** or **her business** dismiss a person; send a person away. [OE *bisignis* (as BUSY, -NESS)]

ACTIVITY 2

1. An American president once said, 'The business of America is business'. Explain the senses in which he uses the word.

2. Find the meaning of the following words in your dictionary and write them in the space provided:

   dyslexia ....

   expletive ....

   banal ....

   bizarre ....

   obdurate ....

   obeisance ....

   paean ....

purblind ....

ingot ....

mayhem ....

polyglot ....

3. Find the following in your dictionary and write them in the space provided:

Monetary unit in Argentina ....

Monetary unit in Israel ....

Monetary unit in Denmark ....

Ninth letter of Greek alphabet ....

First letter of Russian alphabet ....

Number of millimetres in one inch ....

Number of kilometres in a mile ....

What is a peck? ....

Number of acres in one square mile ....

Number of yards in one mile ....

Pronunciation

Most dictionaries will give you an indication as to how words are pronounced. A dictionary can only give you an accepted pronunciation. It is very unlikely that there is any word that has only one pronunciation. English is a living language which is growing and changing, and the world itself would be a very dull place if everyone pronounced every word in exactly the same manner. Sometimes your dictionary will give more than one pronunciation.

ACTIVITY 3

1. Find out how your dictionary suggests that the following words should be pronounced and write the pronunciation in the space provided:

   temporary ....   Thomas ....

   veterinary ....   Thames ....

   controversy ....   Tipperary ....

   February ....   supple ....

   Wednesday ....   garage ....

2. Form small groups and make a list of ten words that are pronounced in different ways in different parts of the country.

Thesaurus

As well as a dictionary you should also have a thesaurus available to you at work. It will help you use the correct word for every occasion. If you use the same word again and again in a short document, it can lead to boredom so a thesaurus is necessary to allow you to add variety to your writing.

A thesaurus groups words which are related or which have similar meanings. An index at the back of the thesaurus guides you to the right group of words. Suppose you want to find a short or different way to describe the sort of loan that helps a person buy a house. First you look up the word *loan* in the index of the thesaurus. In the index to *Roget's Thesaurus* (London: Longmans, 1966), you will find the following:

Loan
lending 784n
borrowing 785n

The number is not a page reference; it is the number of a particular entry in the thesaurus. The 'n' for noun after the reference indicates that in both these instances the equivalent nouns for *lending* and *borrowing* are listed. Since you are looking for a word to express the idea of a 'loan' in the context of borrowing for house purchase, you must turn to reference 785 in the thesaurus. There, in *Roget's Thesaurus*, you will find the following:

785. Borrowing – N. *borrowing*, request for credit, loan application; loan transaction, mortgage 803 n. *debt*; hire purchase, never-never system; pledging, pawning; loan, repayable amount, debenture 784 n. *lending*; infringement, plagiarism, copying 20 n. *imitation*.

Vb. *borrow*, touch for; mortgage, pawn, pledge, pop, hock; get credit, take on loan, take on tick; hire-purchase 792 vb. *purchase*; run into debt 803 vb. *be in debt*; promise to pay, float a loan; invite investment, accept deposits; borrow, or steal; plagiarize, infringe 20 vb. *copy*.

hire, rent, farm, lease, take on lease, take on let, charter.

The word you require is *mortgage*.

Synonyms

A synonym is a word that is similar in meaning to another word, e.g. cold/chilly, big/large, small/tiny.

ACTIVITY 4

Write synonyms for the words listed below in the spaces provided. The first letter for each word is given to help you.

mysterious	s	cold	i ....
profit	g	hard	s ....
harsh	c	youth	a ....
evil	m	girl	c ....
stay	r	nest	h ....
difficult	c	question	q ....
unbelievable	i	inflame	a ....
anger	i	ignite	l ....
coarse	r	liberal	f ....
desire	w	net	r ....
clear	t	change	a ....
proud	h	see	p ....
reveal	d	shout	h ....
potent	p	remedy	c ....
forbid	d	position	s ....
yearly	a	puzzling	b ....
tedium	b	terrible	a ....
fat	o	throw	f ....
disaster	c	try	a ....
wealth	a	hide	c ....
dark	d	jovial	h ....
courtesy	m	journey	t ....

Antonyms

Words of opposite meaning are called antonyms, e.g. good/bad, clean/dirty, big/small.

ACTIVITY 5

Write antonyms for the words below in the spaces provided. The first letters are given to make your task easier.

leave	a	abstain	i ....
wicked	g	betray	p ....
abandon	s	benefit	l ....
hate	l	defeat	v ....
stay	g	defer	e ....
cleverness	s	definite	i ....
shout	w	hardy	w ....
beautiful	u	heavy	l ....
question	a	hide	e ....
excellent	t	high	l ....
blame	p	insipid	t ....
certain	u	inspire	d ....
deep	s	intellectual	u ....
respect	d	painstaking	c ....
clear	c	principal	i ....
scatter	g	probable	u ....
abbreviate	l	reckless	c ....
abhor	e	raw	c ....
ability	i	silly	w ....
stand	s	absent	p ....

Homonyms

Words that sound alike but are spelled differently and have different meanings are called homonyms, e.g. advice/advise, ally/alley, alter/altar.

ACTIVITY 6

Find homonyms for the following words and write them in the spaces provided:

air	....	aisle	....
all	....	aloud	....
arc	....	bail	....
bard	....	beach	....
bear	....	calendar	....
concert	....	eight	....
elude	....	ewe	....
eye	....	sail	....
scene	....	stair	....
sum	....	sun	....

IPA *Yearbook & Diary*

Very often in the course of your work you will need to know the names, addresses and secretaries of various organisations. You may need to know who is chairperson of a certain company. The Institute of Public Administration (IPA) *Yearbook & Diary* will answer all these questions and every business should have at least one copy.

The IPA *Yearbook* is very useful for anyone working in Irish business. This yearbook is a comprehensive directory of Irish life covering the private as well as the public sector. Its information ranges from county councils to embassies; private companies to government departments; religious orders to youth organisations; statistics on agriculture, industry and population to holidays in EU member states. It is issued yearly and is constantly updated. It may be somewhat expensive for a student, but if you go along to some company one of the managers will probably give you an old copy and this will do you for the present. Much of the information would not change from year to year. However, at work you would need an up-to-date copy.

ACTIVITY 7

Using the IPA Yearbook & Diary *find the following information and insert it in the spaces provided:*

1. The population of Munster ....
2. The population of Leinster ....
3. The percentage of the population from 0-14 years

   in Ireland ....

   in Belgium ....

   in Germany ....

   in UK ....
4. Number of hectares in Ireland engaged

   in agriculture ....

   in pasture ....

   in tillage ....
5. The value of dairy products in Ireland ....
6. The value of sugar beet in Ireland ....
7. The number of people in Ireland engaged

   in services ....

   in industry ....

   in agriculture ....
8. Who is the County Manager in Carlow? ....
9. Show how the purchasing power of the pound (punt) has declined since 1922 ....
10. What is the address of the Censorship of Publications Board? ....
    ....
11. What were the average weekly earnings in industry for each of the past ten years? ....
12. How many miles is it from

    Athlone to Carlow? ....

    Clonmel to Wexford? ....

    Dublin to Derry? ....

    Waterford to Tullamore? ....

    Ennis to Ballina? ....

    Sligo to Dublin? ....

    Tralee to Cork? ....

    Letterkenny to Dundalk? ....

13. In Pay-Related Social Insurance describe

    Class A ....

    Class B ....

    Class C ....

14. If it is 10.00 a.m. in Ireland, what time is it

    in Paris? ....

    in Athens? ....

    in Madrid? ....

    in Bonn? ....

    in New York? ....

    in Singapore? ....

    in Seoul? ....

    in Tokyo? ....

    in Calcutta? ....

15. Who is the MP for Fermanagh and South Tyrone? ....

An Post Services

It may be your task at work to deal with the post. You must be aware of the various costs charged by the Post Office and the variety of services available. The Post Office issues a little booklet with all this information.

An Post Services is a small booklet detailing the various services of An Post (the Post Office). It replaces what used to be called *The Post Office Guide*. It is, indeed, only a brief summary of the services available but should be sufficient for the needs of most offices. However, full details of all services available may be obtained by contacting your local head post office, or the GPO Dublin. Full details can also be obtained by consulting *Eolaí an Phoist*, Volumes 1 and 2, available from your local head postmaster, or The Controller, Dublin Postal District, if you reside in Dublin.

ACTIVITY 8

By using An Post Services, *indicate whether the following are true or false by putting T or F in the spaces provided:*

1. An Post will transmit, free of charge, packets containing literature specially adapted for use of the blind ....

2. Mail van drivers and postmen in rural districts will carry light packets or medicines from a doctor to a patient. ....
3. Savings certificates may be purchased in units of £50. ....
4. Index-linked savings bonds are issued in units of £50. ....
5. The cost of a colour TV licence is £70. ....
6. A dog licence costs £5. ....
7. An Post operates a philatelic service. ....
8. An Post is not legally liable for anything transmitted by post. ....
9. An Post recommends the sender putting his/her name and address on envelopes. ....
10. An Post does not operate an express delivery service. ....
11. An Post operates a direct marketing service. ....
12. There is no airmail service to Europe for printed papers or small packets. ....
13. PostPhoto is a service whereby you can have your picture taken by An Post. ....
14. Freepost means An Post will sometimes allow you to post free of charge. ....
15. SAL stands for Surface Account Letters. ....
16. An Post operates a cash-on-delivery service. ....
17. Money orders are available from all head post offices. ....
18. Postal orders cannot be used to send money to foreign countries. ....
19. The cost of sending a postcard is 22p. ....
20. POP stands for Post Office Preferred. ....

| Wordgloss |

Another book which would be useful is *Wordgloss* by Jim O'Donnell, published by the Institute of Public Administration in 1990. It gives definitions and uses of words and terms used in common speech and which speakers rarely define. Such terms are *laissez-faire*, a draconian measure, forensic evidence, *caveat emptor* and caucus.

ACTIVITY 9

Use Wordgloss *to find the meaning of the following:*

balance of payments, carpet-bagger, charisma, primus inter pares, codicil, compos mentis, cornucopia, Delphic, demagogue, fiscal rectitude, lobby, maverick, parochialism, prolific, separation of powers, sinecure, white paper.

Review

1. Use your dictionary to find the origin of the following words: argue, bikini, bilingual, bomb, cholesterol, courier, bank, leaflet, previous, knave.
2. Find all the possible synonyms for the following words: girl, boy, student, business, children, parent, secretary, bold, fastidious, discreet, hinder, summary, compute, teacher.
3. How many public holidays are there each year in the Republic of Ireland and how are their dates determined?
4. What is Faxpost?
5. What is Swiftpost?
6. What service does An Post call SDS?

Pitfalls

In 1976 the *Daily Telegraph* drew attention to a notice in a Dublin laundrette that read: Please remove your clothes as soon as all the lights are out.

Confusing words

persecute	prosecute	observance	observation
expedient	expeditious	flaunt	flout
perspicacity	perspicuity	erotic	esoteric
statue	statute	stature	status

Quiz

'Men used to be children.'

When the Abbey Theatre put on *The Great Hunger* by Tom MacIntyre in Leningrad, this is how the phrase 'Ahah, the men's the boys' was translated for the Russian audience.

What do you think it means?

Spellings

The words most commonly misspelled are highlighted.

facsimile	festivity	fourth
fallacy	fierce	fraud
familiar	fiercely	fraudulent
fascinate	**financial**	**friend**
fatality	forcible	fugitive
fatigue	**foreign**	fulfil
favourable	foretell	**fulfilled**
feasible	forfeit	fulfilling
February	forgotten	**fulfilment**
feign	**forty**	fullness
ferocious	fought	funeral

READING 2:
FINDING INFORMATION – BASIC RESEARCH

Introduction

1. How many people are at work in Ireland at present?
2. How many students sat the Leaving Certificate this year?
3. Who do you contact if you want to have an exhibition stand at this year's National Ploughing Championship?
4. How many people are unemployed in the EU?
5. Where would you get a copy of the Irish Constitution?
6. Who got the highest number of votes in the last election to the European Parliament in this country?
7. How many new cars were bought in January of this year?
8. When did the last inhabitants leave the Blasket Islands?
9. How many people between the ages of 14 and 18 live in Co. Carlow?
10. How many people emigrated from Ireland last year?

'Where can I find . . .?' This question is asked constantly at work. A good employee needs to be able to find information quickly and accurately. Good decisions are based on good information.

Due to modern technology an enormous amount of information is now available. So much information is available that we sometimes tend to be almost overwhelmed with books, newspapers, periodicals and computer printouts.

Some types of information are more difficult to find than others. The information required by questions 1-9 at the beginning of this chapter is easy to find for anyone with the required skill. Question 10 is more difficult.

Information about the future always presents a difficulty. How many new babies will be born between the year 2000 and 2010? Nobody knows with certainty, but estimates must be made. The government must plan school buildings and teacher training for the future.

The birth rate in Ireland rose during the 1970s. It was estimated that it would continue to rise during the 1980s. Based on these estimates the government began producing extra primary school teachers and made a big investment in facilities at Carysfort Training College in Co. Dublin. But the birth rate began to decline in 1981 and within a few years Carysfort was closed.

So information on the future is difficult to predict, but most other information which is useful is usually available if we know where to find it.

Sources of information

The library

Your local library is generally your first source of information. The librarian will explain the types of information available and the classification system.

The Business Information Centre, Ilac Centre, Henry St, Dublin 1, is of particular interest to people being trained for secretarial and business positions. This centre is run by Dublin Corporation and caters for the needs of business and industry. It provides a quick and efficient reference service to organisations and individuals seeking the kind of information that is obtained from dictionaries, encyclopaedias, periodicals, and national and international directories. A wide range of company and financial material is also available. Files of press cuttings, annual reports and a collection of statistical data are available. For a reasonable cost, photocopies of material can be obtained, subject to the usual copyright restrictions.

Because libraries usually have an arrangement to lend books to one another, joining one library gives access to several.

When using information, it is important to acknowledge the source. On no account should a quote be taken from a document without giving the reference. Even if it is not a direct quote but only a summary of material, the original source should be acknowledged.

ACTIVITY 1

1. What is the library classification number given to computers?
2. Who wrote the book The Past is Myself?

3. List five different facilities which your local library offers.
4. List ten periodicals taken by your local library.
5. Find two books in your local library about the Spanish Civil War. Write down the title, author, date of publication and classification of each book.
6. Name two books under the following classifications: 826, 350.8, 651.78, 823.8.
7. What classifications are used for the following subjects: communications, speech, plastics, shorthand?
8. Go to the reference section of your local library and write down the titles of two reference books.
9. What books have you in your local library by the following authors: W. B. Yeats, Peter Drucker, Garret FitzGerald, T. S. Eliot, Charles McCarthy?
10. Write down the titles of two magazines of business interest which your local library stocks. Find out from the librarian how back issues are stored.
11. What classification would the following books receive: The Tools of Social Science, The Concise Oxford Dictionary, Writing the Executive Report, Modern Irish Poetry, English for Business and Secretarial Students?
12. Does your local library stock tapes, cassettes, slides and videos?
13. Who is the editor of The Sunday Tribune?
14. Has your library a book written by Ernest Gowers?
15. Who was Minister for Justice in Ireland in 1973?

Newspapers

Many newspapers store their old numbers on microfilm, and will be glad to allow you to examine them. Newspapers and magazines often have an advantage over books in that they tend to be more up to date.

Reference books

In addition to the books mentioned in Chapter 6 which you should always have available to you, certain other books can be a great help in collecting information. A good starting point is an encyclopaedia such as the *Encyclopaedia Britannica*. This will usually give you a good introduction to the subject and refer you to other books. The following reference books are of particular importance to people working in business:

Books in Print is published annually by Bowker and details all books in print in the USA.

Cumulative Book Index, Whitakers, England. This attempts to include the title and author of all books published in English throughout the world.

Guide to Current British Journals, David Woodworth, 2nd edition, Library Association (2 vols), 1973

Guide to Reference Material, A. J. Walford (ed.), Library Association (3 vols); Vol. 1 Science & Technology (1980), Vol. 2 Social and Historical Sciences (1982), Vol. 3 Generalities, Language, Arts and Literature (1986)

How to Find Out: A Guide to Sources of Information for All, G. Chandler, Pergamon, 1982

Whitaker's Almanack, first published in 1869, presents information about public affairs, government, industry, finance, commerce and the arts in Britain (published annually).

Whitaker's British Books in Print is published annually by Whitaker. This was originally called *British Books in Print*. It provides the only British list of all the books in print and it lists all the different publishing houses at the beginning of the book. It records all the books in print in Britain at the end of March each year and publication takes place in October. It is a four-volume set. It is now also available monthly on microfiche.

A World Bibliography of Bibliographies, T. Besterman, Societas Bibliographica, 1966

Yearbooks and directories

Administration Yearbook & Diary, see Chapter 6

CIF Directory and Diary – directory of the construction industry

Dublin Corporation Yearbook and Diary

Dublin Port and Docks Yearbook

Education Directory and Diary

Environmental Health Officers Association Yearbook

Food Ireland Directory

Irish Computer Directory and Diary

Irish Exporters Yearbook and Diary

Student Yearbook and Directory

Several other yearbooks and directories are published, and the Business Information Centre in the Ilac Centre will have them in stock.

Journals/periodicals

Accounting Ireland (bi-monthly) – journal of the Institute of Chartered Accountants.

Books Ireland (monthly, except January and August) – provides news on books and libraries.

Business & Finance (weekly) – general business journal.

Catering and Licensing Review (monthly).

Checkout Magazine (fortnightly) – information on food trade in Ireland.

CIS Report – Construction Information Service (weekly) – provides information on commercial, industrial, foreign investment and public building projects.

Engineers Journal (monthly) – official journal of the Institution of Engineers of Ireland.

Industrial Relations News Report (weekly) – provides coverage of industrial relations issues.

Inside Business (monthly) – magazine of Chambers of Commerce of Ireland.

Ireland of the Welcomes (bi-monthly) – produced by Bord Fáilte.

Iris Oifigiúil (twice-weekly) – gives details of Acts passed and official orders being enforced.

Irish Banking Review (quarterly) – review of economic trends.

Irish Building Services News (10 issues a year).

Irish Hardware Magazine (monthly) – all information on hardware trade.

Irish Marketing Journal (monthly) – general marketing magazine.

Irish Travel Trade News (monthly) – information on travel.

Irish Women (quarterly) – produced by the Irish Countrywomen's Association.

An Leabharlann, The Irish Library – journal of the library associations in Ireland and Northern Ireland.

Management (monthly) – general information on management.

Motoring Life (monthly) – news on the motor industry.

Retail News (monthly) – official magazine of RGDATA.

Statistical Bulletin (quarterly) – contains information collected by the Central Statistics Office.

Technology Ireland (10 issues a year) – covers all matters technical.

Trade Statistics (monthly) – up-to-date statistics on trade.

Organisations

Organisations such as government departments, local authorities, semi-state bodies, companies, trade and other professional organisations are usually very helpful in providing information. You should contact them in good time by writing to the information officer or other relevant person.

Government departments

Government departments are valuable sources of information. Address your query to the minister or to the secretary of the appropriate department. If information is urgently required, your local TD may be able to speed up the matter.

Embassies

There are seventy embassies accredited to Ireland. In addition, twenty-eight countries are represented by honorary consulates in various parts of Ireland. Some countries, e.g. France, Italy, Spain and Germany, maintain permanent cultural institutes in Dublin. All of these places are good sources of information.

European Union

The European Union maintains offices in each of its member states and these are a valuable source of information. The European Commission has an office in Dublin as does the European Parliament. Direct your enquiries to the head of information.

Local administration

Sources of information under this heading are:

- Local authorities – urban councils, county councils, corporations, town commissioners.

- Regional authorities – there are eight of these and they began operations in 1994.

- Regional tourism organisations – there are six of these and they were established by Bord Fáilte.

- Health boards – there are eight such boards.

- Vocational education committees – there are thirty-eight such committees and they provide and manage community colleges and vocational schools.

- County enterprise boards – they foster economic development in the various counties.
- Central and regional fisheries boards – there are seven regional fisheries boards.
- Harbour authorities – these are responsible for the operation and maintenance of their harbours.

State-sponsored bodies

State-sponsored bodies can be divided into five categories according to the nature of their work:

(a) commercial, e.g. ESB

(b) developmental, e.g. Bord Fáilte

(c) health, e.g. Comhairle na n-Ospidéal

(d) cultural, e.g. RTÉ

(e) regulatory/advisory, e.g. National Economic and Social Council.

Financial institutions

Financial institutions in Ireland can be divided into the following:

(a) Central Bank

(b) Associated Banks, e.g. AIB, Bank of Ireland

(c) non-Associated banks, e.g. Ansbacher Bankers Ltd

(d) hire purchase finance institutions, e.g. Smurfit Finance Ltd

(e) building societies, e.g. EBS Building Society

(f) insurance companies, e.g. Standard Life

(g) venture capital institutions, e.g. ACT Venture Capital Ltd

(h) credit card companies, e.g. Diners Club International

(i) stockbrokers, e.g. Butler & Briscoe

(j) European Union financial institutions, e.g. European Investment Bank

(k) International Financial Services Centre, e.g. Gandon Securities Ltd.

Major companies and co-operatives

Most companies, both public and private, will be willing to help you with research. Address your letter to the personnel officer or the public relations officer.

The top five hundred companies are listed in *Business & Finance* each year. There are more than eighty thousand companies in operation according to the Companies Office in Dublin Castle. Ninety-nine per cent of them are private companies with fewer than fifty shareholders.

Trade, professional and other organisations

The following are just some of the organisations which would provide business-related information:

- Chambers of commerce: most towns have a chamber of commerce which provides useful local business information.
- Trade unions: these are always a good source of information on employees' attitudes, levels of employment, wages and working conditions. For information of a broader nature contact the Irish Congress of Trade Unions.
- Muintir na Tíre: will supply information on rural areas.
- Irish Business and Employers Confederation (IBEC): represents industry in all matters.
- Institute of Public Administration: provides training, education and research as well as publishing books and periodicals dealing with Irish government.
- Irish Management Institute: provides a comprehensive programme of management development and training. It holds conferences, seminars and publishes books. It is a very useful source of information on Irish business.
- Credit unions: an excellent source of information on people's spending habits.
- Irish Farmers Association: will supply information on agriculture.
- Irish Creamery Milk Suppliers Association: will also supply information on agriculture.
- Irish Countrywomen's Association: particularly valuable for local information. Records have been well preserved by this organisation and would be very useful in researching women's attitudes during various times in this century.
- Irish Computer Society: will supply information on all areas in computers.

Social, cultural and political organisations

May be divided into the following:

- Health organisations, e.g. Asthma Society, Coeliac Society.

- Irish language associations, e.g. Comhaltas Ceoltóirí Éireann, Cumann na bhFiann.
- Political parties, e.g. Fianna Fáil, Fine Gael, Labour, Workers Party, Democratic Left, Progressive Democrats, Green Party.
- Women's interest groups, e.g. Cherish, Soroptimists, Women in Technology and Science (WITS).
- Youth organisations, e.g. National Federation of Youth Clubs, Foróige.
- Other social, cultural and political interest groups, e.g. ACRA (Central Body for Residents Associations), Consumer Association of Ireland, GAA, IRFU, FAI, Royal Dublin Society (RDS), Royal Irish Academy.

Interviews

When the object of research is to gauge attitudes or to collect opinions, then interviewing knowledgeable and interested persons is an appropriate procedure. Information gathered in this way, however, must be cautiously sifted.

It should always be remembered that people have a tendency to tell an interviewer what they think the interviewer wants to hear. However, interviews have the following advantages over questionnaires:

(a) People often enjoy being interviewed, while filling in a questionnaire is considered a chore.

(b) If a response needs to be clarified, it can be done immediately.

(c) A person's behaviour or attitude can be observed during an interview, and this can often convey useful information.

However, in an interview a person needs to be aware of factors which may distort the information:

(a) the tendency to find what one wishes to find;

(b) intrusion of interviewer who may interpret the information given on the basis of personal experience;

(c) tendency of interviewed person to modify her ideas and behaviour to meet the known expectations of the interviewer.

This type of interview demands careful planning. The following steps should be taken:

(a) write to person concerned requesting interview;

(b) give full details of purpose, format and approximate duration of interview;

(c) give outline of areas to be covered;

(d) request permission to tape interview if necessary.

When conducting an interview you must have some means of recording responses if you are not using a tape recorder. The usual method is to have a form where the responses can be recorded easily.

Fig. 1 – Sample interview form

Name of Interviewee: _____ Position: _____

Place of Interview: _____ Date: _____

Time Begun: _____ Ended: _____

Number of People Employed: _____ Men _____Women   Total: _____

Comments:_____
_____
_____

Number of Employees Who Left in 199?: ___ Men _____ Women Total: _____

Comments:_____
_____
_____

Reasons for Leaving: _____ Retirement _____ Going to Other Jobs

_____ Not Happy _____ Dismissed _____ Other

Comments:_____
_____
_____

Reasons for Dismissal: _____ Sub-standard Work _____ Poor Attendance

_____ Dispute _____ Other

Comments:_____
_____
_____

Questionnaires

Where information of a statistical nature is required, a questionnaire will be useful. The advantages of using a questionnaire for gathering information are:

(a) capable of reaching a large audience

(b) same questions are asked of each person

(c) questions asked in same order

(d) answers are easy to tabulate.

The disadvantages are:

(a) person may misunderstand question

(b) person may not return questionnaire at all

(c) person may return uncompleted questionnaire.

When drafting a questionnaire the following rules should be observed:

(a) Identify the purpose of the questionnaire in very specific terms. What precisely are you trying to discover?

(b) It should be easy to understand. Draw up a sample questionnaire first and pre-test it on a small number of people.

(c) Questions should be objective. Do not begin a question with 'Do you agree that . . .' This is called a leading question; it suggests that you should agree. Write instead 'With which of the following do you agree . . .'

(d) Questions should be capable of being answered with a minimum of effort. Multiple choice, fill-ins and 'Yes/No' options are attractively simple to answer. You should not, of course, give a biased list from which to choose.

(e) Present your questions in logical order.

(f) Number each question.

(g) Send out each questionnaire with a covering letter outlining the purpose of the survey, emphasising the importance of completing and returning it promptly.

Fig. 2 – Sample questionnaire

CAREERS SURVEY OF AWARD RECIPIENTS 199?

REGIONAL TECHNICAL COLLEGE
KILKENNY ROAD
CARLOW
TEL: 0503-31324

Careers Survey

Dear Graduate,

We are conducting a survey of our former students. We hope you will complete the enclosed questionnaire, as we expect that the result will be of great benefit to us in evaluating and planning our Courses. The results will also be of great interest to you and we plan to send you a resumé of our major findings. This will enable you to compare your career with those with whom you studied here.

We are contacting all students who completed the Course for which they registered and we hope that the response rate will be very high. If you have any queries about the survey, you may contact us at the College and we will be delighted to help you.

A stamped addressed envelope is enclosed and we would urge you to complete the questionnaire today and return it to us immediately.

Many thanks for your help.

Yours sincerely,

Juliann Coogan, Brenda Murphy, Michelle McGroarty

SECTION 1: GENERAL INFORMATION – TO BE COMPLETED BY ALL RESPONDENTS

OFFICE USE ONLY

1. Surname
2. First Name
3. Permanent Home Address
   - Line 1
   - Line 2
   - Line 3
   - Line 4

Code No.

4. Location Code
5. Age in Years
6. Sex (Enter Code in Box)
   - Female = 1
   - Male = 2

7. Award obtained in 199? ....   Please place relevant Code in Box

   - 1 = One Year Certificate
   - 2 = National Certificate
   - 3 = National Diploma
   - 4 = College Diploma
   - 5 = Marketing Institute of Ireland
   - 6 = Royal Society of Arts
   - 7 = London Chamber of Commerce
   - 8 = ACCA
   - 9 = Degree

   Please write the exact title of your Award

   ....
   ....

8. Present Situation

Please read the categories listed below and then place relevant Code in Box. ☐

1 = Full-time employment, i.e. you have already commenced or are due to commence full-time employment either in a temporary or permanent capacity.

2 = Part-time employment, i.e. you are working less than normal hours.

3 = Work experience scheme, i.e. you are engaged on a work experience scheme organised by FÁS or any other statutory body.

4 = Further studies, i.e. you are primarily engaged in further studies.

5 = Seeking employment, i.e. you are unemployed, and are not engaged in any form of work experience scheme, or further studies, and you are actively seeking employment.

6 = Other, i.e. you are not engaged in or seeking employment for reasons such as ill health, travel, domestic circumstances, etc.

SECTION 2: TO BE COMPLETED BY RESPONDENTS WHO ARE OR WHO HAVE BEEN IN EMPLOYMENT SINCE RECEIVING AWARD

1. Please write the exact title of your job ....

   Please specify the primary duties
   and responsibilities of this position ....

2. Was the qualification you obtained a requirement for appointment to your present position?

   Please enter relevant Code in Box

   1 = Yes   2 = No   ☐

3. Was the course you took relevant to the job which you are now doing?

   Please enter relevant Code in Box

   1 = Very relevant   2 = Relevant   3 = Unsure
   4 = Largely irrelevant   5 = Irrelevant   ☐

4. To be completed only by those in full-time employment.

   Present Salary (Per Annum)   Please enter relevant Code in Box   ☐
   1 = Up to £4,999   2 = £5,000 – £5,999   3 = £6,000 – £6,999
   4 = £7,000 – £7,999   5 = £8,000 – £8,999   6 = £9,000 – £9,999
   7 = £10,000 – £10,999   8 = £11,000 – £11,999   9 = £12,000 +

5. Name of company or person with whom you are employed. If self-employed state 'self-employed'.

Address of Employer

(Office Use)

SECTION 3: ANY OTHER COMMENTS?

....
....
....
....

Interpreting information

Interpreting information is a delicately balanced affair. Nobody is totally free from bias; acknowledgment of this fact is a necessary preliminary to objective interpretation. A useful corrective to personal bias is to ask a friend with different political, economic and ideological views to interpret the facts and then to compare the interpretations.

A good example of differences in interpretation appears in a review titled 'How Much Intolerance Exists in the Republic?' in *The Irish Times* of 6 August 1977. In the article, Dr Conor Cruise O'Brien is writing a review of *Prejudice and Tolerance in Ireland* by Fr Michael McGreil. The response to questions on the Irish language are tabulated as follows:

Desired situation

(1) Principal language of use (as English is now)	8%
(2) Bilingualism with Irish as the principal language	10%
(3) Bilingualism with English as principal language	33%
(4) Preservation of spoken Irish only in Gaeltacht and/or preserved for its cultural value as in music and art	34%
(5) Irish language should be discarded and forgotten	15%

Fr McGreil brackets the first three responses and comments: 'Situations Nos. 1-3 imply a revival of the Irish language (the choice of

51%) in order that it become a spoken language throughout the country.' But Dr O'Brien comments that 'the 33% who make up the ingeniously amassed 51% said nothing about the "revival of Irish"'. Bilingualism, Dr O'Brien points out, does not necessarily mean revival of Irish; it may mean a few Irish phrases on certain occasions.

The second example appears in response to the question 'Would you say that the religious beliefs in which you were brought up influenced your growth or development as a person?' The responses are tabulated as follows:

Perceived influence of religious beliefs in which respondent was reared:

Degree of Influence	Actual %	Cumulative %
(1) Essential help	55.3	
(2) Important but not essential	13.7	81.1 (positive)
(3) Helped somewhat	12.1	
(4) Neither help nor hindrance	15.2	15.2 (neutral)
(5) Hindered somewhat	2.6	
(6) Serious hindrance	0.7	3.7 (negative)
(7) Grave hindrance	0.4	

Fr McGreil says 'the perception of religious beliefs as being essential or important aids to personal development by over 80% of the sample speaks for itself'. But Dr O'Brien does not agree with that interpretation. He says an equally legitimate interpretation is the following:

religion essential 55.3%

religion not essential 44.7%

These differences in interpretation in dealing with the same figures show how two people with different outlooks can view figures differently.

ACTIVITY 2

1. How would you find out how many chambers of commerce there are in Ireland?
2. Where would you discover how many publishers there are in this country?
3. What periodical would be useful if you were thinking of changing your car?
4. Which government department would you contact to find out when will new Gardaí be recruited?
5. You wish to complain about pollution of your local river. To whom would you complain?

6. Give the name and address of the organisation to which you would write to find out how many workers in Ireland are members of trade unions.

7. Find out how many books mentioned in this chapter are in your local library.

8. Draw up a form for recording an interview you are going to have with the secretary of your local chamber of commerce. You are going to ask about membership, fees, amount of participation, attendance at meetings and projects being undertaken at the moment.

9. You are going to do a report on how students choose their careers. Explain the method of procedure you would use.

10. You are doing a report on emigration. You are confining it to the final-year class in your own college. Your main emphasis is to find out the reasons for emigration and whether or not the potential emigrants intend to return to Ireland again. Draw up the questionnaire you would use.

11. A public library produced the following statistics at the end of the year:

Books borrowed by the public	50,000	100.0%
Books borrowed by members aged 5-13	12,500	25.0%
Books borrowed by members aged 14-18	15,000	30.0%
Books borrowed by members aged 19-35	6,250	12.5%
Books borrowed by members aged 36-50	4,000	8.0%
Books borrowed by members aged 51-65	7,250	14.5%
Books borrowed by members aged 66+	5,000	10.0%

    Write an interpretation of the figures.

12. The same library also produced the following figures. Of the total number of books borrowed:

    15% were children's books

    45% were fiction

    20% were history

    10% were literature (poems, plays, etc.)

    5% were politics

    5% were others.

    Write an interpretation of these figures.

Review

1. Find out if your local newspaper has back copies of each of its issues. Is there an index to help you find topics quickly?
2. What facilities and services has your local library for children?
3. What help can your local library give you if you want to study German?
4. Your college is thinking of investing in a new general encyclopaedia. You are asked to draw up a report on the type of encyclopaedias available and make a firm recommendation as to which one should be purchased.
5. How many yearbooks and directories does your local library stock?
6. What is the difference between the Associated Banks and non-Associated banks?
7. What are some of the advantages of carrying out interviews rather than using questionnaires when doing a survey?
8. What is a leading question?
9. Why do people interpret information differently?
10. What measure can you take to guard against prejudice and bias when interpreting information?

Pitfalls

quite

Quite means completely, entirely, absolutely. *Quite* is an adverb. For example, 'He is *quite* a hero.' You should not write '*Quite* a number of people were present.' The word *quite* is not an adverb in that sentence. You must say 'A large number of people . . .' or 'A great many people . . .'

It is true that *quite* is sometimes used colloquially to mean 'to a large extent'.

Confusing words

requisite	requisition	superficial	superfluous
resume	resumé	temperate	temporary
social	sociable	ultimate	ultimatum

spacious   specious   unsatisfied   dissatisfied
stimulant   stimulus   memoir   memorandum

Quiz

There are two words in English that contain the five vowels (aeiou) once in their alphabetical order. What are they?

Spellings

The words most commonly misspelled are highlighted.

gaiety	gigantic	grieve
gaily	glacier	grievous
garage	glossary	grotesque
gauge	gorgeous	grudge
generosity	gossiping	guarantee
generous	govern	**guard**
genius	**government**	**guardian**
genteel	governor	guess
genuine	gracious	guest
geography	**grammar**	guidance
gesture	grandeur	guide
ghastly	gratitude	gymnastics
ghost	grief	
giant	**grievance**	

READING 3:
READING CRITICALLY

Summary

'The good die happily; the bad unhappily.
That is the story of Western Literature.'
This is Oscar Wilde's summary of Western literature.

An old king who was at death's door asked to be told the history of man. His minister for education told him:

'They were born, they lived and they died.'

A summary requires you to state the main message in a passage or speech in fewer words than the original. It means that you must understand the passage, be able to extract the main points and reproduce these in your own words.

It is an essential skill for business and secretarial students. The practical value of the summary is that it saves time and labour for someone else. A good summary must be accurate, concise and presented in readable form.

In business, summarising is a practical skill. You may have to summarise correspondence, minutes of meetings, reports, fax messages, telephone messages and statistics.

If instructions for the summary in examination questions state not more than 110 words, then marks will be deducted for exceeding that number. On the other hand, if it is to be approximately 110 words, it is permissible to write a summary between 100 and 120 words.

Avoid faulty proportioning, i.e. two-thirds of your summary dealing with one-third of the original passage. Do not use direct questions, figurative language or illustrations which appear in the original if you can avoid it. If the original is in direct speech, the summary will have to be in reported speech.

Converting direct speech into reported speech

(a) Omit quotation marks. For example:

Direct – Oscar Wilde said 'To love oneself is the beginning of a lifelong romance.'

Indirect – Oscar Wilde said that to love oneself was the beginning of a lifelong romance.

(b) Verb tense changes. For example:

Direct – He said 'I will be late.'

Indirect – He said that he would be late.

Direct	Indirect
'I am interested.'	He said he was interested.
'I will go.'	He said he would go.
'I can do it.'	He said he could do it.

(c) Changes in pronouns. The first person (I/we) usually changes to the third person. For example:

Direct – The judge said to the accused, 'I cannot hear you.'

Indirect – The judge said to the accused that he could not hear him.

(d) Changes in time and place. Events and places become more distant in indirect speech. For example:

Direct – He said 'I was here yesterday.'

Indirect – He said that he had been there the previous day.

Direct	Indirect
here	there
this place	that place
now	then
these	those
tomorrow	the next day
last year	the year before

(e) Commands and questions. Commands and questions must be rephrased. For example:

Direct – The teacher said 'Stop talking.'

Indirect – The teacher told them to stop talking.

Direct – 'Why are you crying?' the woman asked the little girl.

Indirect – The woman asked the little girl why she was crying.
(f) All indirect speech is introduced by the word *that*. For example:
Direct – He said, 'I will go.'
Indirect – He said that he would go.

Fig. 1 – How to write a summary

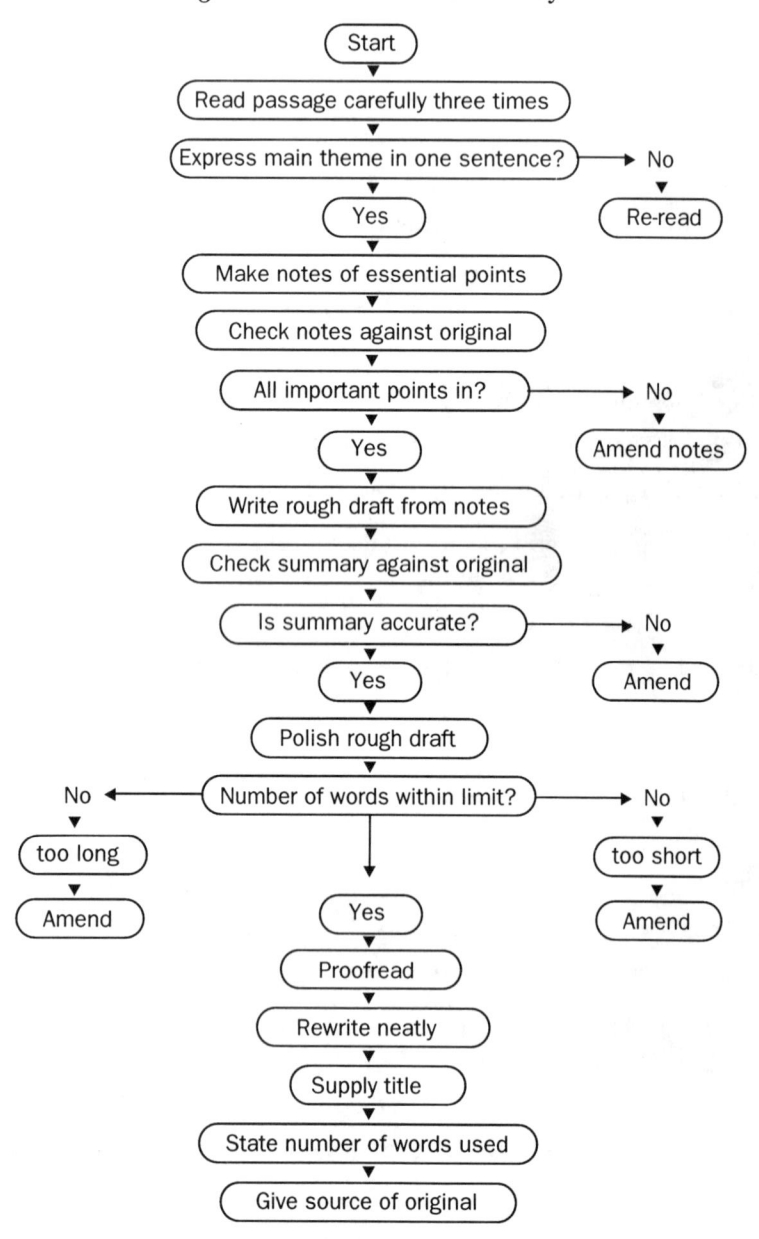

```
                    Start
                      ▼
        Read passage carefully three times
                      ▼
       Express main theme in one sentence? ──▶ No
                      ▼                        ▼
                     Yes                    Re-read
                      ▼
          Make notes of essential points
                      ▼
            Check notes against original
                      ▼
            All important points in? ──▶ No
                      ▼                   ▼
                     Yes             Amend notes
                      ▼
            Write rough draft from notes
                      ▼
          Check summary against original
                      ▼
               Is summary accurate? ──▶ No
                      ▼                  ▼
                     Yes               Amend
                      ▼
               Polish rough draft
                      ▼
 No ◀── Number of words within limit? ──▶ No
  ▼                   ▼                   ▼
too long             Yes              too short
  ▼                   ▼                   ▼
Amend            Proofread              Amend
                      ▼
               Rewrite neatly
                      ▼
                Supply title
                      ▼
          State number of words used
                      ▼
            Give source of original
```

Sample summary

Write a summary of the following passage in 125 words:

In hitting out at the current income tax regulations recently, the Congress of Trade Unions have identified the most *potent* creator of inequality and bad social feeling that is within the Government's power to control. Income tax has progressively spread its *tentacles* over the last decade as prosperity and inflation have brought more people into taxable brackets; but it is an unfair system that totally omits some categories of citizens, leaves others largely free to decide what they will declare, and includes others – the salary earners – up to the hilt, with virtually no means of reducing the amount they pay to the State.

There is no doubt that PAYE was an ingenious solution to a problem that existed twenty years ago when it was introduced. Many young people without ties took the emigrant boat when the tax bill for the previous year came in, and for those who were not so mobile, the annual assessment came as a cold shock to the domestic budget. PAYE has helped the State's cash flow, too, and provides a direct and immediate link between income increases and higher tax liability that makes sense in times of inflation.

But, as the ICTU have argued in their submission on the Government's Green Paper on full employment, it has created a deep sense of grievance – *among workers who are locked into the system* – towards other sections of the community like the many whose incomes are not subjected to anything like as close or continuing a scrutiny as the luckless PAYE victim. It means heavier taxes for those who pay, which in turn increases the sense of injustice that leads to evasion where possible. Many workers on PAYE who are able to do '*nixers*' ask for payment in such a way that tax is not paid, and, in doing so, they feel as justified as the professional man who is paid in cash and declares only the visible part of his income.

(*The Irish Times*)

Theme

The government should change the current PAYE system of taxation which creates inequality and bad feeling among people.

Notes on essential points

1. ICTU has pointed out the greatest creator of inequality – income tax.
2. It is an unfair system.

3. PAYE was a good solution to a problem which existed twenty years ago.
4. PAYE has helped the state's cash flow.
5. Income tax has created a sense of grievance among PAYE workers because others are not subject to the same scrutiny.
6. It means heavier taxes for those who pay.
7. PAYE workers doing nixers feel justified in not paying tax on them.

Rough draft

As the Congress of Trade Unions has pointed out, the most potent creator of inequality and bad social feeling which the government can control is the income tax regulations. The income tax system is unfair because some people are free to decide how much income they will declare, while the salary earner is included up to the hilt. It was a clever solution to a problem which existed twenty years ago, when young people with no ties emigrated when the tax bill arrived. Though PAYE increases the state's cash flow, it has created a sense of grievance because others are not subject to the same close scrutiny as PAYE people. This means heavier taxes for those who pay, it increases their sense of injustice and encourages tax evasion. Those on PAYE who can do nixers seek payment in such a way that tax is not paid and feel justified in doing this. (151 words)

Final draft

Title: Change the PAYE System

As the Congress of Trade Unions has pointed out, the most potent creator of inequality under the government's control is the income tax regulations. It is an unfair system though it was a clever solution to a problem which existed twenty years ago, when young people with no ties emigrated when the tax bill arrived. Though PAYE increases the state's cash flow, it has created a sense of grievance because others are not subject to the same close scrutiny as PAYE people. This encourages tax evasion. Those on PAYE who can do nixers seek payment in such a way that it is not subject to tax and feel as justified in doing this as the professional man who keeps part of his income secret. (125 words)

ACTIVITY I

1. Here are a series of comments about emigration. Read them carefully and sum up the point of view of each in a short sentence:

    (a) Emigration has always been a fact of life in Ireland: this country was never able to support its population. Even back in the centuries after Christ there is evidence of people leaving the country. It is a small place. People tend to leave small places.

(b) This is the greatest problem facing us today. The country is being deprived of its young blood. Who is to give stimulation and come up with new ideas if the young leave? Those left here will be happy with the status quo. We need the young to make us think anew.

(c) Emigration is a good thing. Of course people should leave their own small place. There's a big world out there and the young want to see and experience it. Those who emigrate are all the better for it. Everyone should emigrate at least for a while.

(d) Every government has failed the people of this country. More people left the country than came into it in every decade since the foundation of the state except in the 1970s. Our literature (songs, stories, plays) is crowded with sad scenes of departing loved ones. From the American wakes to the modern equivalent in Dún Laoghaire and Rosslare, our people, whose government has failed them, have left our shores.

2. Make a suitable summary of the article below in no more than 180 words.

The Health and Safety at Work Act 1974

The philosophy of the Health and Safety at Work Act, which was passed in 1974 and came into effect in 1975, was that workers should take an active part in the efforts to maintain health and safety at their workplace. The Act aimed to involve everyone, management and employees, and to make all conscious of the importance of safety awareness and of effective care for safety and health. Under the Act, duties were placed upon a wide range of people, including: employers, directors, managers, secretaries and similar officers, employees, and 'other persons' including members of the public.

The employer owes duties to his own employees and it is important for the employee to be aware of the duties of the employer simply because the 'duties' of the employer form the 'rights' of the employee.

The health and safety information which the employer is required to provide for employees concerns possible hazards or any precautions necessary in connection with their work. It might include the issue of a copy of company or departmental safety rules and regulations, the procedures to be followed in the event of a fire or accident, and the method by which employees may raise with management any questions relating to their health and safety. The instruction and training in health and safety matters which the employer has a duty to provide may be given in the company or 'off-the-job' in some other place such as a college of further education. As far as 'supervision' is concerned, this applies not only to junior staff but to all employees whatever their position. Supervision may, for example, be necessary when an employee is learning to operate a new machine or item of office equipment.

The employer has other important duties to his employees. He must issue to employees a written statement of general policy with respect to the health and safety at work of his employees, together with the organisation and arrangements for carrying out the policy.

An employee must take reasonable care for his own health and safety, and that of other persons who may be affected by what he does or what he omits to do at work. Someone who lit a cigarette while filling a container with flammable liquid would not be taking reasonable care either for his own safety or that of other persons. Such a thoughtless act may sound unlikely to occur, but there was an actual incident concerning two girls in an office who were killed within seconds when a one-gallon can of flammable liquid was accidentally knocked over and the vapour ignited by an open-bar radiant electric heater. As another example, an office worker who took receipt of a new guillotine and failed to assemble and fit the guard supplied by the manufacturer would be omitting to do something which would affect the safety of others at work.

Every employee has a legal duty to co-operate with his employer in matters of health and safety and therefore failure to follow procedures such as fire drills, to attend safety courses provided, or to wear protective clothing supplied by the employer are examples of failure to co-operate.

Failure to fulfil the duties outlined in the Health and Safety at Work Act is a criminal offence, and it is not only the employer who may be prosecuted and punished – the employee is also liable to the same penalties.

So far, about 40 directors of companies have been found guilty of criminal offences under the Health and Safety legislation and attention has been drawn to businessmen's ignorance on this aspect of the law. Many of those prosecuted were unaware of precisely what their responsibilities under the law involved. It is probably true to say that many employees are also unaware of their duties and responsibilities.

In the report of the Robens Committee, the major conclusion was that accidents are caused by apathy. The way to combat this and provide more effective safety awareness is, they concluded: 'by an accumulation of influences and pressures operating at many levels – from board room to shop floor – through education and training, better information and advice, through practical co-operative organisation and action; also, where necessary, with legal sanctions'.

Everyone with a responsibility (legal or moral) to pass on information to personnel in a workplace must review, tighten up and improve the ways in which he or she attempts to achieve this.

Managements must realise they have a responsibility not only to know about the 1974 Act and safety policy themselves but to play a constructive part in passing on their knowledge.

Companies must make safety and health one of their major concerns, must admit to failings of their organisation in terms of information flow, take an objective view of these failings and set about improving them.
(London Chamber of Commerce Private Secretary's Certificate)

3. Give the passage below a title and summarise excluding the first and last paragraphs in about 110 words.

In addition to the layout and capital resources employed by the insurance industry, its operations affect the economy in three ways. First, insurance is the most important method of handling many of the pure risks encountered by individuals and firms. The extent to which insurers are prepared to accept the transfer of risks, and the rates of premiums charged, thus have important effects on the allocation of resources. Secondly, both life and general business involve the accumulation of substantial funds which are then available for long-term investment in industry. Lastly, the industry is the largest net contributor of invisible earnings to Britain's balance of payments.

Life is uncertain and every individual and firm is exposed to a wide variety of risks which may give rise to losses ranging from the insignificant to the catastrophic. The rational approach is to employ methods of handling such risks that will reconcile the twin objectives of obtaining protection against financially embarrassing losses and of minimising the total long-term cost.

If, as is usually the case, it is not possible to avoid a risk entirely, steps can often be taken by means of various prevention measures to reduce either the probability of loss or the size of the loss should it occur. Then any remaining risk can be either borne by the individual (or firm) or transferred elsewhere. Insurance provides for the latter. In return for an agreed premium, the insurer undertakes to meet all or part of the financial losses resulting from the occurrence of the insured event. Insurance, it is thus said, substitutes certainty for uncertainty.

Commercial insurance is able to fulfil this function by pooling the premiums of a large number of policy holders. Provided the insurer is able to underwrite a sufficiently large number of fairly homogeneous risks, and that past results provide a valid guide to the future, the fund will be adequate to meet the claims of those who suffer loss, and the underwriter will be able to operate with a low degree of risk. Thus, the policy holder will have gained by eliminating his risk and – by combining a large number of units – the insurer will have reduced the general risk in society.

Therefore, by means of insurance, firms are able to operate with a greater degree of security and without the need to set aside scarce funds to meet unexpected losses. Likewise, the dislocation and waste of resources which would result from bankruptcy of firms caused by serious losses is reduced, and small firms are placed at less disadvantage in the handling of risks, compared with their larger competitors.

>Of equal importance is the reaction of firms to risk. In the absence of insurance some firms might not be prepared to undertake certain forms of production or would be forced to reduce the scale of their activities.
>
>It is impossible to quantify the total value of such benefits or, indeed, to imagine a modern economy without insurance. The only generalisation possible is that the social benefits arising from insurance extend well beyond total private benefits.
>
>(London Chamber of Commerce Private Secretarial Certificate)

4. Summarise the following passage in about 200 words. It was written by Neil Holman in a 1986 edition of the journal Management.

>The paradox of the Irish economy is that we need to both cut wasteful and unproductive expenditure, public spending and yet increase investment in areas where expertise is already proven and where real growth prospects can be identified.
>
>Additional government spending cannot cure the disease of unemployment. The rise in government borrowing and in personal taxation over the past 13 years have mirrored the rise in unemployment from 53,000 in 1973 to 240,000 in 1986. Personal spending power has been reduced in order to finance excessive public expenditure. Ironically and tragically this reduction has been the greatest single contributor to job losses in recent times. Much of government expenditure damages rather than protects those still in work. But now there is developing an increasing public awareness that high public expenditure does us limited good and that expenditure will have to be drastically curtailed if the economy is to recover.
>
>Our political masters approach this problem from a different perspective. They are, after all, the authors of the 'high spending, high borrowing, high taxation' script that we are now acting out: promise increased spending to get elected, borrow as much as you can get away with to finance that spending and then (reluctantly) raise taxes to finance the balance. But we have now nearly reached our national overdraft limit and those taxpayers left in work have made it clear that they will accept no further increases. So from government's point of view, political and economic pressures dictate that it is no longer expedient to borrow and that the only remaining alternative is a programme of cuts in expenditure.
>
>But cut what? Debt service – impossible! Public sector pay – hardly. Although the growth in numbers in the public service has been contained, the pay bill has not, nor is it likely to be in the short term. The bill for social welfare benefits will only start to reduce when unemployment starts to fall which means that first of all taxes have to be cut. In other areas of social spending, such as health, economies may well be possible through increased efficiency – but to be realistic, worthwhile economies cannot be achieved overnight.

Most early cuts will have to be achieved in that first billion of public spending from which state agencies and state-sponsored bodies derive their funding. There are obviously areas from which worthwhile cuts can be achieved with minimal pain to the economy. But most cuts, essential though they are, can be expected to cause some degree of discomfort, and again ironically and I suppose, tragically, the discomfort will occur in the areas most needing support – the areas, in other words, which have no strong lobby but in which many of our future strategies for economic success can be identified – areas where at present there are no votes. There are no votes in science and technology, none in research and development. But these are the very areas that need a voice equal to that of Austin Deasy's trinity of powerful lobbies: the Church, the farmers and the GAA.

There are no votes in science and technology but there are jobs. In order to maintain and expand our industrial base we need to manufacture and export technology-based products developed here in Ireland. There are too few Irish companies able to do this. The profile of the Irish industrial sector is unbalanced. We rely heavily on low-tech, home-owned industries depending on the home market and high-tech, foreign-owned industries that typically concentrate their Irish operations on assembly type operations and put little emphasis on produce development and marketing. There is little scope for employment expansion in the nation's bakeries or soft drink bottling plants. Although our overseas-owned industries are at present substantial contributors to the economy, they are potentially vulnerable for a number of well chronicled reasons, not least of which is changes in tax regulations in their home countries. Current US tax proposals bear witness to this.

Investment in R & D is investment in the future. Because it does not tend to produce quick results it receives less than its fair share of state resources (and less than its sensible allocation of private sector investment). We need investment in R & D. We need to know where our science and technology expertise can best be deployed. We need to convert our human and technological resources into jobs, not dole queues. It is time the script was rewritten.
(National Certificate in Secretarial Studies Year 1, Carlow RTC)

Comprehension

A summary tests your ability to gain an overall understanding of a passage while comprehension questions give you the opportunity to show a deeper understanding of the passage. People working in secretarial and business positions constantly have information before them which must be understood and assessed quickly. Practice in comprehension will develop this skill.

Tips for comprehension
- Read the passage through three times.
- Read the questions on the passage carefully.
- Refer each question back to the passage as you frame your answers.
- Write the answers accurately and concisely.
- Check answers.

Types of comprehension questions
Comprehension questions may:

(1) test your understanding of particular words and phrases;

(2) test your understanding of facts in the passage;

(3) seek explanation in detail of an important point in the passage;

(4) ask you to read between the lines to understand the tone;

(5) allow you to comment on the style in which it is written;

(6) allow you to give your own opinion on some major element in the passage.

Sample comprehension questions
We will use for comprehension the passage from *The Irish Times* which we used for our sample summary (see page 95).

- Sample comprehension question (1)

The first comprehension question on the passage asks you to explain the words in italics:

(a) *potent* – powerful

(b) *tentacles* – talons or claws

(c) *workers who are locked into the system* – employees who are caught in the tax net and have no means of escape

(d) *nixers* – odd jobs apart from one's main occupation carried out sometimes with some secrecy.

- Sample comprehension question (2)

The next type of question tests your understanding of facts in the passage:

What is PAYE?

PAYE stands for 'Pay As You Earn'. It is a system whereby the amount of income tax to be paid by an individual is deducted from his wage or salary in weekly or monthly contributions.

What is a Government Green Paper?

It is a document produced by the government to begin and/or encourage discussion on a particular topic. It generally sets out the various points of view on an issue.

- Sample comprehension question (3)

This next type of question asks for explanation in detail of some important point:

What, according to the writer, are the advantages and disadvantages of PAYE?

Advantages

It helps the state's cash flow.

It ensures tax is paid by would-be evaders.

It ensures that as a person's income increases so does his tax liability.

Disadvantages

Workers in the system have virtually no means of reducing the amount they pay.

It creates a sense of grievance among those on PAYE against those whose incomes are not scrutinised so carefully.

It encourages tax evasion.

- Sample comprehension question (4)

This type of question asks you to read between the lines to understand the tone of the passage:

Do you think the writer of the passage is earning a salary on which he pays PAYE?

Yes, because the passage has an aggrieved tone. The writer uses terms such as 'the most potent creator of inequality and bad social feeling' and also the word 'tentacles' in the passage. He feels discriminated against because he says non-PAYE people are not subjected to the same careful scrutiny.

- Sample comprehension question (5)

This question allows you to comment on the style of the passage:

Comment on the use of the phrase 'the luckless PAYE victim'.

The use of the two negative terms 'luckless' and 'victim' shows clearly where the writer's sympathies lie. It shows his very strong feelings as they are highly emotional terms. The person on PAYE has a job and is not really 'luckless' or a 'victim' at all. It is an example of the writer using emotional language to get the reader on his side.

• Sample comprehension question (6)

The next type of question allows you to give your personal opinion:

Do you agree or disagree that there are inequalities in the tax system?

The point of view you present here is not important so long as you can produce evidence for it. A reiteration of the points in the passage is not what is expected. The question offers a chance to present your own view of the matter.

ACTIVITY 2

1. Read the following passage and then answer the questions below.

   Service Sector Must Stop Seeing Itself As Servile Sector

   It was supposed to be Jim Slater, in scornful mood, who once referred to the manufacturing industry as 'thing-makers'. No doubt, for purpose of effect, he was overdoing the derision. But an attempt to shake the **pedestal** upon which manufacturing industry is sometimes tempted to pose should not be dismissed because it was expressed in so tasteless a fashion. There is room for a slight realignment of attitude to manufacturing.

   The suggestion apparently contained within the 'thing-maker' **epithet** is that manufacturing is a profitless pursuit for witless people. This is entirely wrong. It is as far out of line as the suggestion that all clever and right-thinking businessmen should concern themselves solely with **commercial and financial manipulation**.

   But there is the germ of a new idea contained within it. For many years there has been a sort of **industrial apartheid**. Manufacturing industries were always seen as shining white and totally acceptable. The service industries always seemed to be **relegated** to a second place in that they were somehow lesser beings.

   When measured in their direct contribution to the economy, to export revenue or to the country's balance of payments, there are certainly some service industries which appear to offer very little save a fair profit for their participants. But there are many which, when looked upon as generators of employment, stimulators of skills and simple makers of money are anything but second class.

   Neither, when the relevant figures are examined, can there be much argument against the service industries' show of growth and durability. The service sector grows while the manufacturing does not. And there seems to be no suggestion that the service industries are growing at the expense of manufacturing. It can fairly be argued that the new style of manufacturing is causing the service industries to grow stronger.

Yet, in an often unsubtle way, **manufacturing industry sees itself at the top of the pecking order**. It is hard to understand why manufacturers look upon their support services in the condescending way that a man who has built a house looks upon the man who has come to repair the plumbing.
(The Irish Times, Ronnie Hoffman)

(a) Explain the highlighted words and phrases used in the passage.

(b) Rewrite the title of the passage in your own words.

(c) What is meant by the 'service industry'? Give three examples of service industries.

(d) 'The service sector grows while manufacturing does not.' Explain why this is happening.

(e) Do you agree or disagree with the point of view of the passage? Give reasons to support your answer.

2. Read the following extract from a booklet entitled Extending Your House, published by the Consumers' Association, and answer the questions which follow it:

Most gas appliances must be separated from any combustible material in the structure of the building either by a non-combustible material or by an air space.

The flue requirement of gas appliances often depends on the size of the room. Some appliances do not connect directly to a flue: a gas cooker does not, nor a water heater below a certain size – for instance, a sink water heater. You can install a gas water heating appliance without connecting it to a flue only if the room is !arge enough and has a specified amount of permanent ventilation. In a bathroom a gas water heater should be of the room-sealed type with a balance flue.

(a) A householder fixes a gas water heater directly on to a brick wall. Is this permitted? Give reasons for your answer.

(b) A householder proposes to install a gas cooker in a very tiny kitchen which lacks ventilation. Is this permitted? Give your reasons.

(c) A householder fixes a sink water heater over the hand basin in his bathroom. There is no flue. Discuss how one should interpret the regulations on this point; is there any ambiguity?

(d) A householder shows the foregoing regulations to a builder, who says he has not read them before. What evidence do you notice which might indicate that a builder is, or is not, likely to have seen this extract?

(London Chamber of Commerce Private Secretary's Certificate)

3. A secretary has been invited to visit a college to speak to a secretarial class on 'The Role of the Secretary'. Below is the text of the talk he gave together with some of the questions he was asked. Using the material given in the text answer the questions:

In this talk I am not going to try to achieve the impossible – to make any of this class into a perfect secretary instantly – but I will try to tell you what I think is required of someone to become a good secretary and what I see the role of the secretary to be. It seems logical at the very outset to enquire why become a secretary? As a member of a secretarial class like this one you should try to answer this important question. It might be easier to be an usher, a programme seller, a clerk, a copy-typist or a seamstress in jobs which make no special demands on the individual who is content to be a mere cog in a large machine. These jobs, and many like them, although they are useful and necessary, do not make claims on initiative or bring anxiety, responsibility, understanding, the need for study and a willingness to participate in something in which personality plays a vital part.

Why, then, should you contemplate becoming a secretary? In the top echelon the secretary can look for a good reward, but the status that such jobs can confer must be earned by dedication and a remarkable degree of competence. There is a vast and ever-widening difference between a secretary and a typist. Whereas the secretary is, in effect, an extension of the personality of his/her executive, the typist is the detached user of a piece of machinery.

Ambition has much to do with the choice of becoming a secretary – the sort of ambition that stems from a desire to advance in one's profession and to find openings that provide the facilities for promotion. There are several strata of secretaries, such as junior secretary, senior secretary, personal or private secretary, executive secretary or personal assistant. Many people who euphemistically describe themselves as secretaries are little more than shorthand-typists, but the secretary in any of the capacities mentioned is very much more: the secretary is a skilled executive and interpreter of his/her superior's thinking and he/she is often the executant of that thinking, especially so in the absence of the superior.

If you are genuinely interested in a career as a secretary you will have to reconcile yourself from the beginning to the fact that true secretarial work is going to require skills which are far in advance of normal requirements of routine office work. The functions are different and much more demanding and this becomes even more obvious as you advance from junior secretary stage and pass on through the stage of working for perhaps several junior managers, to the position of executive secretary or personal assistant to a senior manager whom you will help to make decisions and whose representative you might be on a variety of occasions.

Many would-be secretaries fail to achieve their goals. Realising the implications of the work, the demand it can make for the sacrifice of spare time for study, and the responsibilities that have to be carried, not a few resign themselves to remaining typists or clerks and do not pursue the aim which interested them originally.

Those who persist in their design do so largely because they recognise that they have in themselves what it takes to become a competent secretary and they have the determination to succeed, even though they have not had a chance to be fully aware of the responsibilities involved. Such people succeed because they deserve to succeed. Even so, much thought should be given to the prospects, the scope for advancement, the possibility of being appreciated and not being taken for granted, as well as the danger of being overlooked.

Some intelligent people will doubtless look for other areas of work where they are more likely to be recognised. But why, indeed, should anyone contemplate becoming a secretary in the first place?

Job satisfaction should be the spur because where there is job satisfaction, there is competence; where there is competence, appreciation usually follows; and where there is appreciation, there is improved status carrying better pay, conditions and prospects, but above all, there is the assurance of happiness in one's job and this ought to be your main ambition.

(a) (i) Please explain why you referred to the job of programme seller.

   (ii) What features do you think this job has in common with a copy-typist?

(b) Please explain what you meant by the expressions:

   (i) The secretary is an extension of the personality of his/her executive.

   (ii) The typist is the detached user of a piece of machinery.

(c) What difference is there in the responsibilities of those who merely call themselves secretaries and those who can genuinely be described as secretaries?

(d) For someone genuinely interested in becoming a secretary how would you differentiate between the demands of a secretarial post and those of routine office work?

(e) Why do you think that so many who set out to become secretaries do not realise their ambitions?

(f) Sum up why you think anyone should consider becoming a secretary.

(London Chamber of Commerce Private Secretarial Certificate)

| **Other sample passages** |

Reviews

To write old wrongs

By Charles Townshend

Rebel Hearts.

Journeys Within the IRA's Soul

by Kevin Toolis, Picador £15.99

The 25-year Northern Ireland war had a baffling quality, like a blind-man's buff in which everyone was blindfolded and the buffets were deadly. The lack of mutual comprehension seemed obvious, at least to outsiders. In Britain, the question 'what makes the IRA tick?' may not have gone altogether unasked, but was certainly not asked as persistently as it should have been. Even so, it was probably asked more often than the question 'what makes the British state tick?' was asked by the IRA. Negotiations, we must now hope, will begin a process of discovery, but there is a long way to go.

Pamela Kane: convicted IRA terrorist on her release in February 1995 after 8 years

Kevin Toolis, who has reported the conflict for a variety of British, Irish and American journals since the early 1980s, provides an unusually clear signpost for this journey. Aside from his purplish title (befitting his other job as a screenwriter for Universal Pictures), this is a sombre and honest personal investigation. It is sometimes very personal: witness the uneasy analysis of his motives in dating the sister of an IRA man whose death in an SAS ambush he was investigating. Was she, he wonders, a special sexual prize, as the sister of 'an I-R-A M-A-A-N'? His precise rendering of the northern drawl conveys how the dark glamour of the gunman, the mystique of the rebel, simultaneously grips and repels him.

Toolis begins from his family roots: displaced Achill islanders living in Edinburgh, making an annual return through the gauntlet of armoured patrols and checkpoints to the bare strand at Dookinella with its little monument to a priest executed for taking part in the 1798 rebellion. The resilience of Irish republicanism slowly impressed itself on him. As he says, no other western political movement is so tenuously grounded in political reality, so consciously espouses a doctrine of self-sacrifice, promises so much pain and death to its followers and offers so little in return. So why does it go on?

A Unionist will unhesitatingly answer, because Fenians are evil, heartless, homicidal criminals, and will deduce from Toolis's origins that he is one of them. To others it will not seem so simple. He may have a 'rebel heart', but his mind and conscience revolt at the grim, pointless roster of 'stiffings', individual assassinations, that make up the overwhelming bulk of the 'armed struggle'. Time and again the suffocating pressure of vendetta overwhelms him, as when he gets to hear the ghastly tape-recording of the final confession of a 'tout' – an IRA man who became an informer to protect his wife from police harassment – to the IRA 'court' which would shortly blow his head to bits and dump his body in a lovely country lane.

Most of his book is an attempt to grasp, through patient study of individual IRA volunteers and their families, the reasons why such a struggle carried on for so long. In the case of Harlow-born Frankie Ryan, Toolis looks for 'a moment of epiphany in Frankie's life that would explain his transformation from an Essex lout into an IRA bomber, but there was no such moment'. A rich chapter explores the attitudes of a leading republican family: big brother Pat, the lawyer who defended IRA prisoners, was denounced by Douglas Hogg in the House of Commons and shot dead soon after by loyalists, and the other three IRA men of varying deadliness.

All share one simple conviction – that the armed struggle is war, legitimised by deep historic wrongs. As Ryan's widow put it, 'It's a war isn't it? They shouldn't have treated Catholics like second-class citizens.' Clearly, the statement 'this is war' is not so much military as political – an assertion of unflinching determination never to give in. Yet 'war', in Ulster, is a treacherous notion which obscures the hopelessness of killing Protestants as a means of convincing them of the need for Irish unity, by disguising sectarian killings as attacks on British rule.

Toolis worries away at this problem, especially in his vivid analysis of Martin McGuinness and the IRA leadership. Can the IRA make peace? Can an organisation built on refusal to compromise accept less than its ideal? Toolis sees clearly that any settlement will depend on the reputation of McGuinness, who is (so far) absolutely trusted by the IRA rank and file. Yet his sharp portrait of the incorruptible republican, 'almost robotically repeating the same narrow verbal formula', lacking any of the 'expressive nuances that guide us to the mental state of our fellow humans', leaves plenty of room for doubt. McGuinness owes his ascendancy to his capacity to out-argue others, rare in a group whose normal argument is 'We know we're right and if you don't lay off we'll shoot ye'. But this capacity has yet to be tested on the real enemy. If Toolis is right that this street-fighter turned guerrilla statesman has not moved far from his roots, negotiating with him may be less than rewarding.

The Independent on Sunday, 4 June 1995

Questions

1. Analyse the title of the review.
2. Discuss the use of the word 'terrorist' in the caption to the picture.
3. What do you think is Townshend's view of the IRA?

Sinead smiles and sways for a privileged few

Review: Nell McCafferty

Sinead O'Connor was given a rapturous reception at her powerful comeback performance in Dublin's Tivoli Theatre on Friday night, a couple of years after she had announced her retirement from rock. Among those who gathered in the tiny, intimate, standing-room only venue were those who had come from Cork, Mayo, Galway and the midlands, some of whom had paid £30 to touts for tickets with a face value of £11.

Their word-perfect singalong to some of the tracks from her latest album 'Universal Mother', as they stood at her feet, swayed and held lighted matches aloft in the dark room, brought several rare flashes of that famous dimpled smile from the hitherto unhappy wild child of rock. She seemed content and at ease, giving a virtually private performance to a privileged few.

Ms O'Connor, who wore a simple white blouse over a pair of leather trousers, has dispensed with the trademark shaven head and now wears a closecut, glossy caul of hair, evidence, she has said, of a new peace of mind. She was escorted to the concert by Roscommon-born John Waters, the newly-bearded, long-haired, author of *Jiving at the Crossroads*, who is known as the man who 'put cool into culchie'. Mr Waters wore a flowered shirt. Ms O'Connor, who has attempted several reconciliations with estranged husband John Reynolds, dedicated the song 'John, I love you' to 'all the Johns in her life'.

The bar closed as the concert began at 30 minutes after midnight, in strict accordance with a notice which declared the singer's wish that no alcohol would be served after that time. A prolonged ovation greeted her unannounced arrival onstage after which she plunged straight into a performance that continued for 90 minutes. Seemingly undaunted by years of publicly proclaimed suffering, the hauntingly beautiful young woman danced and sang her way through a wide-ranging selection. There was gentle, undimmed defiance in her delivery of 'Red

Football', with a supportive audience chanting the refrain 'I am not a crocodile in the Dublin zoo . . .'

After a pair of what looked like men's black briefs were thrown onstage, the singer announced with a wicked grin that she would like more knickers 'from men or women, it doesn't matter, as long as they're cleanish'.

When Paddy Moloney came onstage to play the tin whistle for her encore, a rendition of 'Raglan Road', a near-perfect silence brought to a close one of the sweetest, simplest, happiest nights in a long time.
The Sunday Tribune, 4 June 1995

Questions
1. Is Nell McCafferty sympathetic to Sinead O'Connor? Give reasons for your answer.
2. Why does the author dwell on the clothes of the singer?
3. Is the use of the words 'privileged few' a criticism of O'Connor?

A courageous quest for justice
By Susan McKey
Betrayal of Trust
By Chris Moore
Marino Press £6.99

While Father Brendan Smyth's leering spectre hangs once again over the Dáil, this book sets out to remind us that what is important is that men who prey on children must be stopped. It should be read by all of those currently haranguing each other across the chamber, and by all the cardinals, bishops, priests and abbots who refused over the years to take responsibility for a man they employed to keep the faith, and who instead destroyed it.

In January last year, UTV reporter Chris Moore met a young West Belfast man to talk about a story. Shortly afterwards, Moore got a call from the man's partner who said she had another story to tell. This call plunged him into more than a year of intensive research,

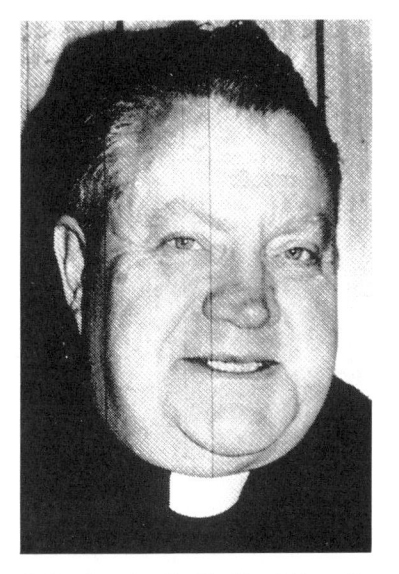

Father Brendan Smyth, his sickly smile is what is remembered of him by one of his victims

which took him all around Ireland, to Italy and the US. He made a stunning documentary, which has already won three major awards, and wrote this book, which deserves similar acclaim.

The woman told him that she had seen Fr Brendan Smyth on the news. It was a report on his appearance in court in Belfast to face child abuse charges he had evaded in 1991 by skipping bail and returning to his abbey in Cavan. The RUC had been unable to persuade either the abbot or the Republic's Attorney General to return him to the North for trial.

The woman said she had been abused by Smyth in the 70's. Moore was put in touch with a network of other families victimised by Smyth as far back as the 1950's. He heard of monstrous betrayals. One woman had learned that while she was making dinner in her kitchen, happy in the knowledge that her long time friend, Fr Brendan, was playing with the children in the living room, he was sexually assaulting them. The words 'cover up' began to be used in the West Belfast living rooms where Moore met these people. A woman told him that she had been abused by Smyth in the 70's in a Catholic grammar school, that her parents had complained to the church authorities – and that this was the same school in which another girl had been abused by Smyth more than a decade later.

Moore heard stories of horrific cruelty – a six year old whose mother had killed herself was taken into care and straight into the clutches of Smyth, a child beaten by a nun for making allegations against him. He heard of broken marriages, of suicide attempts, of people who felt like lost souls haunted by what one described as Smyth's 'sickly smile'. Perhaps most shocking of all, he learned that Smyth's abusive activities had first been noted within the church in the 1940's when he was a teenager, and that complaints against him had gone to the highest levels. Cardinal Daly had been approached on several occasions going back to the late 80's. In a sensitive and hard hitting preface, Fr Kevin Hegarty comments that 'in light of the clergy's long expressed idealisation of the family as the most vital social unit, the revelation that these families were not protected by the church, were instead its victims, has been staggering'. Hegarty concludes bleakly that while the church emphasises the dignity of the individual from conception to death, more energy is expended on the rights of the unborn, than on children after they are born.

Books about sexual abuse can be voyeuristic, and in themselves abusive. Moore at all times keeps his focus on the courageous quest for justice which led those abused by Smyth to trust him with their stories in the first place. He has spoken of the fear that by asking an insensitive question of someone who had been abused, he might open a door into the darkness which it might not be possible to close. Instead he has poured light into the darkest secrets of the Catholic Church and those who uphold its authority at the price of its soul.

Father Smyth is still a priest, while many of those his employment enabled him to devastate are no longer practising Catholics. This book is investigative reporting at its finest.

Susan McKay is a staff journalist with The Sunday Tribune.

The Sunday Tribune Magazine, 4 June 1995

Questions

1. Analyse the caption to the picture.
2. Discuss the use of the words 'leering spectre' in the opening sentence of the review.
3. Is Susan McKay reviewing the book or giving her own personal reaction to the subject of the book?

The Easter Rebellion,

by Max Caulfield (Gill & Macmillan, £12.99)

Max Caulfield's book, now over 30 years old, broke new ground at the time, since it cut through much of the propaganda and mythology from both sides about the 1916 Rebellion. In particular, his account of de Valera's rather eccentric and unsoldierly behaviour at Boland's Mill caused annoyance and even offence at a time when many older people still believed that Dev possessed military talents as well as political ones. This is sound professional reportage, with many eye-witness accounts garnered at a time when survivors of the era were much thicker on the ground than they are today. Though they were amateur soldiers at best, with limited training and virtually no battle experience, the Volunteers put up a good fight, even if many or most of the troops facing them were almost as green as themselves. The Dublin Castle administration was totally wrong-footed by the Rising – Lord Wimborne, the Viceroy, resigned and Augustine Birrell's political career was finished, while the military generally assumed that the rebel leaders were in the pay of Germany. General Maxwell, whose reputation had already suffered in the Dardanelles campaign, managed to offend all sides and ultimately was banished to a military command in Northern Ireland. Connolly, once again, emerges as the brain of the enterprise, a fact generously acknowledged by Pearse. The hyper-emotionalism of the whole event was further heightened by the fact that the first World War was already nearly two years old, and had claimed the lives of many Irishmen as well as British.

Brian Fallon

The Irish Times, 3 June 1995

Questions

1. What was the 'propaganda and mythology' of the 1916 Rising?
2. Explain the reference to de Valera?
3. What does the reviewer mean by saying 'This is sound professional reportage . . .?

Business writing

Banks withdraw overdrafts

Sudden removal of facility leaves customers exposed

Some bank customers with long standing overdrafts with their banks have been surprised recently to discover that the facility has been withdrawn pending new application.

A number of cases have been brought to *Family Money's* attention in which customers who claim to have good relationships with their banks and who did not abuse the terms of their overdrafts were informed that they would have to reapply for the facility.

In the case of AIB, an application form was enclosed with a very terse letter in which considerable information about the customer's spending and borrowing position was sought. 'On receipt of same we will be in a position to review your facilities for the coming year', stated the letter.

A number of other readers have complained that overdrafts, which in the past had been rolled-over from year to year, have expired without the account holder being informed, leading to embarrassment as cheques bounced or ATM cards were rejected due to lack of funds in the account. Overdrafts were usually quickly re-established when the customer complained, but usually only in person to the lending manager.

Spokesmen for AIB and Bank of Ireland both told *Family Money* that there is no formal bank policy regarding annual re-application of existing overdrafts. The renewal of an overdraft is within the discretion of the branch manager: some will allow a facility to roll-over for a couple of years before the customer's position is formally reviewed. When a new manager is assigned the review process may occur. If a customer is not keeping to the conditions of the facility they can certainly expect an annual review or a request to re-apply.

AIB's spokesman told us that it is not unusual for a branch manager to seek up-dated information from a customer before an overdraft is renewed, particularly if a number of years has passed since a review. 'It does not reflect any negative judgment on the customer's financial position to ask them to fill out a detailed application form', he said.

While at least one of our readers believed his bank was using his overdraft renewal as a marketing opportunity, the Bank of Ireland spokesman suggested an alternative reason.

'Branches are now virtually autonomous sales units that must justify every penny they lend and take in. A lot of customers have overdrafts that they seldom if ever use, but the branch must make provision for this money anyway. If you have enough people in this position you might be talking about a million pounds being tied up that could be lent out more productively. The customer who seldom uses the overdraft might really be better off with a different facility.'

Where overdrafts have expired without the customer being informed was described as 'bad service' and 'inexcusable' by both bank spokespersons. 'This should never happen, and in most cases the facility is usually extended until the manager can meet the customer', we were told.

The Irish Times, 3 March 1995

Questions

1. What is an overdraft facility?
2. What is Family Money?
3. Discuss the reasons given for the withdrawal of overdraft facilities by the banks' spokesmen?

Barings: life after the collapse

How could so much be lost so quickly? Could it happen here?

By John Hennessy

After the Barings collapse, the questions on the lips of every business person this week are how could so much be lost so quickly. And could it happen to me? The facts about the Barings disaster are still emerging and we may never know the full story. However, it seems clear that a number of significant factors contributed to the collapse, including the enormous size of the risk taken by the dealer in question; inadequacy of controls over the execution and report of dealing activities and significant adverse market movement affecting the exposed positions over a short period of time.

The story is a dealer was permitted to open up a huge exposure through substantial trading in a derivative instrument, and controls were not effective enough to prevent calamity.

Why are Derivatives so risky?

Barings is not the first major financial disaster arising from the use of derivatives. IG Metallgesellschaft – a German trade union, Proctor & Gamble, Orange County in the US and Kidder Peabody are just some of the organisations which have suffered enormous losses while playing with derivatives.

It might therefore sound somewhat unusual that combined worldwide activity in derivatives rose by almost 50 per cent to over $4 trillion in the first half of 1994 compared to the previous six months. This activity continues to increase. It must be noted that most trading in derivatives takes place with the objective of reducing or eliminating risk rather than creating it.

Much has been written in recent days about the complexity of derivatives. Although some derivative transactions are highly complex, the vast bulk of activity in derivatives is of a straightforward nature.

Put simply, companies normally use derivatives to buy certainty by fixing interest rates and/or exchange rates for future transactions and so reducing or eliminating exposure to volatility in these rates.

Dealers take a different approach. They effectively create a market in derivatives by selling the products to the end-users. Part of their activities are focused on matching the needs of different end-users and off-setting the exposures created by separate deals.

Dealers are also engaged in true trading or speculating and this is the area of biggest risk. Dealers engaged in trading take positions in which they consciously open up exposures, effectively betting on anticipated movements in the instrument underlying the derivative in which they are dealing.

It is these trading activities which need to be subject to the tightest of controls because of their inherently risky nature.

Could it happen here?

What are the lessons for corporate end users and dealers in financial institutions in Ireland? The key lies in the need to monitor and control very tightly the use of derivatives in the organisation.

A very large number of Irish companies are end-users of derivatives. This is particularly so because of the nature of Irish business which depends to a large extent on export markets for sales and on foreign companies for the provision of raw materials and other supplies.

These factors, combined with the need to borrow to fund activities, open up immediate exposures to volatility in interest rates and foreign exchange rates. Irish corporates are therefore significant users of certain derivatives products (principally forward interest rate agreement, forward foreign currency contracts and interest rate swaps).

For these companies, although not taking dealer-type risks, expensive mistakes can be made. In order to avoid these risks, specific procedures and controls must be put in place. In particular, corporates should ensure that:

- A clear strategy for the use of derivatives is set at the very top of the company, specifying that treasury activities are confined only to hedge existing and anticipated exposures or, if the Board so decides, that speculative positions can be opened up subject to specific predetermined limits.
- Derivative strategy is linked to the company's business needs and all members of senior management understand and approve company policy in this area.
- Treasury activities are subject to the separation of duties necessary to ensure that they are recorded and reported regularly by individuals other than those engaged in taking treasury decisions.

Financial institutions and others engaged in trading activities need additional procedures which centre around the independent recording and reconciliation of transactions entered into by dealers.

These procedures must be combined with sophisticated systems which allow the immediate reporting of exposures, the measurement of the sensitivity of these positions to movements in the underlying instruments and the comparison of exposures with predetermined limits.

No system is perfect in that, without on-line real-time systems which can impose limits before transactions are consummated, exposures can only be reported after the event.

Given the size and profile of losses associated with derivatives in recent years, it is not surprising that the topic of control over derivative usage has received considerable attention. The most useful source of best practice in this area is the report of the Group of 30 (G30) a group of bankers and regulators based in Washington and led by Paul Volcker, the former Chairman of the Federal Reserve Bank. The July 1993 G30 Report entitled *Derivatives: Practice and Principles* contained twenty major recommendations which together define best practice for both dealers and end users of derivatives.

Since the publication of this report two major surveys have been carried out by Arthur Andersen on behalf of the G30 in order to measure compliance with the recommendations. The results of the most recent survey, published in 1994, were based on responses from 250 major organisations.

In general, the survey showed a very high level of acceptance of the G30 recommendations of best practice and a clear intention to implement them. 58 per cent of respondents who are dealers in derivatives had already used the G30 Report to benchmark their own risk management practices and a further 30 per cent plan to do so over the next year. The corresponding percentages for end-users were lower, a total of 50 per cent have either already benchmarked their practices or plan to do so in the near future.

The best advice to Irish derivatives users is: benchmark your organisation and take immediate steps to achieve best practice.

John Hennessy is a partner in Arthur Andersen's Audit and Business Advisory Practice in Dublin and he leads the firm's Financial Services Industry Group.

The Irish Times, 3 March 1995

Questions

1. What was Barings?

2. Why did it collapse?

3. What is meant by the last sentence of the article?

Satire

Real Ireland

Aodghán Feeley

A phone call from BBART (Bobby Ballagh Against Royal Tours) was enough to steel my resolve and have me springing into action. Bobby, an old friend of mine, was direct and to the point. 'Aodghan', he cooed. 'You're the only man I can think of to get things moving in the Midlands. I also want you as national coordinator. Just think,' he continued dreamily. 'You and your friends in Mullingar will form MART, my Cork friends are already setting CART in motion and several free-thinking nationalists of the old school in Fethard-on-sea have set up a ginger group.'

'To be called?', I inquired.

'Currently operating as FosART', he replied. 'But I think FART has more . . .'

'Force?', I suggested.

'Relevance to the cause', he replied.

And so, within an hour of Bobby's call I had assembled the core group of MART. There was no time to lose so we immediately set about preparing plans for the 'bussing' of the Mullingar MARTers to Dublin. Labhras 'Imperial Leather' Ui Laoghaire, with his fine track record as FCA adjutant, pedagogue and fearless republican, was appointed to the 'hot seat' as transport coordinator. My spanking new (87MH) cream-coloured Lada Riva 1600 which has just replaced my beloved mauve Marina, will take the bulk of the MARTers with the over-spill crammed into Labhras' remarkable 1974 Chrysler avenger. Briege 'Bioethics' Brannigan, our local WAH co-ordinator, vowed to cycle all the way from Mullingar.

The core group, comprising myself, Brother Cathal and Labhras then headed off for a late night meeting of AART (Athlone Against Royal Tours), held in the Lough Derg Room of the Prince of Wales Hotel. A popular gathering, considering the filthy night that was in it, was gathered there and all seven, including us

MARTers resolved to throw our full weight behind Bobby Ballagh and my old friend Kevin 'Belted Earls' Boland.

Then back home where Breda had a fine supper of gammon rashers, batch loaf, Little Chip marmalade and piping hot Campbell's tea waiting for us.

At the time of writing she had laid out what Brother Cathal calls my 'ensemble' for the protests: my brown suit with (proper) Fainne and pioneer pin, my cream nylon shirt with the delicate floral design picked out in a brown pin-stripe, my black clerical rain coat and sheepskin hat and a spare pair of brown Terylene slacks. I think I can safely say that I will cut a dapper figure in front of the cameras of the world's press. Of course there is a long and uninterrupted tradition of protest against royal visits in the Feeley family. My uncle, the republican and martyr, Corny O'Malley, threw at least one egg at the general direction of George V on the Merrion Road in 1911 (the same year as his father, Paschal, established the Irish Vigilance Association).

My father, Sylvester 'Vesty' Feeley travelled to Dublin for the 1911 royal visit and cheered loudly when the window of Yeates's in Grafton Street was put in with a well-aimed half brick. In later years he claimed to have supplied the weapon, carried all the way from Kinnegad.

And so, in the autumn of my years, at a time when I had despaired of having any opportunity to protest at a royal visit, my hour has come and I can carry on the torch for a later generation of Feeleys and O'Malleys. And I will be doing this with the Greatest Living Irishman, Kevin Boland, the only public figure who has had the vision and the guts to describe this royal tour as 'sinister'. All I can say now is that Sinn Fein's silence on this important matter suggests that they have already begun to sell out.

The Sunday Tribune, 11 June 1995

Questions

1. Do you think Aodghán Feeley is the author's real name? Why?

2. The author entitles his article 'Real Ireland'. What does he mean?

3. Do you think he has an uncle called Corny O'Malley?

Pictures

Belfast Barriers

Nine months after the ceasefire, the city of Belfast still lives in the shadow of continued surveillance and military reminders of the Troubles.

Photographs and text by Alan O'Connor

Springfield Road Barracks. A walkway which passes down the side of the barracks. Since the ceasefires there has been much pressure for the removal of such fortifications to which the RUC reply is 'Public opinion will always be taken into account wherever possible, but it must be remembered that all security measures are a response to the threat of life and limb.'

New Barnsley RUC station. Known locally as 'Henry Taggart' due to a linen mill which previously occupied the same site, this fortification was regularly attacked by the IRA from the neighbouring Ballymurphy housing estate.

Springfield Road RUC station. 'Security arrangements are constantly reviewed in light of the current threat assessment. A number of measures have already been introduced in response to the continuing absence of overt terrorist activities. We will continue to monitor the situation in respect of other measures which may be possible.' – RUC press statement. The metal barricades to the left and right of the police station are to protect it from rocket propelled grenades.

The Sunday Tribune Magazine, 4 June 1995

Questions

1. Do you think these pictures are effective? Why? Why not?
2. Why are images of children used in the pictures?
3. What, in your opinion, is the message of the pictures?

Review

1. Why are summarising skills useful for working in business?
2. What is the difference between direct speech and reported speech?
3. Turn the following into reported speech:
   (a) In his address the chairman said, 'This has been a successful year for our company, but we hope that in future things will be even better.'
   (b) 'We will meet here next week', he said.
   (c) He declared, 'I ask you, can this go on?'
4. How do you render the following in reported speech?

now	today	last week	tomorrow
here	mine	next week	ourselves
us	may	can	last year

5. What is meant by reading between the lines of a passage?
6. How do you gauge the tone of a passage?
7. Find two reviews of the same book and compare them.
8. Find two different pictures of the same event and compare them.

Pitfalls

Dutch auction

Sometimes when a general election is being held the political parties are accused by the media of turning it into a *Dutch auction* for the votes of the people.

This use of the term *Dutch auction* implies that the political parties are making higher and higher bids for the votes of the people. This is an incorrect use of the phrase. A *Dutch auction* is applied to a situation in which the price is reduced step by step as opposed to the usual kind of auction where the price is increased.

Confusing words

arc	ark	ail	ale
alley	ally	hail	hale
annalist	analyst	banded	bandied
ante	anti	beau	bow

Quiz

What is the answer to this riddle?

He went to the wood and caught it,

He sat down and sought it.

Because he could not find it

Home with him he brought it.

Spellings

The words most commonly misspelled are highlighted.

harassed	hesitation	humanity
harassing	hideous	humiliation
having	hoist	**humorous**
healthiness	honest	**humour**
hearth	**honorary**	hungry
heather	honour	**hurriedly**
height	honourable	hymn
heighten	horizon	**hypocrisy**
heir	horizontal	hypocrite
hereditary	**horrendous**	**hypothesis**
heroes	hospital	

WRITING 1:
IN WORDS THERE IS POWER

Vocabulary

It is possible to communicate messages without using words. These are called non-verbal communications. In business, however, and indeed in life, words are very important and your success as a communicator will, to a great extent, depend on your ability to use words. You should always strive for conciseness and accuracy. Do not be happy to use just the first word that enters your head. The English language may have several other words that are more appropriate to your situation. By constant practice your ability will improve.

The following activities are designed to increase your word power.

ACTIVITY 1

Express the meaning of each of the following phrases in a single word. The first letter of each word is given to help you.

happening each year	annually
a person seventy years old	s ....
a person one hundred years old	c ....
a non-drinker	t ....
celebration of an event that happened one hundred years ago	c ....
occurring at the same time	s ....
not capable of being heard	i ....
not enough	i ....
cannot be rubbed out	i ....
not capable of being explained	i ....

a person who collects stamps	p ....
a person who writes plays	p ....
a person who carves in stone	s ....
a book that has been shortened	a ....
a person who pleads in court	b ....

ACTIVITY 2

In the blank spaces in the continuous passage below, insert the appropriate words from the list provided at the end.

Why is the industrial .... problem in Ireland so acute? Do Irish workers have a self-destructive ....? Is the good of the .... put before selfish .... gain any longer? All strikes are .... settled. Why cannot they be solved sooner rather than later? It is well known that the .... a strike goes on the more .... it is to settle. The great problem is that each side refuses to .... for fear of losing face. To find a .... that each side can agree to without losing dignity is the .... to many of the strikes which occur at present. One of the .... questions to be decided is whether the findings of the Labour Court should be .... But what happens if people refuse to .... by the Labour Court findings? Should they be fined or ....? If the latter, will many people see them as ....? Despite all the talk about the problem of strikes there seems to be general .... when it comes to solving the problem. If all .... people involved with the problem would sit down and work ...., surely a solution could be found which would not .... the .... of any party.

Words to insert:

principles	eventually	relations
longer	personal	community
difficult	formula	solution
vital	binding	conscientious
compromise	abide	jailed
apathy	impulse	diligently
martyrs	compromise	

Always use simple words rather than complex words. Use familiar words rather than unfamiliar ones.

ACTIVITY 3

For the words below insert a more commonly used word in the blanks provided:

approximately	....	promulgate	....
accomplished	....	masticate	....
ameliorate	....	employment	....
cognisant	....	diminish	....
demonstrate	....	expensive	....
modification	....	terminate	....

Confusing pairs of words

ACTIVITY 4

For each of the following sentences choose the correct word in the brackets.

1. The (coarse, course) was (formally, formerly) approved.
2. The actress missed her (cue, queue) because she was short of (breath, breathe).
3. The (current, currant) affairs programme could not be seen because the electrical (current, currant) was switched off.
4. The (site, sight) of the house was in a terrible state because of the weather.
5. The mother heard the telephone (ring, wring).
6. It is very difficult living in a (desert, dessert).
7. The car accident had a terrible (effect, affect) on him.
8. He was delighted he (passed, past) his examination.
9. What are the responsibilities of county (councils, counsels)?
10. The boy had a (flare, flair) for music.
11. I left the (stationery, stationary) in the car.
12. My lace was (lose, loose).
13. I really was left with no (alternative, alternate).
14. The guards (disbursed, dispersed) the crowds.
15. The house had (depreciated, deprecated) in value.

125

16. He died of a rare (disease, decease).

17. The (weather, whether) this summer was very bad.

18. She writes in her (dairy, diary) every night.

19. Some people make (elicit, illicit) whiskey.

20. She made the cake from a new (recipe, receipt).

ACTIVITY 5

Choose the correct word for each of the phrases in the left column:

1. The head of a school   (principle, principal) ....
2. A prominent person   (imminent, eminent) ....
3. To quote from a book   (cite, sight) ....
4. A false statement about a person (liable, libel) ....
5. Permission to do something   (aloud, allowed) ....
6. To say 'goodbye'   (bad, bade) ....
7. What hay is made into   (bale, bail) ....
8. Not fertile   (barren, baron) ....
9. A bed in a boat   (birth, berth) ....
10. A type of gun   (canon, cannon) ....
11. A clever device   (ingenious, ingenuous) ....
12. To look for votes   (canvas, canvass) ....
13. A hiding place for treasure (cash, cache) ....
14. To put a spell on someone   (cast, caste) ....
15. To disagree   (dissent, descent) ....
16. The yellow of an egg   (yoke, yolk) ....
17. To forego a claim   (wave, waive) ....
18. To praise   (complement, compliment) ....
19. Go before   (proceed, precede) ....
20. A problem that cannot be solved (insolvent, insoluble) ....
21. A wind coming through the door (draft, draught) ....

22. Further up the mountain   (hire, higher) ....
23. It belongs to them   (their, there) ....
24. A small part of a play   (scene, seen) ....
25. To be diplomatic   (discrete, discreet) ....
26. This is an offence   (steal, steel) ....
27. To leave a country   (immigrate, emigrate) ....
28. Thickly populated   (dents, dense) ....
29. A large animal   (guerilla, gorilla) ....
30. The principal city   (capital, capitol) ....

Business terms

Every trade, profession and occupation has its own specialised terminology. It is evident that groups of specialists must, among themselves, use a special language so that they can speak and write accurately on their subjects. Technical language is often called jargon. Jargon is useful and is a vital aid to efficient communication. However, it is often looked on as a barrier to communication because people tend to use technical words even when speaking to people who have no knowledge of them. Jargon is a valuable and necessary part of the English language and it is vital for the secretary and young business employee to become familiar with the technical language of business. It would be useful to keep a dictionary of commercial terms. However, it is more efficient to be able to use the common language of business without having to refer to a dictionary. The following activities will help to increase your vocabulary of business terms.

ACTIVITY 6

Choose the word from the selection given on the right hand side that most closely matches the definition on the left:

1. Secure payment of sum of money in the event of loss or damage to life   (a) advance (b) insurance (c) asset (d) assurance
2. Gratuity to employees beyond their normal pay   (a) discount (b) interest (c) bonus (d) rebate

3. Sum paid to author for copy of book sold — (a) royalty (b) commission (c) drawings (d) lien

4. Amount by which sum drawn exceeds credit balance — (a) loan (b) mortgage (c) overdraft (d) advance

5. One who buys in the stock exchange hoping to sell at a higher price — (a) broker (b) bull (c) bear (d) stag

6. A list of goods sent — (a) debenture (b) invoice (c) credit note (d) tare

7. Money contributed to keep down the price of commodities — (a) subsidy (b) annuity (c) tariff (d) will

8. Agreement between parties for supply of goods or performance of work — (a) trustee (b) contract (c) monopoly (d) partnership

9. Established custom or popularity of a business — (a) endowment (b) return (c) goodwill (d) turnover

10. Companies coming together to agree on pricing policy — (a) premium (b) actuary (c) usury (d) cartel

11. One who owes money — (a) debtor (b) creditor (c) trustee (d) middleman

12. Sum payable as profit of joint stock company — (a) requisition (b) share (c) dividend (d) annuity

13. Person who winds up, ascertains liabilities and apportions assets of a company — (a) agent (b) receiver (c) liquidator (d) director

14. Instruction to bank to make regular payments — (a) bank giro (b) standing order (c) credit note (d) blank cheque

15. Official examination of accounts — (a) demurrage (b) search (c) audit (d) deed

Foreign phrases

English has borrowed extensively from other languages and occasionally you will come across words or phrases from other languages, especially Latin and French. Your dictionary will provide you with an exhaustive list of these words and phrases, so only the more frequently used ones are given here.

- *ad hoc*: for this special purpose. Used generally in regard to a meeting

called to deal with a specific problem, e.g. an *ad hoc* meeting.
- *à la carte*: used in hotels to describe the menu where each item is priced separately.
- *table d'hôte*: the menus in hotels which have a fixed price for the complete meal.
- *rapport*: in sympathy with. 'He has great *rapport* with children.' He has a great relationship with children.
- *ex officio*: by virtue of office. 'The principal is a member of the board of management *ex officio*.' That means she is a member because she is the principal and if she ceased to be principal she would lose her position on the board.
- *in camera*: in private. 'The court proceedings were held *in camera* as children were involved.'
- *nem. con.*: This is used at meetings when a motion is passed unanimously. The words stand for *nemo contendere* and mean no one disputed the matter.
- *NB (nota bene)*: note well. It is often used at the end of letters or memos to add emphasis to a point.
- *post mortem*: an examination carried out to establish the cause of death.
- *sine die*: 'The meeting was postponed *sine die*.' It means the meeting was postponed indefinitely.
- *per annum*: yearly.

Figurative expressions

The English language is also rich in figurative expressions such as 'sticking out like a thumb', 'the tip of the iceberg' or 'straight from the horse's mouth'. The most common of these expressions are listed below but you will find many, many more in your dictionary.

to buy a pig in a poke (bag)	to buy something without seeing it
a blind alley occupation	a job that has no prospects
a cock and bull story	a story made up to lead you astray
to be under a cloud	to be under suspicion

to cross swords with	to have a dispute with someone
to let the cat out of the bag	to reveal a secret
sour grapes	to be jealous
with a grain of salt	to treat something you heard with some disbelief
to call a spade a spade	to state in blunt terms. A person who is very blunt is sometimes said to call a spade a shovel
a square peg in a round hole	a person in a position that doesn't suit him
at sixes and sevens	to be confused
to bury the hatchet	to forget a grievance

ACTIVITY 7

Write down the foreign phrases or figurative expressions for the highlighted phrases:

1. The meeting was adjourned **indefinitely**.
2. He is the type of person who **speaks in very blunt terms**.
3. **An examination to establish the cause of death** was carried out on the victim.
4. Mary was **under suspicion** after the examination.
5. He was **not really suited to his new position**.
6. Liam and Garret decided to **forget their quarrel**.
7. The motion to ask for an increase in salary was passed **without opposition**.
8. The retired director is paid £10,000 **yearly**.
9. Iseult was advised **not to take the story she heard too seriously**.
10. When the child was in court the proceedings were held **in private**.

Review

1. What is the meaning of each of the following words?

exonerate	facet	denigrate	vulnerable
laconic	habitual	petulant	insinuate

inflation	countersign	uncouth	demurrage
demoniac	disburse	discern	ergonomics
flux	flummery	fudge	gumption

2. What is the meaning of each of the following business terms?

stagflation	deflation	inflation
dumping	share	index
preferential debts	merger	frozen assets
benefit-in-kind	arrears	

3. Find the meaning of the following words or expressions:
   (a) An *ad hominem* argument.
   (b) To be full of *bonhomie*.
   (c) A *coup d'état* took place.
   (d) A *gauche* person.
   (e) To be on tenterhooks.
   (f) Caught between the devil and the deep blue sea.
   (g) To be hand in glove with.
   (h) A chip off the old block.
   (i) To live in a fool's paradise.
   (j) To beat about the bush.

Pitfalls

same

The word *same* is frequently used incorrectly, e.g. 'Your tender has not been accepted, so I am returning *same* to you.' Or 'I received your letter this morning and am forwarding *same* to the manager.'

In each of these sentences *same* is used as a pronoun which it is not. The pronoun *it* should have been used in each sentence. 'Your tender has not been accepted, so I am returning *it* to you.' 'I received your letter this morning and am forwarding *it* to the manager.'

Confusing words

there	their	its	it's
too	two	flair	flare
right	write	feint	faint
there	they're	stationary	stationery
canvas	canvass	hair	hare
due	dew	bare	bear

Quiz

What is the meaning of the word *floccinaucinihilipilification*?

Spellings

The words most commonly misspelled are highlighted.

identify	impulsive	injurious
idiot	inaccessible	**inoculate**
idiotic	incapacity	**inoculation**
ignorance	incense	insensible
illegal	**incidentally**	inseparable
illegible	**incipient**	**install**
illustrious	include	**instalment**
image	incompetent	intelligence
imaginable	inconvenient	intelligible
imaginary	incredible	intercede
imagination	incurred	interference
immediately	indelible	interior
immense	**independent**	interrupt
immigrate	indignant	invincible
immovable	**indispensable**	invitation
impartial	indolent	irregular
impatient	industrious	**irrelevant**
imperative	inferior	**irreparable**
impertinent	**influential**	**irresistible**
impetuous	influenza	irresponsible
impetus	ingenious	irritate
impossibility	inheritance	ivory
imprudence	inimitable	
imprudent	initial	

WRITING 2:
... AND YET MORE POWER

Prefixes

Prefixes are placed at the beginning of words. They are very important in word formation. The word *undress* is composed of *dress* and *un-* placed before it. The prefix varies the meaning of the root word, e.g. a *theist* is a person who believes in a god, but an *atheist* is a person who believes there is no god.

The commonly used prefixes are:

ante- (before) – antenatal, anteroom, antecedent, antedate
anti- (against) – anticlimax, antipathy, antidote
auto- (self) – automobile, automatic, autocratic
bene- (well) – benevolent, benefit, beneficial
bi- (two) – bicycle, bicentenary, bilingual
cent- (hundred) – century, centenary, centigrade
contra- (against) – contradict, contrary, contraband
di- (two) – dialogue, dichotomy
ex- (out) – exhale, exhaust
magna- (great) – magnificent, magnitude
mal- (bad) – malevolent, malicious
micro- (small) – microchip, microphone, microscope
mis- (wrong) – mistake, mishap
pan- (all) – pantheist, panacea
poly- (many) – polygon, polygamy
post- (after) – postpone, postgraduate, post mortem
pseudo- (sham) – pseudonym, pseudo-intellectual
quad- (four) – quadrangle, quadrilateral
retro- (back) – retrospective, retrograde

tri- (three) – triangle, trinity, tricycle

uni- (one) – uniform, unity, unilateral

Prefixes and spelling: be careful of spelling when using prefixes. Note 'disappoint' only has one 's', 'dissatisfy' has two; while 'unaided' has only one 'n' and 'unnecessary', two.

ACTIVITY 1

1. Match the words in the right hand column with the phrases on the left:

    (a) Antenatal   (a) Conversation between two people
    (b) Post mortem   (b) To breathe out
    (c) Autocratic   (c) Having several spouses
    (d) Contraband   (d) He doesn't know if God exists
    (e) Dialogue   (e) Able to speak two languages
    (f) Bisect   (f) Before birth
    (g) Bigamy   (g) Smuggled goods
    (h) Bilingual   (h) Having two spouses
    (i) Malevolent   (i) An object having three legs
    (j) Uniform   (j) To divide in two
    (k) Exhale   (k) Car
    (l) Benevolent   (l) An aversion to something
    (m) Bicentenary   (m) Test to establish cause of death
    (n) International   (n) Dictatorial person
    (o) Polygamy   (o) Evil
    (p) Pantheism   (p) Generous
    (q) Agnostic   (q) Between nations
    (r) Antipathy   (r) God is everywhere
    (s) Automobile   (s) Two hundredth anniversary
    (t) Tripod   (t) Of the same

2. The prefix bi- means two. Match up the words on the left with their meaning on the right:

    (a) Biannual   (a) For use by both ears
    (b) Bilateral   (b) Having two axles

(c) Bimonthly   (c) Occurring twice each year
(d) Bifocal   (d) Occurring every two years
(e) Biennial   (e) Using both hands
(f) Binary   (f) Vehicle with two wheels
(g) Bimanual   (g) Occurring every two months
(h) Bicycle   (h) On both sides
(i) Biaxial   (i) Involving pairs
(j) Biaural   (j) Glasses combining distance and near vision

3. The prefix mis- means bad or wrong. Write the missing words, all beginning with mis- in the spaces beneath:

   (a) The guard said the man was .... in the street.

   (b) The judge said the funds had been ....

   (c) The accountant believed the totals had been ....

   (d) The public felt it was a .... of justice.

   (e) The actor was totally .... in the play.

   (f) Most children are full of ....

   (g) It was unfair of him to .... what I said.

   (h) He should not have .... my statement.

   (i) The judge found him guilty of a ....

   (j) The dress is a total ....

   (k) When I was driving the car I had a ....

   (l) When taking the free he .... the ball.

   (m) I found his speech a ....

   (n) There is no doubt but that the solicitor .... him in court.

   (o) You should try not to .... your words.

   (p) I can't find it so I'm sure I .... it somewhere.

4. The prefix tri- means three. Supply words beginning with tri- for the following phrases:

   (a) A flag with three colours   ....
   (b) A three-wheeled vehicle for children   ....
   (c) Three days of prayer   ....
   (d) Occurring every three years   ....

(e) Having three spouses　　　　　　　..

(f) A group of three　　　　　　　　　..

(g) Having three sides　　　　　　　　..

(h) Having three languages　　　　　..

(i) Figure bounded by three straight lines　..

(j) A three-legged stand　　　　　　..

Suffixes

Suffixes are placed at the end of words. For example, if the suffix -*able* is added to *change*, we have the word *changeable*.

The commonly used suffixes are:

-cide (kill) – suicide, matricide, genocide

-ess (feminine) – abbess, mistress

-fold (times) – twofold, tenfold, a hundredfold

-ful (full) – helpful, beautiful, thankful

-hood (state) – boyhood, manhood

-less (without) – helpless, thankless, hopeless

-ology (study of) – sociology, psychology, biology

-man (person) – craftsman, swordsman, ploughman

-mania (craze for) – kleptomania, bibliomania

-monger (dealer) – ironmonger, fishmonger

-phobia (fear) – claustrophobia, hydrophobia

Suffixes and spelling: suffixes can cause problems in spelling. Note 'movable' but 'changeable'. Also note when to use 'full' and 'ful'.

ACTIVITY 2

1. Using the list of suffixes above, insert the missing word in the following sentences:

    (a) Many people are criminals because of their lost ....

    (b) Hitler was guilty of ....

    (c) The science of society is known as ....

(d) A fear of water is known as ....

(e) Some people just can't keep their hands off things; they are called ....

(f) If you are given a present, you should be ....

(g) A person who sells fish is called a ....

(h) The killing of one's mother is known as ....

(i) He is always collecting books; he is a real ....

(j) Many more students study .... than study chemistry.

2. Match the words ending in -ology on the left with their correct meaning on the right:

   (a) Astrology   (a) The study of God
   (b) Anthropology   (b) The study of water
   (c) Archaeology   (c) The study of language
   (d) Biology   (d) The study of criminals
   (e) Criminology   (e) The study of the stars and their influence on human affairs
   (f) Entomology   (f) The study of insects
   (g) Gynaecology   (g) The study of human antiquities
   (h) Genealogy   (h) The study of the descent of families
   (i) Hydrology   (i) The study of mankind
   (j) Meteorology   (j) The study of climates
   (k) Philology   (k) The study of life forms
   (l) Theology   (l) The study of functions and diseases of women

3. Write down the meaning of the following words ending in -phobia and -mania.

   (a) Anglophobia   ....
   (b) Agoraphobia   ....
   (c) Claustrophobia ....
   (d) Gynophobia   ....
   (e) Hydrophobia   ....
   (f) Zoophobia   ....
   (g) Bibliomania   ....
   (h) Kleptomania   ....
   (i) Megalomania   ....

(j) *Nymphomania* ....

(k) *Chronomania* ....

(l) *Ablutomania* ....

Plurals

The plural form of most words is very simple, just add *s* to the singular. There are some basic rules that will be of some help but they do not cover all the eventualities.

Type 1: Add -*s* to the singular, e.g. girl, girls; boy, boys.

Type 2: Words ending in -*y* preceded by a consonant take -*ies* in the plural, e.g. lady, ladies; holy, holies; deputy, deputies; secretary, secretaries.

When the final *y* is preceded by a vowel, just add -*s*. For example: holiday, holidays; donkey, donkeys.

Type 3: Words ending in -*o* take -*s* in the plural, but sometimes take -*es*, e.g. folio, folios; studio, studios; but be careful of cargo, cargoes; potato, potatoes.

Type 4: Some words ending in -*f* or -*fe* take -*ves* in the plural, e.g. half, halves; life, lives.

Type 5: Some words form plurals by changing the vowel, e.g. foot, feet; goose, geese.

Type 6: Compound words usually form the plural by changing or adding to the most important word, e.g. brother-in-law, brothers-in-law; looker-on, lookers-on.

Type 7: Some words are only used in the plural, e.g. trousers, spectacles.

Type 8: Some words have the same form in the singular as in the plural, e.g. sheep, salmon.

Type 9: Foreign words may form their plurals according to the rules of their original language. However, words in common usage may be allowed to form their plurals according to the rules of English, e.g. formula, formulas, though according to the rules of Latin it should be formulae.

Foreign words

Singular	Plural
agenda	agenda, agendas
analysis	analyses
appendix	appendices, appendixes
axis	axes
basis	bases
bureau	bureaux, bureaus
circus	circuses
crisis	crises
criterion	criteria
curriculum	curricula
datum	data
dogma	dogmas
focus	foci, focuses
fungus	fungi, funguses
gymnasium	gymnasia, gymnasiums
hypothesis	hypotheses
ignoramus	ignoramuses
index	indices, indexes
medium	media (the press, radio and TV)
	mediums (those communicating with the dead)
memorandum	memoranda, memorandums
millennium	millennia, millenniums
nucleus	nuclei
oasis	oases
phenomenon	phenomena
plateau	plateaux, plateaus
radius	radii
series	series
species	species
stadium	stadia
stimulus	stimuli

stratum	strata
syllabus	syllabi, syllabuses
synthesis	syntheses
thesis	theses

ACTIVITY 3

1. Correct all the errors in the following sentences, ensuring that singular nouns are followed by singular verbs and plural nouns by plural verbs:

   Example: 'The media in Ireland has high standards.'

   This can be rendered as:

   'The media in Ireland have high standards.'

   (a) The students are working on their thesis.

   (b) RTE is a news medium.

   (c) Two court-martials were held this morning.

   (d) I always put two spoonfuls of sugar in my tea.

   (e) Powerful physique is one of the criterions for a good Kerry footballer.

   (f) Many people make jokes about mother-in-laws.

   (g) Most women do not have lady's-maids now.

   (h) We have too many good-for-nothings in society.

   (i) The company employs ten salesmen.

   (j) The child fell under the horse's hoofs.

   (k) The woman were delighted when they heard the news.

2. Turn the highlighted words in the following sentences into their plural form and ensure that the verbs are also plural:

   (a) A **lay-by** is useful on a busy road.

   (b) A **radio** is a help to pass the time.

   (c) Many houses have a **piano**.

   (d) What is a **hero**?

   (e) A **loaf** of bread will not go far.

   (f) **Life** is sacred.

   (g) The **thief** was caught.

(h) Put on your **scarf**.

(i) The **staff** of the school was there.

(j) A rainbow is a beautiful **phenomenon**.

(k) The **thesis** was completed last year.

(l) I hear the **echo**.

(m) I saw the **dwarf**.

(n) Put it in the **safe**.

ACTIVITY 4

From the right hand side choose the word or phrase that corresponds most closely to the highlighted word on the left:

(1) A literary **allusion** — (a) correct (b) indirect (c) reference (d) important

(2) **Ambiguous** word — (a) difficult (b) strange (c) double meaning (d) observe

(3) **Amenable** person — (a) criminal (b) foreign (c) responsive (d) silly

(4) **Insipid** personality — (a) outgoing (b) dull (c) happy (d) introverted

(5) **Bravura** performance — (a) hopeless (b) brilliant (c) uninspired (d) mediocre

(6) **Alleviate** disaster — (a) relieve (b) increase (c) explain (d) report

(7) **Blatant** disregard — (a) conscious (b) devious (c) strong (d) thoughtless

(8) **Castigate** unfairly — (a) punish (b) reject (c) demote (d) acquire

(9) **Dogmatic** personality — (a) logical (b) weak (c) illogical (d) forcing opinions on others

(10) A **catalyst** for change — (a) facilitates (b) prevents (c) in favour (d) retards

(11) **Denigrate** the proposal — (a) support (b) castigate (c) defame (d) second

(12) A **cavalier** attitude — (a) bad (b) off-hand (c) proper (d) dangerous

(13) **Concurrent** sentence — (a) long (b) at the same time (c) hard labour (d) complex

(14) A **conciliatory** gesture   (a) open (b) aggressive (c) friendly (d) ambiguous

(15) An **audacious** suggestion   (a) daring (b) outrageous (c) stupid (d) impractical

(16) A **disproportionate** reaction   (a) timid (b) too large or small (c) over-zealous (d) criminal

(17) **Dissipate** your earnings   (a) increase (b) invest wisely (c) control (d) squander

(18) A **prevalent** attitude   (a) correct (b) widespread (c) immoral (d) dangerous

(19) A **prudent** suggestion   (a) foolish (b) wise (c) impractical (d) diplomatic

(20) Of **dubious** value   (a) great (b) precious (c) doubtful (d) useless

Abbreviations

The use of abbreviations is common in all walks of life. It saves time and increases efficiency. You should be familiar with the following ones. If not, you will find some of them in your dictionary.

PAYE, GNP, a/c, ACCA, ACA, COD, PRSI, VAT, AA, BBC, EU, GMT, HMSO, PRO, VIP, SRN, RSVP, BComm, BA, BE, AMIEE, BSc, PhD, CIMA.

The following abbreviations are relevant to Ireland. You will find what they stand for in the IPA *Administration Yearbook & Diary*.

UCC, UCG, UCD, DCU, RTC, TCD, UL, NUI, NCAD, HEA, DIT, NCEA, CAO, RIA, FÁS, ICMSA, IFA, TUI, INTO, ASTI, VEC, ICTU, IBOA, AIB, GAA, FAI, IRFU, IPA, ESB, IEI, IMI, FF, FG, PD, WP, ICA, ESRI, FLAC, MCC, HEDCO, TD, MEP, MD, DG, SIPTU, DL, IBEC, IMPACT, CCI.

Review

1. Find five words, other than the ones mentioned in this chapter, that have prefixes.
2. Find five words, other than the ones mentioned in this chapter, that have suffixes.

3. Find the word for a craze for animals.
4. Find the word for a fear of being alone.
5. Find the plural of the following:

   company, journey, man, child, deer, grouse, trout, fish, chateau, memento, halo, himself, sanatorium, stadium, sheaf, erratum, photo, motto, manifesto, tax.
6. Check that you understand the meaning of the following words:

   unequivocal, avaricious, cursory, opulent, gullible, subtle, invective, lethal, vicarious, tenuous, innocuous, strident, halcyon, derision, dearth, scurrilous, diffident, zenith, anti-climax, placate.
7. What do the following abbreviations stand for?
   RDS, B&I, SDLP, RUC, FCA, USI, UN, NCH, BIM, VHI, PD.

Pitfalls

between among

The words *between* and *among* are often used incorrectly.

Between is used when two people or things are involved, e.g. 'I divided the sweets *between* Iseult and David.'

Among is used when three or more are concerned, e.g. 'I divided the sweets *among* Iseult, David and Una.'

Confusing words

impassable	impassible	judicious	judicial
personal	personnel	aggravate	arrogate
artifact	artifice	average	averment

Quiz

What is a 'Goldwynism'?

Here are three examples:

(1) He bit the hand that laid the golden egg.

(2) Include me out.

(3) A gentleman's agreement is not worth the paper it's written on.

Who was Goldwyn?

Spellings

The words most commonly misspelled are highlighted.

January	jocose	**juicy**
Japanese	jocular	jumble
jargon	jostle	junction
jaunty	journal	jungle
jealous	journalist	junior
jealousy	journey	junket
jeopardy	journeys	junta
jersey	**jubilee**	justice
jester	judge	justification
jewel	judiciary	justify
jeweller	judicious	**juvenile**
jewellery	juice	

WRITING 3:
YOU MUST KNOW THE BASICS

Subject and predicate

'A way a lone a last a loved a long the' (the ending of *Finnegans Wake* by James Joyce).

Words carry meaning but to express our thoughts completely we use sentences. A sentence is a group of words which has a complete meaning. It begins with a capital letter and ends with a full stop, question mark or exclamation mark.

Example

Iseult goes to school.

This is a correct sentence. In all sentences two things are essential:

(1) A subject. The subject is the word or words which stand for the person or thing about which something is said. In our example, *Iseult* is the subject.

(2) A predicate. The predicate is the name given to the part of the sentence which tells you about the subject. In our example *goes to school* is the predicate.

Sentences may be short or long, simple or complex but they must have the two elements mentioned. Sometimes one of the elements may not be in the sentence but may be understood. If somebody snatches your money and you shout 'Stop', is that one word a sentence? Yes, it is. The predicate is 'Stop' and the subject 'you' is understood.

Examples

SUBJECT	PREDICATE
(a) The office	opened at 9 a.m.
(b) Conor	laughed.
(c) *You* (understood)	halt!

(d) *You* (understood) put that down!

(e) Tipperary *is* (understood) the home of hurlers.

Question: Is the ending of *Finnegans Wake* at the beginning of this chapter a sentence?

ACTIVITY I

1. Decide which of the following are sentences and tick YES or NO in the column provided:

	YES	NO
(a) The greatest scoundrel I ever met		
(b) Careful!		
(c) Brown football boots		
(d) In the evening		
(e) Yours sincerely, Enda		
(f) See you tomorrow.		
(g) No parking.		
(h) Post early for Christmas.		
(i) Drifts of snow everywhere		
(j) 'Nonsense!' said the mother.		

2. Pick out the subject and predicate in the following:

    (a) A great man for jokes.

    (b) The manager called a meeting.

    (c) Be sure to keep accurate minutes.

    (d) We all complained.

    (e) A mighty man.

    (f) Please ask if the sales forecast is available.

    (g) It is surprising.

    (h) Don't mention that.

    (i) What a lovely day!

3. Add predicates to each of the following subjects to form complete sentences:

    (a) The river ....

    (b) The setting sun ....

(c) The agenda ....
   (d) The liquidator ....
   (e) The receiver ....
   (f) The view from the window ....
   (g) Winter time ....
   (h) Computers ....
   (i) Silence ....
4. Supply suitable subjects to the following predicates to form complete sentences:
   (a) .... entertained the audience.
   (b) .... decided to adjourn the meeting.
   (c) .... collapsed.
   (d) .... is a dangerous sport.
   (e) .... came to a stop.
   (f) .... flows into the sea.
   (g) .... are to receive an increase in wages.
   (h) .... re-open in September.
   (i) .... is a complete thought.
   (j) .... has a subject and a predicate.

Agreement

The most common error in sentences is lack of agreement. Agreement is concerned with the relationship between a subject and a verb. A verb is the word in the sentence that tells you what the subject does.

Iseult goes to school.
  | \
subject verb

Subject and verb must agree, that is they should both be singular or both be plural. In most cases this is obvious:

'Enda is in school' (subject and verb singular).

'The boys are in school' (subject and verb plural).

Be careful of the following types:

• *Type (i): Two or more singular subjects joined by 'and'*
When two or more singular subjects are joined by *and*, the verb is plural. For example:
'The man and boy are in the car.'
'The student and teacher are happy.'

• *Type (ii): Each, every, any, either, neither*
Each of these words takes a singular verb. For example:
'Each of us should mind her own business.'
'Everyone is going to the match.'
'Either Iseult or Enda is in charge.'

• *Type (iii): None*
None can be looked upon as singular or plural. Strictly speaking it should be singular since *none* comes from the two words *not one*. Because of usage, however, the plural is now generally allowed. For example:
'None of the troops was injured.'
or
'None of the troops were injured.'

• *Type (iv): Subjects not joined by 'and'*
Two or more subjects not joined by *and* take a singular verb. For example:
'The ship, with its crew, was lost.'
'John, with Emma, goes to school.'

• *Type (v): 'One of those who'*
In sentences containing phrases such as *one of those who*, the following verb should be plural agreeing with *who* and not singular agreeing with *one*. For example:
'He is one of those judges who delight in putting people in prison.'
'She is one of those managers who believe in punctuality.'

• *Type (vi): Collective nouns*
A collective noun is the name given to several persons or things of the same kind regarded as one group, e.g. crowd, school, team. Generally speaking, collective nouns are singular and are followed by singular verbs. For example:
'The team is playing on Sunday.'
'The mob is very hostile.'

But it has now come to the point, through usage, that the plural may be used. So we can say the following, depending on whether we want to express the idea of the group or the individuals in the group:

'The committee has (or have) published its (or their) report.'

'The council intends (or intend) to refuse permission.'

NB The important thing is to be consistent in your use of singular or plural. Consistency is the important rule. You should not write, for example, 'The class *is* requested to have *their* notes available' because *is* is singular and *their* is plural.

- *Type (vii): Attraction*

Many writers fall into what is called the *error of attraction*. For example:

'A parcel of books were found' (incorrect).

The subject is *parcel* which is singular, and hence the verb should be *was*. The verb is attracted by the plural word *books* and there is a tendency to use the plural verb. So it should be:

'A parcel of books was found' (correct).

- *Type (viii): Titles of books, articles and poems*

The titles of books, articles and poems are singular and must take a singular verb. For example:

'*The Grapes of Wrath* is excellent.'

'Lamb's *Tales from Shakespeare* is enjoyable.'

It must not be *are excellent* or *are enjoyable* because we are writing of just one book.

- *Type (ix): Nouns with plural form*

Certain nouns, although plural in form, are treated as singular, e.g. *means, physics, news* ('The news is good').

Trousers, scissors and *shears* may be considered singular or plural. They are of course singular when preceded by *a pair of*. *Wages, riches* and *alms* are, however, considered plural. For example:

'My wages are £65 a week.'

Certain words may use the same form for singular or plural, e.g. *sheep, dozen, fish*.

Exception: When two singular nouns joined by *and* refer to the same person or thing, or are closely related in meaning, they take a singular verb. For example:

'Milk and sugar is provided.'

'The tumult and the shouting dies.'

ACTIVITY 2

1. Choose the correct verb in each of the following sentences.

    (a) Enda and Conor is/are going to the match.

    (b) Emma, with John, is/are going to school.

    (c) Bread and water is/are a good diet.

    (d) Shouting and roaring are/is forbidden.

    (e) Openness and frankness are/is expected from all the participants.

    (f) Great love and devotion is/are bestowed on children.

    (g) Hammer and chisel is/are on your desk.

    (h) Garret, with Emma, John, Patrick, and Conor, is/are going to the theatre.

    (i) There is/are bacon and eggs for breakfast.

    (j) The size of the task, and its very complexity, lead/leads people to avoid it altogether.

2. Correct the errors in the following sentences:

    (a) Each of us must do our duty.

    (b) Each member of staff should park their car in the space provided.

    (c) Everyone has their own opinions.

    (d) Everyone is going to the concert.

    (e) Is there anyone there?

    (f) If anyone is going they would want to leave now.

    (g) Either Patrick or Garret are responsible.

    (h) Either Mary, Emma, Dermot or Tom is interested in the topic.

    (i) Is anyone going?

    (j) Neither I nor the stewards was aware of what was happening.

    (k) Neither I nor the steward was at the presentation.

    (l) Neither James nor Michael nor Mary is in a position to make a statement on the matter.

3. Explain why each verb is singular in the sentences below:

    (a) A series of ten questions was asked in the examination.

    (b) The value of your books, letters and notes is considerable.

    (c) A catalogue of descriptions, prices and reference numbers was found in the attic.

(d) A wide variety of apples, oranges and pears is available.

(e) What is the news?

(f) Every Tom, Dick and Harry is doing that.

(g) The scissors is in the drawer.

(h) Your trousers is on the line.

(i) Ten miles is a long distance to go home every evening.

Review

1. What is a sentence?
2. What two elements must a sentence have?
3. How do you find the subject of a sentence?
4. How do you find the predicate of a sentence?
5. What is meant by saying that the subject may be understood?
6. Give two examples of sentences where subjects are understood.
7. What is known as 'the error of attraction'?
8. What is a collective noun and should it be considered singular or plural?
9. 'None of us is going to class.' Is that sentence correct or incorrect? Give reasons for your answer.
10. 'Two fours is/are eight.' Should the verb be singular or plural?

Pitfalls

Comparatives and superlatives

Adjectives describe, or qualify, nouns and pronouns, e.g. 'the clever man'. Adverbs qualify verbs, adjectives and other adverbs, e.g. 'The machine moved very quickly.'

Adjectives can be used to make comparisons:

(a) Positive: 'Their service is *good*' (no comparisons made).

(b) Comparative: 'Their service is *better* than the other company's' (comparing two persons or things).

(c) Superlative: 'Their service is the *best* available' (comparing more than two persons or things).

Adverbs too can be used in this way:
(a) This van brakes quickly.
(b) This van brakes *more* quickly than the old one.
(c) This van brakes *most* quickly.

Confusing words

accept	except	affect	effect
access	excess	aggravate	annoy
adapt	adopt	alter	altar
adverse	averse	alternate	alternative
advise	advice	allusion	illusion

Quiz

Can you explain the following excerpt from the Income Tax Act 1967, section 507?

'For the purposes of the Part, a person shall be deemed not to have failed to do anything required to be done within a limited time if he did it within such further time, if any, as the commissioners or officer concerned may have allowed; and where a person had a reasonable excuse for not doing anything required to be done, he shall be deemed not to have failed to do it if he did it without unreasonable delay after the excuse had ceased.'

Spellings

The words most commonly misspelled are highlighted.

kangaroo	**kidnapper**	knave
karate	kidney	knead
keen	kilogram	knight
keenness	kilometre	knitting
keepsake	**kindliness**	knot
kennel	kindly	know-all
ketchup	kindred	know-how
keyboard	kitchen	**knowledge**
keyhole	kleptomaniac	knuckle
khaki	knapsack	

(12)

WRITING 4:
PUNCTUATION GIVES MEANING

Introduction

Punctuation is not used for ornamentation, but to help the reader understand a passage in the way in which the writer intended. A written text does not have expressions, gestures or vocal inflection to help convey meaning, so written English must depend on punctuation. The main purpose of punctuation is to help the writer convey his ideas clearly and without ambiguity, and to help the reader understand a passage without having to reread it. When we say 'Are you sad?', the pitch of the voice or its inflection shows that we are asking a question, which in writing is indicated by the question mark. All writers must decide what type of punctuation to use to convey their meaning.

Sample 1
'It was the best of times, it was the worst of times, it was the age of wisdom, it was the age of foolishness, it was the epoch of belief, it was the epoch of incredulity, it was the season of Light, it was the season of Darkness, it was the spring of hope, it was the winter of despair, we had everything before us, we had nothing before us, we were all going direct to Heaven, we were all going direct the other way – in short, the period was so far like the present period, that some of its noisiest authorities insisted on its being received, for good or for evil, in the superlative degree of comparison only.'

(Charles Dickens, *A Tale of Two Cities*, Heron Books, Centennial Edition)

Sample 2
'Studies serve for delight, for ornament, and for ability. Their chief use for delight, is in privateness and retiring; for ornament, is in discourse; and for ability, is in the judgment and disposition of business. For expert men can execute, and perhaps judge of particulars, one by one; but the general counsels, and the plots and marshalling of affairs, come best

from those that are learned. To spend too much time in studies is sloth; to use them too much for ornament, is affectation; to make judgment wholly by their rules, is the humour of a scholar. They perfect nature, and are perfected by experience: for natural abilities are like natural plants, that need proyning by study; and study themselves do give forth directions too much at large, except they be bounded by experience.'

(Francis Bacon, 'Of Studies')

Sample 3

'Momentous day. The sun is shining. That in itself is not momentous – merely, for August, surprising.

The house sits sideways to the sea and facing south, so all the rooms are filled with sun. Judging by the haze on the horizon, almost like steam rising off the sea, the sun is shining everywhere, not just on this stretch of the east coast of Ireland, but in Cork, Skibbereen, Galway and Kilkenny; drying up the grass and causing anxiety to the farmers. Weather seems permanently to be causing anxiety to the farmers. Even in England, where I have never been, the sun is shining. We read this in the newspaper which arrives in time for breakfast every morning and keeps Aunt Mary occupied for half an hour or so.

If you climb up the hill at the back of the house, you can see Wales on a clear day. It's not really very exciting, just a grey lump in the distance, but it's somewhere else. Somewhere new. For the last two weeks there has been no sign of Wales at all, just that pale haze steaming gently up into the sky, shutting this island off from the rest of the world.

The morning trains from Dublin have been filled with people coming down from the city to sit on the beach, and paddle and throw stones into the sea, and shout at their children, who change as the hours go by from pale city children to fretful whiners grilled beyond endurance by the unexpected sun. They stay mainly up at the far end of the beach, near to the station and the two small cafés that sell fruit drinks and ice creams, and plates of biscuits and delicious cups of reviving tea. They don't in fact bother us over here at all. Two special trains have to be put on in the late afternoon to bring them back to town, as they don't all fit on the five-thirty from Wicklow. They leave an awful mess on the sand but the tide takes care of most of that. Poor Mr Carroll the stationmaster, however, has a terrible time keeping his station clean and tidy, and is the one person in the village to admit to being glad that heatwaves don't happen too often.

Momentous.

It is my eighteenth birthday.'

(Jennifer Johnston, *The Old Jest*, London: Hamish Hamilton Ltd, 1979)

Sample 4

'Yes because he never did a thing like that before as ask to get his breakfast in bed with a couple of eggs since the City Arms hotel when he used to be pretending to be laid up with a sick voice doing his highness to make himself interesting to that old faggot Mrs Riordan that he thought he had a great leg of and never left us a farthing all for masses for herself and her soul greatest miser ever was actually afraid to lay out 4d for her methylated spirits telling me all her ailments she had too much old chat in her about politics and earthquakes and the end of the world let us have a bit of fun first God help the world if all the women were her sort down on bathingsuits and lownecks of course nobody wanted her to wear I suppose she was pious because no man would look at her twice I hope Ill never be like her a wonder she didnt want us to cover our faces . . .'

(James Joyce, *Ulysses*, London: Vintage Books, 1961)

Discussion on four examples

Each of the four writers above uses punctuation, not just to convey meaning, but also tone and emotion. Dickens begins with a very long sentence and rushes along from one short phrase to another using only commas. This gives the impression of confusion and turbulence. It is a passage full of feeling.

Bacon's 'Of Studies', on the other hand, is a short, concise, closely argued piece. It is an intellectual essay bereft of emotion. It is almost mathematical in its symmetry. There seems to be three reasons or three observations on everything. He uses a number of semi-colons to balance his arguments.

Jennifer Johnston once described herself as 'fairly handy with the comma'. This extract is written in very simple language and uses only the simplest punctuation. In it a young girl is talking to the reader and the simple words and the simple punctuation help to convey youth and freshness.

The final extract is very different from the others. It has no punctuation at all. In fact the final forty pages of *Ulysses* has no punctuation except for the full stop at the end. Joyce is depicting Molly Bloom, thinking to herself, as she lies in her bed in Dublin on the night of 16 June 1904. When we think, we do not use punctuation marks but move from one thought to another and back again without maintaining any particular order. So Joyce, instead of putting in punctuation marks to give meaning, in fact dispenses with them.

But for the rest of us punctuation is very important. If you read the following sentences you will see why:

(a) The prisoner felt the judge was a danger to society.

(b) The prisoner, felt the judge, was a danger to society.

or

(a) Peter said the teacher is marvellous.

(b) 'Peter', said the teacher, 'is marvellous.'

In both sentences the words and the word order are exactly the same, but there is a considerable difference between them. What has caused the difference? The answer is punctuation.

Punctuation makes the meaning of what we write clear to the reader. When we talk, the rise and fall of the voice and the pauses we use help to make our meaning clear but in writing, we have no such aids. Instead we use punctuation.

Explanation of punctuation marks with examples

Full stop (.)

(i) The full stop is used at the end of a complete sentence. For example:

'I will go tomorrow.'

'Carry it over there.'

'I feel fine.'

(ii) The full stop is used after abbreviations, e.g. etc., ave., Sept. It is also used after single letters standing for a word:

'I can type 40 w.p.m.'

'The car does 30 m.p.g.'

Though indeed modern usage allows you to omit the full stops in well known abbreviations such as these.

Abbreviations in common use do not require a full stop, e.g. per cent, memo, Mr, St, Dr. The full stop is also dropped from abbreviations that make a pronounceable word, e.g. FÁS.

(iii) Full stops in a series are used to indicate the omission of words from a passage. Three are used if the omission is from the middle of a sentence, e.g. 'We are experiencing a literary breakdown . . . unlike anything I know of in the history of letters.'

Four are used if the omission is from the end of a sentence, e.g. 'As Dickens wrote, "It was the best of times, it was the worst of times . . . ."'

Examples

The lights turned red. The car stopped.

The teacher is happy. Run quickly.

It started pouring rain. I never saw anything like it.

David is going to school in September. Gillian is still too young.

Capital letter

(i) A capital letter is used to begin every sentence, e.g. 'It was kind of you.'

(ii) All proper nouns, proper adjectives and the first person singular pronoun begin with a capital letter, e.g. America, Tipperary, an Irish horse, I.

(iii) People's titles and ranks are always introduced with capital letters, e.g. Professor Scully, Lord Mayor, Major Kelly, President Douglas Hyde. But lower case should be used for those titles when applied in a general sense, e.g. 'a major in the army'.

(iv) The days of the week and months are introduced with capitals, but the seasons are not, e.g. Sunday, Tuesday, May, July, but spring, summer. However in common usage the seasons are often capitalised.

(v) Buildings, well-known geographical regions and historical events begin with a capital, e.g. Leinster House, the North, the Irish Civil War.

(vi) In titles of books, plays, films, etc., the first word always has a capital, but after that, conjunctions, prepositions and the words *the* and *a* are written in lower case, e.g. *An Only Child, The Lonely Passion of Judith Hearne, Lord of the Flies.*

Examples

Who is that?

How is Bernadette?

I believe in God.

It is Friday.

The Taoiseach spoke at length.

The Anglo-Irish Agreement was signed.

The Minister for Finance attended.

Michael Collins was the Commander-in-Chief.

The North is in turmoil.

Comma (,)

(i) The comma is used to mark off a natural pause at the end of a phrase, e.g. 'When we had seen the fire, we went home.'

(ii) The comma is also used to mark off phrases in the middle of sentences. For example:

'The student, standing just outside the door, heard the teacher laughing.'

'The enclosed book, which you may retain, is sent to you for your comments.'

(iii) If a sentence contains two or more phrases or clauses linked by *and, but, for* or *nor*, then a comma precedes the linking word, e.g. 'He decided to do his lessons first, and then watch television.'

(iv) Commas are used with words and phrases such as *at last, finally, however, of course, in fact, meanwhile, nevertheless*. Here are two examples:

'However, we will do the best we can.'

'It is clear, however, he was not telling the truth.'

(v) Commas are used to separate items in a list, e.g. 'The bag contains books, pencils, ink, paper and envelopes.'

It is not necessary to use a comma before the *and* separating the final two items unless not using it would cause ambiguity, as when one writes: 'At school I studied French, Biology, Physics, Irish, English and American History.' Did he study the subject English or was it English History? It would be clearer to write '. . . English, and American History' or '. . . English History and American History.'

Examples

The boy, with great expectation, waited for the result.

A loud, heavy bang was heard.

People of Tipperary, the famine is over.

The rain having stopped, all went home.

Every day, every week, every year, his mother worries about him.

The question is, who will bell the cat?

Semi-colon (;)

The semi-colon is a longer stop than the comma. It is used in the following situations:

(i) If two sentences or main clauses are logically connected but not joined by a linking word, then they are separated by a semi-colon. For example:

'I went to their last production; it was not very good.'

'The product is selling well; I think it will continue to do so.'

'The firm is doing badly; it will close soon.'

Sometimes these same statements could be written in separate sentences, e.g. 'I went to their last production. It was not very good.'

(ii) The semi-colon is also used to separate items in a list when these are phrases rather than single words, e.g. 'The weather was at its most wintry: dark, heavy clouds that rode quickly across the sky; gusts of wet wind that rattled the slates on the houses; the chill in the air that makes the body shiver.'

Examples

He is very happy; you should be also.

Go home; it would be better.

He was going out the door; otherwise I would not have seen him.

I refused to say what he asked me to say; I felt he had been misinformed.

ACTIVITY 1

Punctuate the following:

1. go home
2. i will do it
3. carlow is a small county cork is a big one
4. the boys waited all night for the train it was very late
5. hurling is a great game i like playing it
6. when we got to the field we could not get in as we had forgotten our money
7. i dont like examinations yet they have to be faced
8. most schools in ireland now are modern not like years ago
9. the leaves on the trees are turning brown now what a pity
10. when i was young we kicked the dead leaves before us as we ran to school

11. the towns main streets are very narrow two cars can barely pass
12. people in general are fairly conscientious at their work i think
13. the all ireland football final is a great occasion for kerry people some others arent all that interested
14. there are many more female than male primary teachers is this a disturbing trend
15. vocational schools are governed by the 1930 vocational education act
16. in ireland we have schools which are privately owned and schools which are in public ownership which gives parents a choice

ACTIVITY 2

Punctuate the following:

1. the organisation known as teagasc deals with agriculture
2. the gaa was founded in 1884 at hayes hotel thurles co tipperary
3. the firm is going to establish an o and m department
4. a car able to travel 60 mpg would be very useful
5. ireland has a great tradition in the short story russia has also
6. the ida tries to attract foreign firms to ireland with a package of attractive grants
7. when the school year finishes students look for work
8. it is always sad i think to remember the last summer of your childhood
9. somebody once said when youve seen one city youve seen them all
10. the enclosed form which you should complete as soon as possible will guarantee you entry
11. he went into the house and closed the door behind him
12. nihe dublin is now a university
13. did he cut his hand with a knife or did he fall
14. he stumbled but he didnt fall
15. ill be there tomorrow however dont expect me to be on time
16. according to you i should win easily
17. he did it yesterday in fact he might have done it the day before
18. never do that do you hear me as long as im around

19. i rushed into the room and i threw books papers pencils rulers and maps on the table

20. the enclosed book which you should read carefully and which youll find interesting was in fact written four years ago and then according to the best information i can find was published immediately well not immediately but as soon as the publisher could manage it after all someone had to proofread it

Colon (:)

The colon used to be looked on as a longer pause than a semi-colon. It is now rarely used in this way. It is now used to indicate that something is to follow.

(i) The colon is used to introduce a list of items, e.g. 'The bag contains the following: hurley, football, jerseys, first-aid kit, sweat bands and a whistle.'

(ii) A quotation, if it is a long one, is also introduced by a colon, e.g. 'The President went to the platform and said: "I want to speak about a very serious matter . . . ."'

(iii) The colon is also used to separate two statements in a sentence which are in sharp contrast to each other. For example:

'If you join us you will succeed: if you do not, you will fail.'

'Kings rule: subjects obey.'

Examples

Man proposes: God disposes.

Send me the following: a pen, a brush, a pencil and some ink.

Then the chairman stood up and said: 'I would like to welcome you all here this evening . . . .'

Good health gives happiness: there is none without it.

Parentheses ()

(i) Brackets or parentheses are used to separate words in a sentence which provide additional information or which explain something about certain words in the sentence, e.g. 'The subjects I like most are history (Irish history) and biology.'

(ii) Brackets are used to explain foreign words, e.g. 'My attitude is *de mortuis nil nisi bonum* (of the dead we speak nothing but good).'

Examples

He gave all he had (it wasn't much) to the cause.

Be there on Wednesday (I'll be there myself) at 3 o'clock.

He'll be running in the Olympics (not that he has much of a chance) for the last time.

When he was at school (a long time ago) he did well.

Hyphen (-)

(i) A hyphen is a joining mark, e.g. brother-in-law, commander-in-chief, up-to-date.

(ii) The hyphen is also used to divide a word at the end of a line, e.g. dis-appointed.

Examples

He is a very with-it person.

He looks very down-at-heel.

She had a hang-dog look.

The word has three syllables, for-mer-ly.

On a typewriter or computer the same key is used to type the hyphen and the dash.

Dash (–)

(i) The dash is used to denote a strongly marked aside. For example:

'Many countries – Ireland was not one of them – won gold medals at the Olympics.'

'Complete the form – and don't forget to sign it – as soon as possible.'

(ii) The dash is also used to bring together several subjects belonging to the same verb, e.g. 'If you buy this house, blinds, carpets and heaters – all will be included in the sale.'

Examples

Send down everything next week – this week if possible.

At the age of ninety – such is old age – he could remember nothing.

Last year – the date is uncertain – we bought it at discount.

Padraig was born in Perth, Australia, today – I'm not sure what time.

Apostrophe (')

The rules for the apostrophe are very simple but cause endless trouble to students.

(i) The apostrophe is used to indicate omitted letters in contractions. It is placed where the omitted letter would appear if the word were written out in full, e.g. do not, *don't*; could not, *couldn't*; was not, *wasn't*; it is, *it's*; they are, *they're*.

(ii) The apostrophe is also used to denote ownership, e.g. the boy's coat, cat's paw, table's leg. Here it is used in the singular.

The *s* can still be used even when the possessor's name ends in an *s*, e.g. Keats's poems, Dickens's novels, St James's feast.

(iii) The apostrophe without the *s* is used if three consecutive *s* sounds come together and make pronunciation difficult, e.g. Moses' Law, Jesus' disciples, St Francis' Day.

(iv) An apostrophe is placed after the *s* in the possessive plural form, e.g. boys' coats, cats' paws, ladies' shoes.

(v) If the plural of a noun does not end in *s*, then *s* is added in the possessive form, e.g. men's coats, women's shoes, children's hats, sheep's clothing.

(vi) Some possessive pronouns do not take an apostrophe, e.g. his, hers, yours, theirs, its, ours, mine.

The word *whose* does not take an apostrophe.

Examples

I won't do it.

I don't like it.

The guard's helmet was knocked off.

Children's hour will begin soon.

Go to the players' entrance.

I'll be there.

It's got a great taste.

Question mark (?)

A question mark is used to replace a full stop when a direct question is asked, e.g. 'When are we going?'

A question mark is not used when the question is indirect, e.g. 'I asked when we were going.'

Examples

Who's there?

What's the matter?

Are you going?

Exclamation mark (!)

An exclamation mark is used after an exclamatory expression, e.g. My God!, Well!, You don't say!

Examples

How the mighty have fallen!

Well, can you beat that!

I don't believe you!

Quotation marks (' " " ')

(i) It is fairly common practice now to use single quotation marks, e.g. He said: 'I will go to catch my train.'

(ii) Double quotation marks are used for a quotation within a quotation, e.g. The father said to the boy: 'Did you tell him "Get lost" as you walked out the door?'

(iii) Quotation marks are used instead of italics or underlining for titles of poems, articles in magazines, journals or collections, or individual stories in a collection, e.g. '"Night in Tunisia" is a good story.'

(iv) Punctuation belonging to the quoted words should be placed within the quotation marks, e.g. He asked: 'Have you read the report?'

A separate paragraph is required for each new speaker in a quotation and every quotation begins with a capital letter, unless the quotation begins in the middle of a sentence, e.g. 'He said he was ". . . tired of life."'

Examples

'I agree', said the chairman, 'but I still think it should be changed.'

'Put it over there', she said.

'What did they do to you?' asked the girl.

'They gave me', he said, 'strict orders, "Nobody to be let in without a ticket."'

'There it is!' shouted the boys.

'I'm not going', said Mary.

'You'll go, or I'll give you something to think about', said her mother.

'Did you say, "Why should I?"' she asked.

'Yes, I did', said Conor, 'and why shouldn't I do it? I'm entitled to my own opinion. I have my rights.'

ACTIVITY 3

Punctuate the following:

1. it should be marvellous go to it
2. down came the rain on went the coats
3. out went the windows in came the snow
4. hes doing very poorly he wont last long
5. off with the coats get down to work
6. work never killed anyone many never recover from it
7. on the table are the following items money cheque books credit cards cancelled cheques and a bank statement
8. dont you think that i said to him going out the door a very remarkable sky
9. put it over there she shouted or ill give you something to think about
10. i didnt say youre a fool did i
11. when were in company with other people am i to do nothing am i
12. the chairman said i now declare this meeting open
13. did you say go at two oclock or did you not
14. judges differ teams lose
15. the president began his speech thus it is a great honour to be here
16. have you seen that play by hugh leonard
17. if you say once more i knew it ill shout
18. it is a sound proverb never put all your eggs in the one basket
19. it is a very true saying that goes the evil that men do lives after them the good is oft interred with their bones
20. history is bunk said henry ford

ACTIVITY 4

Punctuate the following:

1. the thing i like best about living in ireland apart from the people is the mild climate
2. put it in the box the blue box when youre ready
3. youll find it in the warehouse the far corner be careful of it

4. the newsletter will be available on wednesday indeed on tuesday perhaps
5. the grapes of wrath now thats a good play novel i mean
6. did you really say to him get lost
7. didnt you say yesterday i like reading the irish times
8. when liam returned to work his father in law got to hear of it
9. the record book should be kept up to date and always available for the managers inspection
10. womens clothes are very fashionable mens are not
11. childrens personalities should be given free expression
12. his and hers boutique is on the far side of the street
13. it is theirs not mine
14. i asked her have you any money
15. did he say i have no money
16. put on your coat quickly or well never be on time
17. my favourite season is spring
18. who was known as the big fellow
19. the rich said f scott fitzgerald are different from you and me yes said hemingway they have money
20. have you ever been to the west of ireland

ACTIVITY 5

Punctuate the following:

(a) fyodor dostoyevsky was born in moscow in 1821 he was the second of a physicians seven children from 1838 to 1843 he studied at the military engineering college in st petersburg graduating with officers rank he was sentenced to penal servitude in 1849 and spent much of this sentence at a convicts prison in omsk as he was a heavy gambler he often found himself in debt however his second wife whom he married in 1867 helped him to put his financial affairs on a firm footing

(b) capital punishment is not a successful weapon against crime in countries where it has been practised regularly not a great reduction in crime has taken place in fact it has increased capital punishment tends to trigger even more violence to seek revenge on the government which inflicted capital punishment the present prison system is not what it should be the people in these houses of shame as oscar wilde called them require special treatment they certainly should not have to suffer the pain and misery that is sometimes inflicted upon them

(c) the constitution of ireland came into effect in 1937 it is sometimes referred to as de valeras constitution it was of course voted on by the electorate and a majority was in favour the constitution provides for a president two houses of the oireachtas known as the dail and the senate and also provides for the independence of the judiciary the president is commander in chief of the armed forces appoints judges and the members of the government the taoiseach must keep the president informed on all matters of state as far as is known this is not done very thoroughly one taoiseach said he met the president every now and then but their discussions were often about the cartoons in dublin opinion.

ACTIVITY 6

Punctuate the following:

(a) a member of the house of commons once asked george stephenson supposing now one of these engines to be going along a railroad at the rate of nine or ten miles an hour and a cow were to stray upon the line and get in the way of the engine would that not be a very awkward circumstance it would indeed said george for the cow

(b) well i met someone like you somewhere he said firmly and i have an hour to kill and i was wondering would you like to come and have a hamburger so that we can think where it was you look as if you have nothing to do either you could read the evening paper i said because i am so extremely kind i would never hurt anyones feelings i wouldnt tell him to get lost that he was an inoffensive bore ive read the evening paper i said i was silent well make up your mind he said its starting to rain do we have a hamburger or dont we its stupid standing here getting wet

(Maeve Binchy, 'My First Book', The Irish Times)

(c) finally on 31 march i set out to meet cardinal dalton of armagh he was a pleasant withdrawn scholarly looking man our conversation was stilted formal and with the exception of one brief period banal and inconsequential the cardinal gave the impression that he was politely wondering what on earth he was doing sharing his luncheon table with this odd earnest young man who was clearly preoccupied with an abstruse and awkward health problem the sole gain for me was the pleasant hock with the fish at luncheon which i had arrived just in time to share with the cardinal i suspect that he accepted the ordeal and decided to offer it up as did i there was but one reference by me and none by him to the mother and child service

(Noel Browne, Against the Tide, Dublin: Gill and Macmillan, 1986)

(d) and when he came to himself he said how many hired servants of my fathers have bread enough to spare and i perish with hunger i will arise and go to my father and will say unto him father i have sinned against heaven and before thee and am no more worthy to be called thy son

Review

1. 'Quotation marks ("quotes") or inverted commas are the most troublesome marks in punctuation; and the irony of the thing is that we could easily do without them. In fact, we did until the end of the eighteenth century.'

   (G.H.Vallins, *Good English*, London: Pan, 1951)

   What do you think?

2. James Joyce in *A Portrait of the Artist as a Young Man* used no quotation marks. Use quotation marks to punctuate this passage from it.

   – Well, my little man, said the rector, what is it?

   Stephen swallowed down the thing in his throat and said:

   – I broke my glasses, sir

   The rector opened his mouth and said:

   – O!

   Then he smiled and said:

   – Well, if we broke our glasses we must write home for a new pair.

   – I wrote home, sir, said Stephen, and Father Arnall said I am not to study till they come.

   – Quite right! said the rector.

   Stephen swallowed down the thing again and tried to keep his legs and voice from shaking.

   – But, sir . . .

   – Yes?

   – Father Dolan came in today and pandied me because I was not writing my theme.

   The rector looked at him in silence and he could feel the blood rising to his face and the tears about to rise to his eyes.

   The rector said:

   – Your name is Dedalus, isn't it?

(James Joyce, *A Portrait of the Artist as a Young Man*, London: Viking Press, 1956)

3. See if you can punctuate *Activity 6 (d)* in the manner in which James Joyce used punctuation in *A Portrait of the Artist as a Young Man*.

Pitfalls

its it's

The confusion of these two words is one of the most common errors in English.

Its, without an apostrophe, denotes possession.

Examples

The dog broke *its* leg.

The government at *its* meeting yesterday made the decision.

The class decided in *its* own interest to study hard.

It's is a contraction of *it is*. The *i* of the *is* is omitted and the apostrophe is inserted instead.

Examples

It's a fine day.

It's the best I have ever seen.

It's great to be alive.

Confusing words

already	all ready	break	brake
altogether	all together	cite	sight
appreciable	appreciative	course	coarse
bazaar	bizarre	compliment	complement
congenial	congenital	comprehensive	comprehensible

Quiz

So now you are very good at punctuation? Then try the sentence below. It can be done.

'That that is is that that is not is not but that that is not is not that that is nor is that that is that that is not.'

Spellings

The words most commonly misspelled are highlighted.

label	lantern	ledger
labelling	latitude	legacy
laboratory	laud	**liaison**
labour	laudable	**livelihood**
labourer	laugh	loose
lament	laughter	**lose**
lamentable	laundry	**losing**
landscape	lawyer	**lounge**
language	**league**	**lying**
languid	lecturer	

WRITING 5:
STARTING A LETTER

Introduction

The ability to write a good letter is a skill essential to all secretaries and junior business executives. The letter is an important means used by a firm to keep in touch with customers and suppliers. It has been truly said that a firm's letters are its ambassadors. Customers form an impression of a firm from the layout, content and tone of the letters it sends out. If a bank were to send out letters poorly typed, poorly constructed and containing spelling and grammatical errors, clients would soon lose confidence in its efficiency. Letters should be written on good quality paper, the letterhead should be attractive and the address on the envelope should be neatly and correctly typed.

In every letter:

- spelling must be perfect
- grammar must be perfect
- punctuation must be perfect
- typing and layout must be perfect.

Always proofread your letter.

There are three basic layouts for business letters: the fully blocked, the blocked and the indented. Each firm adopts its own particular layout. Indeed, the terms used for layout sometimes overlap. What we are calling the blocked style is sometimes called the semi-blocked style.

Fully blocked style

In the fully blocked style everything begins at the left hand margin.

Fig. 1

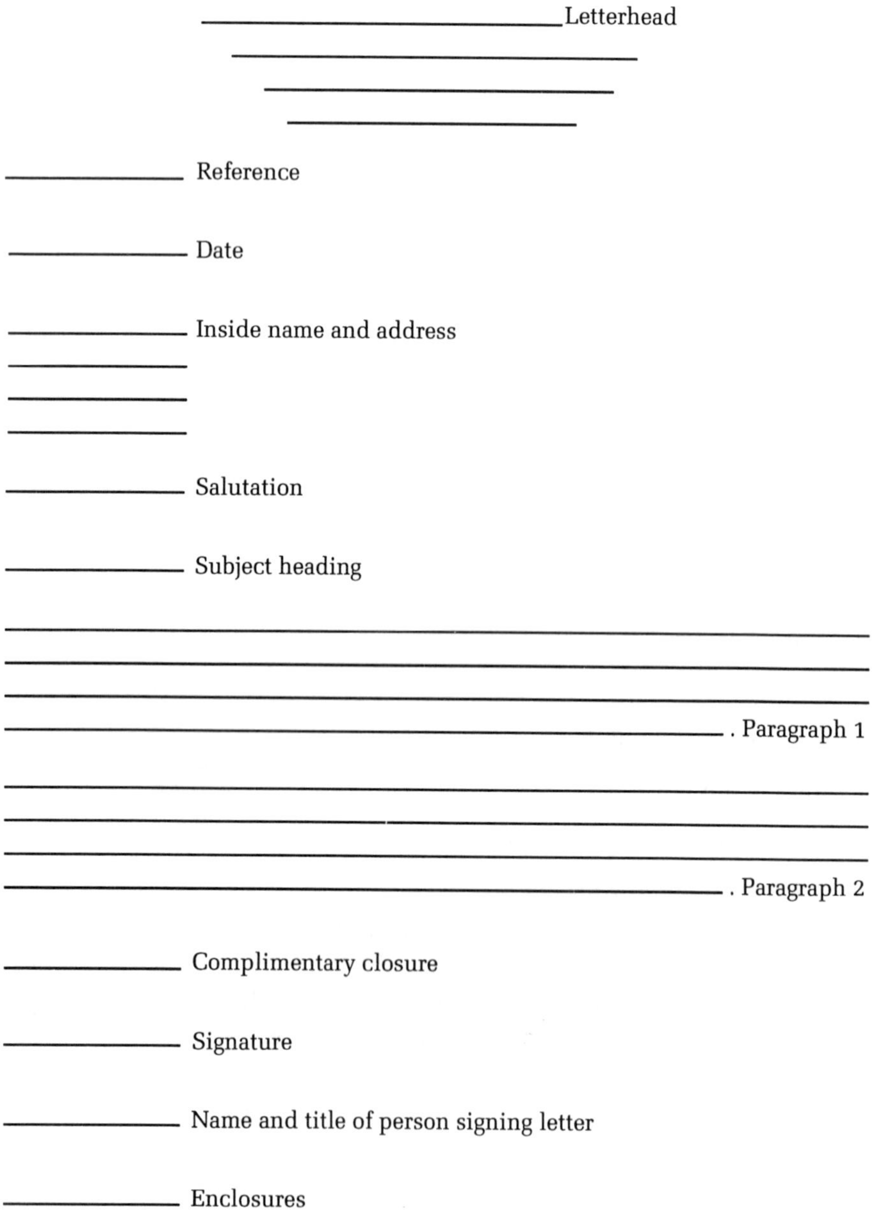

_____ Letterhead

_____ Reference

_____ Date

_____ Inside name and address

_____ Salutation

_____ Subject heading

_____ . Paragraph 1

_____ . Paragraph 2

_____ Complimentary closure

_____ Signature

_____ Name and title of person signing letter

_____ Enclosures

Fully blocked layout

Fig. 2
S & SK MARKETING
Kilmeany
Carlow
Telephone (0503) 32507, Fax (0503) 07235

Our Ref: e. mc/sk

Date: 18 March 199?

Mr Ruairi Kelly
35 High Street
Kilkenny

Dear Mr Kelly

FULLY BLOCKED LETTER STYLE

I am sorry for the slight delay in replying to your letter of 9 March, but the unusually heavy fall of snow meant that the electricity had been unavailable for several days.

We can certainly design a letterhead for your new company and, in fact, I have enclosed some samples for your comments. I would advise you to use the Fully Blocked Layout Style for your letters as it is being adopted by many firms now and is considered very modern. It simply means that every line of a letter, including date, inside name and address, headings and complimentary closure, begins at the left hand margin. This letter is in the Fully Blocked Style.

It is common also in modern business letters to use what is called 'Open Punctuation'. This means that no punctuation is used outside the body of the letter unless it is absolutely essential. You will notice that in this letter I have used no punctuation marks in the date, inside name and address, salutation and complimentary closure.

After you have had a chance to look at the sample letterheads, I will make arrangements to call to see you to discuss them. I look forward to helping you and wish you success in your new venture.

Yours sincerely

Emma McGrane

Enc.

Blocked style

In the blocked style everything begins at the left hand margin except the date, complimentary closure, signature and name and title of person signing letter.

Fig. 3

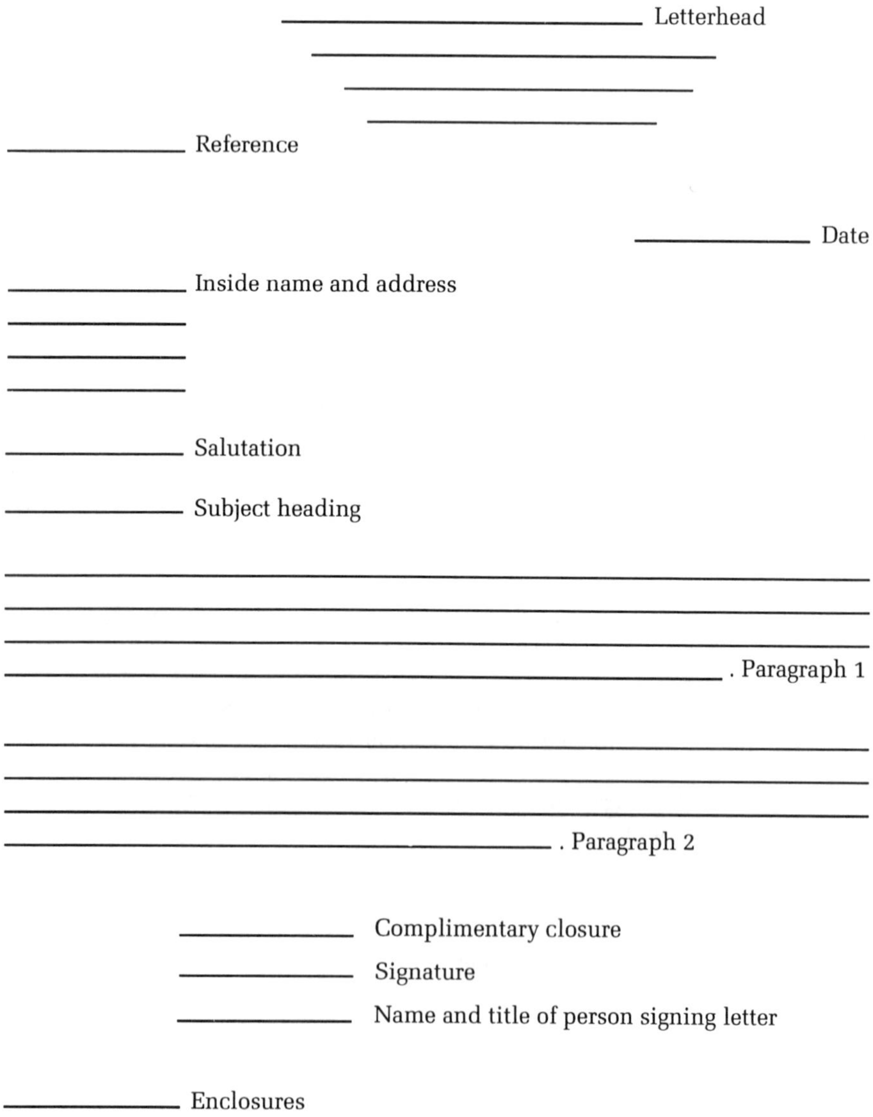

_____ Letterhead

_____ Reference

_____ Date

_____ Inside name and address

_____ Salutation

_____ Subject heading

_____ . Paragraph 1

_____ . Paragraph 2

_____ Complimentary closure
_____ Signature
_____ Name and title of person signing letter

_____ Enclosures

174

Blocked layout

Fig. 4

O'Shea & Murphy Ltd
Timber Merchants
Kickham Street
Tipperary
Telephone (062) 42227, Fax (062) 27242

Your Ref: ks/fc
Our Ref: bs/mc

Date: 19 February 199?

FOR THE ATTENTION OF MR MICHAEL PURCELL

John Ryan & Sons
Builders
Friar Street
Cashel
Co Tipperary

Dear Sirs

Thank you for your letter of 15 February. We have great pleasure in enclosing details of the complete service we offer to builders.

Range
We keep in stock a complete range of foreign and native timber and can supply your order usually on the day it is placed. We also stock doors and windows in teak, pine and red deal. These are made to standard size, but in our workshop, we can have them made to whatever dimensions you wish. Though we are known as 'Timber Merchants', we also stock slates, tiles, bricks, and indeed, everything that the builder requires.

Delivery
We will deliver to any part of the country and there is no charge for this service.

Terms
All bills to be paid within 30 days of date.

I enclose a selection of our brochures which will give you further details. If you have any further queries please do not hesitate to contact us as it is our aim to give you an efficient service.

Yours faithfully

Malachy Murray
(Sales Manager)

Enc.

Indented style

The indented style is not now used very frequently. It is very attractive as it gives the letter a balanced look. Many people claim the indenting of paragraphs makes for easy reading. However, the indenting of paragraphs is time-consuming.

Fig. 5

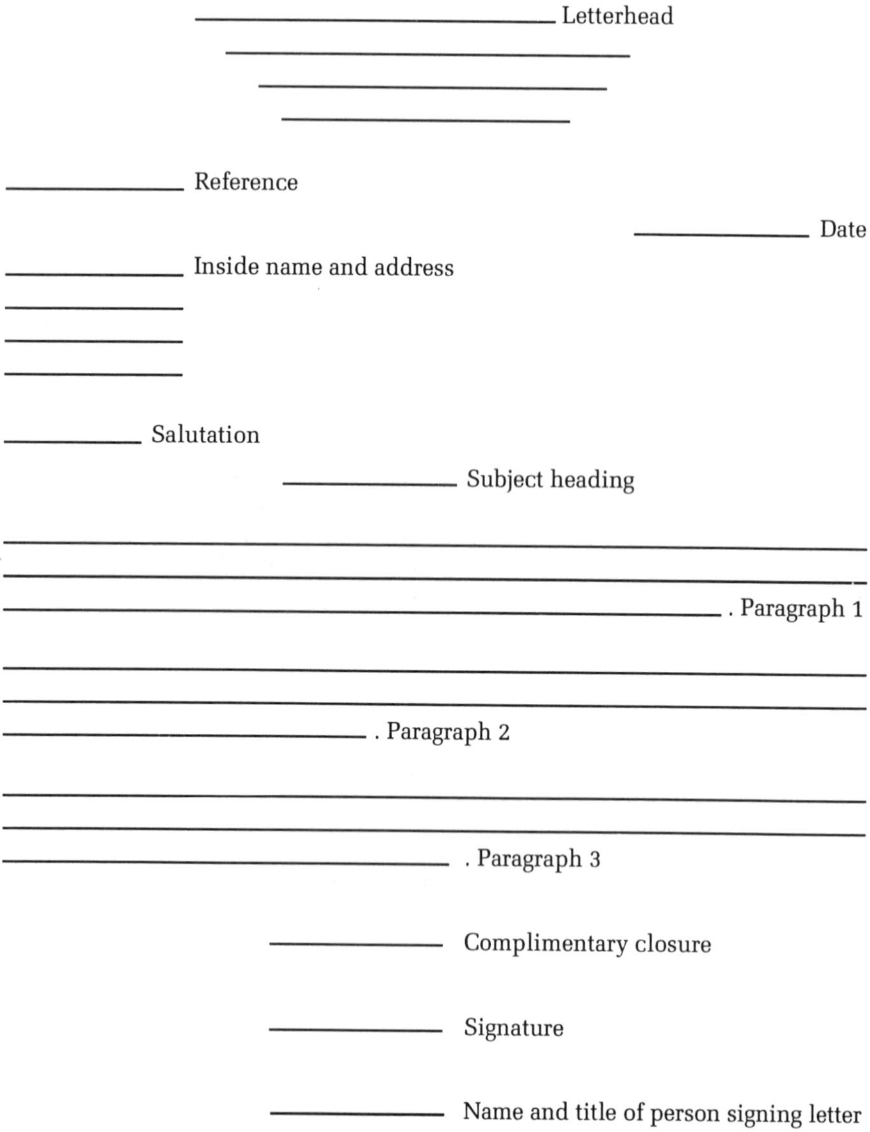

_____ Letterhead

_____ Reference

_____ Date

_____ Inside name and address

_____ Salutation

_____ Subject heading

_____ . Paragraph 1

_____ . Paragraph 2

_____ . Paragraph 3

_____ Complimentary closure

_____ Signature

_____ Name and title of person signing letter

Indented style on headed notepaper

Fig. 6

Collins & O'Doherty (Tax Consultants)
55 Tullow Street, Carlow
Telephone 0503-31601
Fax 0503-60113

Our Ref: jc/sk

14 September 199?

Mr John Kennedy
Main Street
Castledermot
Co. Kildare

Dear Mr Kennedy

Tax

    I thank you for your letter of 12 September asking us to help you sort out your tax problems.

    You are aware that the government has brought in a new system of tax for people in your position. It is called 'Self-Assessment'. This new system puts the onus on you to decide how much tax you are required to pay in any one year. The Revenue Commissioners do not, as in the past, send you a document stating how much you should pay. The Revenue Commissioners will investigate in detail a certain percentage of the returns made in this way and heavy penalties will be imposed on those who do not pay the correct amount of tax.

    Perhaps if you could call to our office next week we could begin to draw up a tax return for you. Please bring all relevant documents with you such as cheque books, receipts, accounts books, etc. and we will start working on your case right away.

Yours sincerely

Eoghan Murray
(Accountant)

The main features of the indented layout on headed notepaper (Fig. 6):
- the date is placed at the upper right hand side of the page;
- headings are centred;
- the reference and the name and address of the person to whom the letter is being sent (the inside name and address) appear on the left side. The inside name and address is not now indented as that would be very time-consuming;
- the first line of each paragraph is indented;
- the 'Yours sincerely' (complimentary closure) is centred.

Indented style on unheaded notepaper

Fig. 7

                                                         The Moate
                                                           Kilfeacle
                                                       Co. Tipperary

                                      14 September 199?

Ms Iseult Cooney
63 Marley Heights
Rathfarnham
Dublin 14

Dear Ms Cooney

                            Solid Fuel Cooker

    Thank you for your letter inquiring about installing a solid fuel cooker in your new house.

    It is difficult for me to recommend the one that is most suitable for your needs. All the models on the market are very popular and perhaps the best thing for you to do is to talk to people who have been using solid fuel for a number of years.

    I will call over to your house on Thursday evening at around 7.30 pm and look at your kitchen and chimney to see how much work is involved. I'll be able to give you a price at that time.

    I have installed a number of solid fuel cookers in the Knocklong area, and I'll tell you the names of people you might talk to about this method of heating when I see you on Thursday.

                              Yours sincerely

                              Patrick Lonergan

The main features of the indented style on unheaded notepaper (Fig. 7):

- the sender's address is placed in the upper right hand side of the page and is progressively indented;
- the inside name and address appears on the left hand side of the page;
- the first line of each paragraph is indented;
- the complimentary closure is centred;
- headings are centred.

Elements of a letter

References

Spaces for references are usually provided for in a letterhead. When replying to a letter it is discourteous and inefficient not to quote the reference on the letter with which you are dealing. The reference will enable your correspondent to locate the appropriate file quickly. Sometimes the initials of the person signing the letter and the typist's initials are used as the reference.

Date

The date should always be written or typed in full, e.g. 5 July 199?. It is not necessary to put *th* after the 5. Never write the date in figures, e.g. 5/7/9?. This is discourteous as it gives the impression that you are in a hurry. It can also be confusing as in the USA the order of the date is month, day and year, whereas we follow a different order – day, month, year.

For the attention of

Some companies adopt the rule that all correspondence should be addressed to the company and not to individual persons by name. The sender of a letter may wish it to reach a particular person. This can be achieved by using FOR THE ATTENTION OF at the left hand margin and two single spaces below the date. No punctuation is necessary. To type it in capitals and not underscore is the modern way of doing it.

Inside name and address

Place the inside name and address two single spaces after FOR THE ATTENTION OF or two single spaces after the date if there is no FOR THE ATTENTION OF.

Salutation

Every letter begins with a greeting. If you are writing for the first time to the secretary of a company, you should begin your letter with 'Dear Sir/Madam'. Your correspondent's first name should be used only if you know him well. If in doubt about the form of salutation, it is always best to err on the side of formality. A woman may be addressed as 'Dear Miss Connolly', 'Dear Mrs Connolly', 'Dear Ms Connolly' or 'Dear Madam', depending on the situation. In a circular letter 'Dear Sirs' or 'A Chara' may be used.

The message
The message should be brief and to the point. If the information to be conveyed can be given in three sentences, then there is no need to write four.

Complimentary closure
The complimentary closure used will again depend upon the relationship with the person to whom you are writing. Only two complimentary closures are in present use. The rule to follow is simple. If the letter begins with 'Dear Sir' or 'Dear Madam', it should end with 'Yours faithfully'. If it begins with the name of the person, e.g. 'Dear Mr Gallagher', end it with 'Yours sincerely'. The initial *f* of 'Yours faithfully' and the *s* of 'Yours sincerely' should not be in capitals.

Signature
The letter should be signed under the complimentary closure. Always use the same signature. Do not sign yourself 'Catherine Lonergan' on one letter and 'Mary C. Lonergan' on another. As a general rule a title is not used in a signature. For example, to sign oneself 'Doctor Michael Hogan' is incorrect.

Name of signatory
Type the name of the person to sign the letter under the signature.

Designation
The official position of the person signing the letter should be placed below his name.

Enclosures
Two single spaces after the designation type 'Enc.', or 'Encs' if more than one paper or document is to be enclosed with the letter.

Open punctuation
All letters should be punctuated in the normal manner. However, many firms now use what is called 'open punctuation'. The sample letters in this chapter are examples of this. No punctuation is used in the reference, date, inside name and address, salutation and complimentary closure. The full stop is also omitted from an abbreviated word unless it appears at the end of a sentence.

Commercialese
Avoid the use of what is called 'commercialese' – language such as Re your letter of, Your letter to hand, We beg to inform you, as per your instructions, etc.

Summary

Careful layout: attention to every detail.

Content: brief and to the point.

Tone: adopt a tone suitable to the subject matter.

Accuracy: be careful of spelling, punctuation.

Expression: simple and direct.

Use good quality paper.

Display and type perfectly.

Always proofread.

Ensure address on envelope is correct.

ACTIVITY 1

1. The following phrases are sometimes referred to as 'commercialese'. Rewrite them in acceptable English:

    Re your letter of 15 inst., We beg to inform you, We beg to acknowledge, Your letter to hand, As per instruction, We are in receipt of, We have to acknowledge, The favour of an early reply will oblige.

2. In the following letter you are required to (a) lay it out in fully blocked style, (b) rewrite the body of the letter to make it more understandable, and (c) correct any other errors you find.

International Insurance Company Ltd
14-17 Dawson Street, Dublin.
Telephone 01-6765322

Ref. gs/ms   Date: 22/3/9?
Mr Oliver McGrane
22 Oaklawns
Terenure
Dublin

        Re: Motor Insurance No. AC 105/23/45676

Dear Mr McGrane

    I have pleasure to enclose herewith the above numbered Certificate to renewal date, duly prepared as per your instructions and trust you will find same in order.

    I appreciate your valued support for which I thank you and shall look forward with confidence to a continuation of this as well as your further valued business which will receive prompt personal attention.

    Always at your service, I remain,

                Yours faithfully

                James Mackey
                Claims Manager

Enc.

3. Rewrite the following impersonal sentences in a more personal form:

(a) It is pointed out that registration will conclude at 5.00 p.m.

(b) Delivery of goods will be accepted next Wednesday.

(c) It is regretted that this mistake occurred.

(d) Sincerest apologies are offered for this unfortunate incident.

(e) Enclosed is a copy of our prospectus.

(f) Ensure that payment is made before the end of the month.

(g) All regulations must be observed.

(h) Payment of all outstanding debts would be appreciated.

(i) The Company extends thanks for orders received on 20 March 199?

Review

1. What are the advantages of arranging a letter in the fully blocked style?
2. What is the purpose of a reference on a letter?
3. Why should the date always be written in full?
4. What is open punctuation?
5. What is the purpose of having an inside name and address?
6. "'Except of me, Mary, my dear, as your valentine and think over what I've said.

   My dear Mary, I will now conclude."

   That's all', said Sam.

   'That's rather a sudden pull up, ain't it, Sammy?' inquired Mr. Weller.

   'Not a bit on it', said Sam, 'she'll wish there was more, and that's the great art o' letter writing.'

   (Charles Dickens, *Pickwick Papers*)

   What do you think of this advice from the point of view of business letters?

Pitfalls

The problem of the unattached or dangling participle is common, e.g. 'Having received your letter, it will be answered today.' The participle *having received* has no corresponding subject (noun or pronoun). 'Sitting within my orchard, a serpent stung me', says the ghost of Hamlet's father to a surprised Hamlet. It would seem from this that it was the serpent, and not Hamlet's father in the flesh, who was sitting in the garden. If care is not taken to attach a participle to a noun or pronoun, we may have absurd sentences like the following: 'While writing this, the telephone rang.'

Confusing words

contemptible	contemptuous	dessert	desert
council	counsel	disease	decease
credible	credulous	emaciated	emancipated
decent	descent	eminent	imminent
device	devise	equable	equitable

Quiz

Here is a famous sentence attributed to an Irish politician, Sir Boyle Roche, in 1798:

'I smell a rat; I see it floating in the air, and if it is not nipped in the bud, it will cause a conflagration which will deluge the world.'

Why do you think it is famous?

Spellings

The words most commonly misspelled are highlighted.

magician	margarine	mechanic
magnetise	**marriage**	**medicine**
magnetism	martial	**Mediterranean**
magnificence	martyr	melancholy
maintain	martyrdom	melodious
maintenance	marvel	merciless
majority	massacre	metropolis
management	mathematics	microphone
maniac	meagre	migrate
manoeuvre	meagrely	militarism
manufacture	measurement	millionaire

mimic
mimicking
miniature
minority
minstrel
minutes
miraculous
miscellaneous
mischief
mischievous
missile

moisture
monarch
monstrous
moreover
mosque
mosquito
motto
mountaineers
mouthful
movable
multiplication

multiply
murmur
muscle
muscular
museum
musician
mutineer
mysterious
mystery

WRITING 6:
COLLECTING MONEY

Introduction

Letters requesting payment, as with all other letters, must always be polite. Many customers may have quite valid reasons for not paying their accounts. The goods supplied may have been faulty or damaged; the cheque may have been lost in the post. It is always wise to assume that there is some valid reason for not paying. There is always the possibility that your own accounts department has made an error.

A collection letter has two aims:

(i) to collect the money owed

(ii) to retain the customer's goodwill.

Firms have their own methods for dealing with outstanding debts. Some may phone the customer and discuss the matter; some may call in person and try to collect at least part of the debt. It may also be preferable in some cases to accept part payment in full settlement of the account. It is better to get some of the debt cleared than to get none of it. Most firms are very slow to take legal action because of the expense and the adverse publicity.

We will now outline a method of collecting money, but it must be remembered that this is just one method and that there are several other ways.

Step-by-step process of collecting money

Fig. 1 – Letter ordering goods
Michael Branagan & Sons Ltd
Builders
75 Main Street
Donnybrook
Dublin 4
Tel 01-4941327

Ref. mc/mb

29 September 199?

Kevin Byrne & Sons
Builders Providers
Lower Churchtown Road
Dublin 14

Dear Mr Byrne

I wish to order 10 tons of cement and would ask that it be delivered immediately to Castletroy where I am building at the moment. Turn right on the Tipperary/Limerick road and the site is about a quarter of a mile from Castletroy Golf Club on the right side of the road.

Yours sincerely

Michael Branagan

This order could also be taken over the phone.

Step 1: End-of-month statement

Most firms will give thirty days' credit, so at the end of October Mr Branagan will simply get a statement of his account.

Fig. 2 – End-of-month statement

Kevin Byrne & Sons
Builders Providers
Lower Churchtown Road
Dublin 14
Tel 01-4896543
Fax 01-4678534

Customer

Mr Michael Branagan
(Builders)
75 Main Street
Donnybrook
Dublin 4

First Statement   Date 31/10/9?

Order No.	Quantity	Description	Unit Price	Total
11570	10 tons	Cement	£7.00	£1,400
			Discount 5%	70
			Amount Outstanding	£1,330

30 Days	60 Days	90 Days
£1,330	nil	nil

Step 2: Second end-of-month statement

If the outstanding amount is not paid during November another statement is sent at the end of the month.

Fig. 3 – Second end-of-month statement

Kevin Byrne & Sons
Builders Providers
Lower Churchtown Road
Dublin 14
Tel 01-4896543
Fax 01-4678534

Customer

Mr Michael Branagan
(Builders)
75 Main Street
Donnybrook
Dublin 4

Second Statement   Date 30/11/9?

Order No.	Quantity	Description	Unit Price	Total
11570	10 tons	Cement	£7.00	£1,400
			Discount 5%	70
			Amount Outstanding	£1,330

30 Days	60 Days	90 Days
£1,330	£1,330	nil

Step 3: First collection letter

If the amount is still not paid a first collection letter must be sent. This will simply state the amount owed and ask for payment.

Fig. 4 – First collection letter

Kevin Byrne & Sons
Builders Providers
Lower Churchtown Road
Dublin 14
Tel 01-4896543
Fax 01-4678534

Ref. kb/js

5 December 199?

Mr Michael Branagan
(Builders)
75 Main Street
Donnybrook
Dublin 4

Dear Mr Branagan

ACCOUNT NO 11570

On checking our records we note that the above account of 29 September 199? has not been settled. The enclosed statement shows the outstanding balance to be £1,200.

We look forward to any early payment of this amount and also to receiving your next order.

Yours sincerely

Kevin Byrne
(Manager)

Enc.

Step 4: Second collection letter

If no reply has been received to your first collection letter, a second, firmer in tone, must be sent. It would, of course, be unusual for a reputable builder to have no contact whatsoever with his supplier over a three month period. It must be remembered that most people pay their debts, otherwise business could not continue to operate.

The second collection letter should be sent about two weeks after the first one. Adopt the following procedure:

(i) firm tone, but polite

(ii) refer to previous applications for payment

(iii) ask if there is some reason for delay

(iv) ask for payment.

Fig. 5 – Second collection letter

Kevin Byrne & Sons
Builders Providers
Lower Churchtown Road
Dublin 14
Tel 01-4896543
Fax 01-4678534

Ref. kb/js

16 December 199?

Mr Michael Branagan
(Builders)
75 Main Street
Donnybrook
Dublin 4

Dear Mr Branagan

ACCOUNT NO 11570

We do not seem to have received a reply to our letter of 5 December requesting payment for the above account. The amount outstanding is £1,200.

We cannot continue to offer our very competitive prices and generous discounts unless our customers settle their accounts within the agreed time limits. Perhaps there is some explanation for non-payment. If so, you should contact us immediately.

We look forward to receiving your remittance without delay.

Yours sincerely

Kevin Byrne
(Manager)

Step 5: Third collection letter

If no payment is received and no reply or contact of any kind is made after your second collection letter, another letter must be sent. Some firms at this stage might make a personal visit to the holder of the outstanding debt. A personal visit is much more persuasive than a letter, and an explanation for non-payment can be obtained there and then.

In the third collection letter you must make it clear that you intend to pursue the matter with urgency and point out the steps you intend to take to collect the money. The letter should include the following:

(i) detail earlier efforts to collect payment

(ii) use fair and reasonable tone

(iii) set reasonable deadline for payment

(iv) state further action if request is ignored

(v) regret the necessity for the letter.

Fig. 6 – Third collection letter

Kevin Byrne & Sons
Builders Providers
Lower Churchtown Road
Dublin 14
Tel 01-4896543
Fax 01-4678534

Ref. kb/js

3 January 199?

Mr Michael Branagan
(Builders)
75 Main Street
Donnybrook
Dublin 4

Dear Mr Branagan

ACCOUNT NO 11570

You ordered 10 tons of cement from us on 29 September 199?. We delivered your order immediately. It is now over three months since the cement left our premises and we have still not been paid. We wrote to you on 5 December and 16 December requesting payment of the outstanding amount which is £1,200. We have received no reply to either of our letters.

This matter has gone on so long that we must now press for immediate payment. We cannot offer our keen prices and credit facilities if customers do not settle their accounts within the specified time limits.

We must point out, therefore, that if the account is not settled by 20 January we will have no choice but to place the matter with our legal advisers.

Yours sincerely

Kevin Byrne

(Manager)

Step 6: Final collection letter

If no reply is received to this third collection letter, it is reasonable to assume that the customer either cannot, or will not, clear his account. A brief letter informing him of the action taken should be sent out.

Fig. 7 – Final collection letter

Kevin Byrne & Sons
Builders Providers
Lower Churchtown Road
Dublin 14
Tel 01-4896543
Fax 01-4678534

Ref. kb/js

23 January 199?

Mr Michael Branagan
(Builders)
75 Main Street
Donnybrook
Dublin 4

Dear Mr Branagan

ACCOUNT NO 11570

We have not received a reply to our letter of 3 January requesting payment of your outstanding debt. The amount owing is £1,200.

We stated in that letter that if payment was not received by 20 January we would be forced to hand the matter over to our legal advisers. We have now taken that action and they will be dealing with this matter.

Yours sincerely

Kevin Byrne

(Manager)

We have now seen the complete process that a firm might go through in attempting to collect an outstanding debt. As has been pointed out before, this is just one method of collection and must not be taken as the only way.

ACTIVITY I

1. One of your best customers, who has always paid you promptly, now has an account of £620, overdue for two months. Write a letter requesting payment.

2. Three weeks have gone by and your customer with £620 overdue still has not settled his account. Write him a second letter.

3. You receive an immediate reply to your letter concerning the £620. Your customer tells you that he will not be able to pay for about eight weeks. Write him a letter granting him the extended credit.

4. A customer of the firm for which you work owes £1,150. Several letters have been written to him requesting payment. He always replies and promises to pay as soon as possible. However, payment has not arrived. You are now asked to write a final letter telling him that if he does not pay within ten days, you will be forced to place the matter with your solicitor.

5. Your customer who owes £1,150 has replied to your letter and promised to pay his outstanding debt. However, within the ten days his payment has not arrived. You are to write him a letter informing him that the matter has now been placed with your solicitor.

6. Write a letter to one of your customers who has a small debt outstanding but is making no effort to pay it. The collection of such a small debt is not important but the manager feels there is a principle involved.

7. You sell goods on the understanding that payment will be made within thirty days. A new customer bought goods six weeks ago but payment has not been received. Write her a letter setting out your terms for payment.

8. Mealy & Lanigan, who have been good customers of A.D. Electronics for a number of years, now owe £5,250. This sum has not been paid within the usual trade terms and a standard reminder has brought no results. As accounts manager of A.D. Electronics, write a tactful letter dealing with the situation.

9. A good customer has an outstanding debt of £7,650. Despite a number of reminders she has not settled her account. Now she has placed a new order for goods worth £1,345. Write a letter asking her to come to your premises for a discussion of her outstanding debt before deciding to fill the new order.

10. Reply to the following letter:

>   Michael Ryan & Co. Ltd
>   The Square
>   Ballylanders
>   Co. Limerick
>   062-72124
>
> 8 October 199?
>
> Peter Looby & Sons Ltd
> Galbally
> Co. Limerick
>
>
> Dear Mr Looby
>
> I was annoyed to receive your letter of 3 October threatening to hand over my outstanding account to your solicitor.
>
> You must know surely that my wife had been very ill and died just two weeks ago. It is surely beyond the bounds of common humanity that you should send such a letter at such a time. Words can scarcely express my feelings about your action.
>
> I demand an immediate apology.
>
> Yours sincerely
>
> Michael Ryan
> (Manager)

11. A customer in Germany, who has always paid his account by banker's draft, has not sent his latest payment. It is ten weeks overdue. You wrote to him a month ago but received no reply. Write him another letter requesting payment.

Varying the terms of payment

When a customer does not, or cannot, meet the terms of payment he may request that the terms of payment be changed. This request would have to be accompanied by strong reasons for the present difficulties and a commitment to pay by a definite date.

Fig. 8 – Request to defer payment

O'Connell & Scully Ltd
13 Davis Street
Clonmel
Co. Tipperary
Tel. 052-31442

Ref. bs/ps

15 October 199?

James Keating & Co.
Dublin Road
New Inn
Co. Tipperary

Dear Mr Keating

With reference to your letter of 1 October asking for payment of £8,000 which is still outstanding on our account with you, I would ask you if I could defer payment for two months.

We are not experiencing any special difficulties here at the moment, but a fairly large tax liability had to be discharged recently and this has meant that we have had to defer certain payments which we would normally make immediately. This tax liability will not be as large in the future and so should cause no problems next year.

I hope that you can see your way to granting my request to defer payment for two months.

Yours sincerely

Patrick Scully
(Manager)

Fig. 9 – Granting deferment of payment

James Keating & Co.
Dublin Road
New Inn
Co. Tipperary
Tel. 062-72114

Ref. cd/jk

20 October 199?

Mr Patrick Scully
Manager
O'Connell & Scully Ltd
13 Davis Street
Clonmel
Co. Tipperary

Dear Mr Scully

Your letter of 15 October requests deferment of payment for two months of £8,000 which is outstanding on your account.

While we appreciate your difficulties, we feel that to defer the full payment is not the appropriate action to take since the goods supplied to you were given at a very keen discount. This action would also damage your good credit reputation.

We would suggest the following:

1. Pay £2,000 immediately;
2. Pay £2,000 on 20 November;
3. Pay the balance of £4,000 on 15 December.

Any deferment of payment beyond the schedule suggested above would not meet with our approval.

I look forward to receiving your cheque for £2,000 within the next few days.

Yours sincerely

James Keating
(Manager)

ACTIVITY 2

1. A good customer has an outstanding debt of £1,200. Every effort has been made to collect it, but, it seems, he is short of money. In his last letter he suggests that he will pay £300 now and try to pay another £300 in two months. Write a letter to him stating whether you will accept his suggestion or place the matter with your solicitors.

2. A customer has a very small debt of £100. Every month or six weeks he comes in and pays £5. It will take about two years to clear this small debt if this continues. Write him a letter asking him to clear this account immediately.

3. One of your customers who was paying off a large debt in monthly instalments has stopped doing so. Write her a letter asking the reason for non-payment.

4. A customer has deducted 5 per cent from his final payment. Write a letter to him pointing out that the amount must still be paid.

5. You have bought goods from your regular supplier. You owe £2,500. You now find that you are unable to pay this amount when it falls due. Write a letter to your supplier asking her to vary the terms of payment.

6. One of your customers has the habit of always deducting a few pounds when settling his account. The amount involved is not significant, but he has always been given the full discount. What action will you take?

7. A customer had an outstanding debt of £100. He says he cannot pay. He suggests that you take his racing bike, which he purchased a few months ago, in lieu of payment. Write a letter to him dealing with this matter.

8. A customer who has always paid her account has now run into financial difficulties. She has written to you to point out that she sees no prospect of being able to pay her outstanding debt of £1,100. She is very apologetic about this and asks you to understand her position. Write her a letter dealing with her situation.

Review

1. What are the two aims of collection letters?
2. Why are firms reluctant to take court action against customers who do not pay outstanding debts?
3. 'It is much better to visit a person who does not pay his bills than to send letters.' Discuss.
4. One way to avoid outstanding debts is to demand cash for every transaction. Why do many firms not demand cash, and indeed, extend generous credit facilities?
5. 'Collection letters should always be polite and courteous.' Why should you be polite and courteous when someone has refused to pay you what he owes?
6. Why is it always wise to assume that there is a valid reason for non-payment?

Pitfalls

less fewer

Less and *fewer* are often confused. *Less* is used to denote quantity, and *fewer* to denote number. For example:

'*Fewer* people than usual attended the seminar.'

'There was *less* snow this year than last year.'

Confusing words

formally	formerly	elicit	illicit
infer	imply	envelop	envelope
flair	flare	bought	brought
border	boarder	cannon	canon
cash	cache	cast	caste

Quiz

Can you form ten words from the word BRANDY? The new words need not contain all the letters of the word BRANDY.

Spellings

The words most commonly misspelled are highlighted.

narrate	necessity	**niece**
narration	negative	notice
narrative	neglect	**noticeable**
national	negligence	notification
nationalism	negligible	notify
naughty	**negotiable**	nourish
navies	**negotiate**	novelty
navy	neighbour	nuisance
necessarily	nephew	numerous
necessary	nervous	nymph

WRITING 7:
LETTERS OF COMPLAINT

Introduction

Letters of complaint call for tact and diplomacy. The reason for writing a letter of complaint is so that the matter may be corrected. Most people do not complain just for the sake of complaining. Many complaints are genuine, for example:

(i) the end-of-month statement may be incorrect;

(ii) the wrong goods may have been sent;

(iii) the goods may have been delivered late;

(iv) the goods may have been damaged in transit;

(v) the quality of the goods supplied may have been less than expected.

When writing a letter of complaint, though you may feel angry, this should not appear in your letter. Your supplier may not be responsible for whatever happened.

Writing a letter of complaint

When writing a letter of complaint the following rules should be observed:

(i) Always make your complaint at once as delay weakens your case.

(ii) Begin by regretting the need to complain.

(iii) Give all the details such as order number, date, quantity, etc.

(iv) Explain why you are dissatisfied and point out the inconvenience caused.

(v) If possible, suggest how the matter can be rectified.

(vi) Do not try to place the blame; it is up to your supplier to investigate the complaint.

(vii) Assume that your supplier will want to put matters right.

(viii) Never be unreasonable or rude as you may create ill-will.

Fig. 1 – Sample letter of complaint

New City Secondary School
Shannon
Co. Clare
Tel. 065-21248

Ref. Account No. 05431423

6 April 199?

The Editor
Longford Publications Ltd
Main Street
Longford

Dear Sir

Your representative, Mr Edmund O'Donnell, came to our school at the end of February to display your new school books for the coming year.

I expressed an interest in examining three books which I might adopt for my classes in the coming year. Mr O'Donnell agreed to send me the three books, and I was under the impression that these books would be considered complimentary copies. The books

(i) *English for the New Junior Certificate*, J. K. McArdle, £6.50

(ii) *Bookkeeping for the New Junior Certificate*, John Hinds, £8.50

(iii) *A New Approach to English*, Patrick Lonergan, £6.00

arrived on 16 March.

However, I have just today received a bill of £21 for the books in question. If I am to retain these books, I will have to buy them personally as there are no funds in our school for such purchases. However, I would again emphasise that Mr O'Donnell told me they would be considered complimentary copies.

I regret to have to complain about this matter, but this is the *third* time this same difficulty has arisen with your company. I would ask you therefore to cancel the bill in question.

Yours faithfully

Siobhan Doyle
(English Teacher)

Replying to letter of complaint

Suppliers should be glad to hear from customers who have complaints because it provides an opportunity to rectify them. It gives a chance to retain the customer's goodwill and it points out weaknesses in the product or service.

When replying to a letter of complaint adhere to the following guidelines:

(i) Assume that the customer *may* be right.

(ii) Always acknowledge the complaint promptly and assure your customer that the matter is being investigated.

(iii) If the customer made a mistake and the complaint is not in order, point this out politely.

(iv) If you are to blame, accept responsibility, apologise for the inconvenience caused, and promise to put matters right.

(v) Establish a friendly co-operative tone in your letter.

Fig. 2 – Sample reply accepting complaint

Longford Publications Ltd
Main Street
Longford
Tel 043-46582   Fax 043-39921

Ref. Account No. 05431423

9 April 199?

Ms Siobhan Doyle
New City Secondary School
Shannon
Co. Clare

Dear Ms Doyle

Thank you for your letter of 6 April. Your understanding of what our representative, Mr O'Donnell, said to you is quite correct. The three books in question are indeed complimentary copies, and, therefore, there is no charge to you.

We have had some difficulty with the programme which we are using on our computer. It has been issuing bills to everybody who receives books, even people like yourself who are sent complimentary copies. This problem has been rectified in the past week and, we hope, will not occur again.

We would appreciate your comments on the three books you received, and hope that you will be adopting them for your courses next year.

I apologise for the inconvenience which this matter has caused, and enclose an end-of-month statement which shows your account to be clear.

Yours sincerely

Michael Hanly
(Managing Editor)

Enc. 1

You may sometimes have to reject a complaint. If it is necessary, do so briefly and politely and retain a friendly, co-operative tone. While rejecting a complaint you must still retain the customer's goodwill so that she will do business with you again. Point out gently that the customer is wrong, or that there has been some misunderstanding.

Fig. 3 – Sample reply rejecting complaint

Longford Publications Ltd
Main Street
Longford
Tel 043-46582   Fax 043-39921

Ref. Account No. 05431423

9 April 199?

Ms Siobhan Doyle
New City Secondary School
Shannon
Co. Clare

Dear Ms Doyle

Thank you for your letter of 6 April.

There seems to have been some misunderstanding between yourself and our representative, Mr O'Donnell. Copies of books are supplied to teachers on the understanding that they may be retained free of charge if at least twelve copies of the book are ordered for class purposes. This is stated on the invoice which is enclosed with the books.

If you intend to adopt the books for your course next year, you may retain the copies free of charge. Fill in the enclosed form stating where you will be placing your order. The same rules apply in regard to the other books for which you have been charged. If, however, you are not adopting a particular book at the present time but would like to retain it for yourself, you are entitled to the special teachers' discount of 25%.

When you have had a chance to read the books I would be very pleased to have your views on them. A form for this purpose is enclosed with this letter.

I apologise for any inconvenience caused and look forward to your comments on our texts.

Yours sincerely

Michael Hanly
(Managing Editor)

Enc. 1

ACTIVITY I

1. Reply to the following letter:

Midland Bank Ltd
Holburn Place
Mullingar
Co. Westmeath
Tel 044-29844   Fax 044-29438

Ref. Ac No 33211765

16 September 199?

Mr Michael Boland
South Swan Circle
Mullingar
Co. Westmeath

Dear Mr Boland

We observe that your account (No 33211765) is currently operating in an irregular fashion. Your overdraft limit is £600 (six hundred pounds) and at present your account is in debit £1,200. The Bank cannot allow you to operate your account in this fashion. When you exceed your overdraft limit the Bank automatically operates a surcharge. However, customers are expected to operate their accounts within the terms freely agreed with the Bank.

Perhaps you would be kind enough to explain why your account is being operated in this fashion, and what steps you propose to take to reduce your overdraft.

Yours sincerely

Kevin Mahon
(Accounts Officer)

2. You have received a consignment of typing paper but, as the boxes were damaged in transit, most of the paper is wet and dirty. Write to your supplier informing him of this and asking him what he proposes to do to rectify the matter.

3. You are working for the company that received the letter of complaint in no. 2 above. You have investigated the complaint and discovered that the boxes were sent by rail and arrived safely at the station in your customer's town. The paper was collected by an employee of your customer. It seems the damage must have taken place between the station and your customer's

premises. Write a letter to your customer tactfully explaining that the blame does not lie with your company.

4. You ordered twenty football jerseys from a supplier but only fifteen arrived. Write a letter of complaint to your supplier.

5. You have received the letter of complaint in no. 4 above. Write the reply you would send accepting the responsibility.

6. A customer has complained that your telephonist is curt and unfriendly when dealing with enquiries. Write a letter to the customer attempting to retain his goodwill.

7. A customer has complained that the previous three letters she has received contained several errors in basic English. She does not criticise your secretary, but criticises you for signing and sending out such letters. Write a letter of explanation to your customer. Remember you cannot blame your secretary; if he is a poor secretary, you should not have employed him.

8. You have two customers with the same surname and, in error, you have sent a large bill owed by one to the other. Write a letter of explanation to the offended person apologising for the error.

9. Your automatic washing machine has been serviced twice in the past three months but it is still not working properly. Write a letter to the company involved.

10. You have received the complaint in no. 9 above. Write the reply.

11. Reply rejecting the following complaint.

United Manufacturers Ltd
The Green
Clonmel
Co. Tipperary
Tel. 02-71271   Fax 02-71216

Ref. N6538

16 August 199?

The Editor
The Midland Star
Bianconi Drive
Clonmel
Co. Tipperary

Dear Sir

I wish to protest in the strongest possible terms at a news report in your issue of 23 May. You allege that my company is responsible for pollution of the River Suir. We have always been conscious of our obligations to the environment and my plant has been built to the highest standards possible. Every effort is made to ensure that no damage is caused to the river.

I am a member of the Clonmel Tidy Towns Committee which indicates my concern about the environment. Last year my company donated £500 to the Tidy Towns Committee. You can hardly imagine that I would donate money to make the town a better place and, at the same time, pollute the river.

You have put forward no credible scientific evidence for your allegations, and I would ask you to display a prominent withdrawal statement in your next issue.

Yours faithfully

Enda Walsh
(Manager)

12. A customer has written a complaint about the unreliability of your milk delivery service. You have contracted the delivery of milk to a delivery company. Write two letters:

    (a) a reply to the customer,

    (b) a letter of complaint to the delivery company.

13. You were promised delivery of insulation for 33your attic within ten days of placing the order. It is now over three weeks and it has still not arrived. Write a letter of complaint to the suppliers.

14. You receive a reply from the suppliers of the insulation saying that the order is held up because of a dock strike. It has to be imported. However, when you ordered it you were told they had it in stock. Write a letter pointing out that they misled you when you ordered it.

Review

1. In what circumstances might letters of complaint be genuine?
2. Why should you use a restrained tone in letters of complaint?
3. Rewrite the following in a restrained tone:
    (a) I am outraged at your treatment of me.

(b) I demand that you rectify the matter immediately.

(c) I am amazed that your company is still in business since you treat your customers so poorly.

(d) How could your company be so stupid?

Pitfalls

hung   hanged

Should we say 'The man was *hanged* this morning' or 'The man was *hung* this morning'?

'*Hanged*' means killed by hanging. So 'The man was *hanged* this morning' is correct. '*Hung*' is used in a general sense, e.g. 'He *hung* up his hat.'

Confusing words

cell	sell	discreet	discrete
dear	deer	doe	dough
dents	dense	draft	draught
descent	dissent	dew	due
die	dye	dire	dyer

Quiz

It is sometimes possible to take a line of poetry and add a second line which makes the two together amusing. For example:

'I think that I shall never see —

My contact lens fell in my tea.'

Could you add an amusing line to the following?

'When lovely women stoop to folly,

- ——— —— — ——— —— ———.'

Spellings

The words most commonly misspelled are highlighted.

oases	occupy	opposite
oasis	**occur**	opposition
obedience	**occurred**	oppression
obituary	**occurrence**	optimism
obligation	oculist	optimist
oblige	offensive	orchard
obscure	official	orchestra
obstacle	**omission**	ordeal
obstinate	omit	ordinary
obtuse	**omitted**	organisation
obviously	omitting	organise
occasion	onion	original
occasional	**onus**	ornament
occasionally	opaque	orphan
occasioned	**opinion**	ostrich
occupation	opponent	outrage
occupied	opportunity	oyster

WRITING 8:
MEMO, NOTICE, PRESS RELEASE

Introduction

The letter is the best-known means of communication in business. But when you go to work you will discover that there are several other methods of written communication which are commonly used. Some of these are used for internal communication such as the memo; some for external communication such as the press release; and others, such as the notice, may be used for either.

The memo

The memo or memorandum is the chief method of written communication within an organisation. It is frequently a hurried, handwritten message from one department or worker to another department or worker. A more formal memo may be typed. A memo may be sent by just one person to another or by several people to one person. In a firm a manager may send a memo addressed to 'All Staff'. *Memos are usually brief.*

Memos are used to:

(a) confirm arrangements made

(b) issue instructions

(c) convey information that has been requested.

Many firms have printed memo slips which are available to all persons who will have occasion to use them. These slips measure about 20 cm x 12 cm. Since these slips are so small the message must be concise. The usual layout of a memo is shown in Fig. 1.

Fig. 1 – Sample memo layout

Bondonno Manufacturing Company

Memo

To: _____   Date: _____
From: _____
            Subject: _____

_____
_____
_____

Writing a memo

(a) A memo should confine itself to one major point. If you wish to deal with two separate topics, send two memos.

(b) The language of a memo is usually somewhat informal.

(c) Every memo should be dated.

(d) Be concise and direct in your writing and remember a memo contains no salutation or complimentary closure.

(e) Use appropriate tone and always be courteous.

(f) Memos need not be signed or initialled, but more formal memos are usually signed. Job titles may be used instead of, or as well as, names.

(g) Titles such as Mr, Mrs, Ms are generally not used.

(h) If a memo is typed, this is usually done on A5 paper.

(i) A reference is sometimes used.

Fig. 2 – Sample memo

Bondonno Manufacturing Company

Memo

To: Aiden Moran   Date: 26/6/199?
From: Michael McCabe   Ref: bs/sk
            Subject: Video Equipment

I wonder could you look at the video equipment in room 504 and supply me with a list of the items which are obsolete so that we can dispose of them?

mm

If the memo is somewhat long, it may be useful to use headings rather like what one might use in a report.

Fig. 3 – Sample memo with headings

Bondonno Manufacturing Company

Memo

To: All Production Staff

Date: 26/9/9?

From: Head of Production Dept

Subject: Borrowing of Computers

Staff are allowed to borrow computers for use at home under certain conditions.

1. Conditions
   (a) Computers may be borrowed only when not required at the plant.
   (b) They may not be borrowed for more than one week at any one time.
   (c) The borrower is responsible for the computer during the time it is in his/her custody.

2. Borrowing Procedure
   (a) Obtain form from secretary and complete.
   (b) Have form signed by Head of Dept.
   (c) Obtain computer from Computer Technician.

3. Returning Computer
   (a) Return computer to Computer Technician.
   (b) Have form initialled by Computer Technician.
   (c) Bring form to Head of Dept for signature.

Stephen Hogan

ACTIVITY 1

1. Write a memo from the director/principal of your college to the president of the students' union complaining about the amount of litter thrown on the lawns during the fine weather. The principal wants the president's suggestions as to how the problem can be tackled.

2. Reply on behalf of the students' union president to the above memo.

3. You have seen an item at an exhibition which you feel would be of benefit to your firm. Write two separate memos: (a) to the chief accountant of your firm, (b) to the chief engineer of your firm, putting the case for the purchase of this item.

4. Your boss has asked you to write a memo to the supervisor of the cleaning staff conveying his displeasure at the lack of cleanliness around the building.

5. As secretary of the students' union you have been asked by the treasurer to draft a memo to all union officers informing them that no further requests for money can be entertained as the union's bank account is overdrawn.

6. You work for a large company where the manager is concerned at the

haphazard parking around the building. Instead of using the car park provided, some employees park close to the entrance on double yellow lines and thus limit access for delivery vans. Draft a memo to all members of staff informing them that the manager has decided that, in future, cars parked on double yellow lines will have a sticker put on the windscreen with the words 'Parked incorrectly' written on it. Cars which receive a second sticker will be towed to the Garda compound.

7. The personnel officer has received the above memo and having investigated the matter discovers that the car parking facilities are inadequate. She has asked you, her secretary, to draft a memo to be sent to the manager informing him of this and requesting him to defer measures suggested as they may cause displeasure among staff.

8. As manager of an office send a memo to all your staff informing them that punctuality is not as good as you expect.

9. As telephonist in your company send a memo to your boss explaining that your switchboard is constantly unable to deal with the volume of incoming calls.

The notice

A notice should be short, simple, designed in such a way that it attracts attention to itself and placed in a central and easily accessible position.

It differs from a memo in that:

(a) it is not directed to an individual or specific group
(b) it is posted on a bulletin board or other conspicuous place
(c) it does not normally demand a written reply
(d) it need not be signed unless knowledge of the source or transmitter is relevant.

If the notice is informal (see Fig. 4) a variety of means may be employed to attract attention and make it more dramatic. Use of unusual design, bright colouring, large lettering, drawings and cartoons will attract the readers' attention. Some computers are capable of designing very attractive notices.

Fig. 4 – Sample notice

STAFF NEWSLETTER
Have you news? If so,
submit to DEIRDRE WALSH (Rm 527)
before FRIDAY, 13 JUNE.
A newsletter can't survive without news

More formal notices (Fig. 5) need not be quite so dramatic and may use a more restrained tone. These may also be signed.

Fig. 5 – Sample notice

LIBRARY BOOKS

All library books borrowed by staff should be returned before start of summer holidays on 20 June.

Each member of staff is allowed to check out six (6) books for the duration of the holidays.

If this number is insufficient, please discuss the matter with me.

Signed: _____   Date: 1 June 199?

Brendan Crosse
(Librarian)

ACTIVITY 2

1. Draft a notice reminding all staff that cars may be parked only in assigned spaces in staff car park.

2. Draw up a notice bringing to the attention of all staff that the 11.00 a.m. break runs from 11.00 to 11.15. Many of the staff are still on break at 11.30.

3. Design a notice inviting students to join the debating club.

4. Design a notice encouraging students to use the waste bins in the classrooms.

5. Draw up a notice asking employees in your firm not to stub out cigarettes on the floor.

6. Draft a notice, suitable for display on a bulletin board, informing students that the gym will be closed for two weeks.

7. Pay cheques for staff will not be available for collection until 5.30 p.m. They have usually been available at 3.00 p.m. Write a notice informing staff of the change.

8. A social club is to be formed in your firm. Draft a notice for the bulletin board giving details of the arrangements for a preliminary meeting.

The press release

Most firms are now very conscious of their public or corporate image. They need to keep their image before the public as often as possible. This is often done through the use of the press release.

A press release is sent to the media with information on the company. It may be about:

(a) a new person joining the board

(b) a new investment programme

(c) installation of new equipment

(d) opening of new plant

(e) sponsorship of some activity.

Press releases are useful to the media as they set out the facts of whatever is taking place without the necessity of a journalist coming to interview someone.

Writing a press release

(a) It should be adapted to the media that are to receive it. Some press releases are only of use to local newspapers or local radio. To a certain extent it is just common sense to know the type of information the various media will be interested in.

(b) State the date and time for release of the information, e.g. 'Not for publication before 10.00 a.m. 27 June 199?' If the information is to be published immediately, put 'For immediate release' on it.

(c) Put a headline on every press release. This should sum up the contents. The sub-editor may change this.

(d) Emphasis should be on factual information. What happened? When did it happen? Where? Who was involved? Why did it happen?

(e) Use a simple, plain, direct style.

(f) The essentials of the story should be contained in the first paragraph.

(g) Use direct quotes from people involved if possible. These will add variety and colour to the piece.

(h) Keep press releases short.

(i) Sign each one.

(j) Always provide name and telephone number of a contact at the end.

Layout of press releases

(a) Always use company notepaper.

(b) Use double spacing and wide margins. This allows the sub-editor to make changes.

(c) Type 'Press Release' on top.

(d) Each continuation page should have 'more follows' or 'm f' typed at the bottom.

(e) Number each page and put title of press release on each page also.

(f) Type 'ends' at the end of the document.

The final three guidelines are particularly important if the press release is being sent by fax.

Fig. 6 – Press release

Arravale Manufacturing Company
Mooncoin, Co. Kilkenny
Telephone 056-81231
Fax 056-82214

PRESS RELEASE

(For immediate release) Date: 27 June 199?

NEW MARKET FOR KILKENNY COMPANY

A new market, worth £1,000,000. This was the good news announced today by Mr Michael Finn, Managing Director of Arravale Manufacturing Company in Mooncoin, Co. Kilkenny. His company has secured a three-year contract to supply Phlemco, a French farm machinery company, with blades for their harvesters.

Announcing the good news, Mr Finn said that the contract will secure the jobs of the 250 employees and the new technology recently installed will enable the company to fulfil the new order without engaging in an expansion programme.

'We won the order against very stiff competition', said Mr Finn. 'A very big factor was our ability to meet deadlines and our very high level of quality control.'

The French company visited the Mooncoin plant recently and were very impressed with the skills of the employees and the high level of technology available. The first consignments to France will be leaving towards the end of October.

Mr Finn said this success encourages his company to seek further markets in Europe and he himself will be visiting Germany soon to seek new opportunities for Arravale.

ENDS

For further information contact
James Deering
Telephone: Business 062-81231   Home 062-83435

ACTIVITY 3

1. Write a press release on the official opening of Ardnageeha Tools Factory by the Minister for Industry on Thursday 25 June 199?.

2. Neadnanave Manufacturing Company is extending its plant and will be recruiting 100 skilled employees. Invent the details and write the press release. It is not for publication until Tuesday 5 September 199?.

3. South West Business College has made a promotional video and will launch it at a cheese and wine reception on Wednesday 6 December 199?. The video will be sent to all second-level schools, free of charge, in the catchment area. The video was made by Big Land Studios at a cost of £15,000. It is twenty minutes long. Write the appropriate press release.

Review

1. What is the difference between a memo and a notice?
2. In what circumstances should a notice be signed?
3. Give three situations in which you would write a memo.
4. Give three situations in which you would write a notice.
5. Give three advantages of a press release from the point of view of a company issuing it.
6. Give three advantages of a press release from the point of view of the media which receive it.
7. Why should press releases always give a contact name and telephone number?
8. Should the same press release be sent to several media, or should it be adapted to suit each medium?

Pitfalls

two-first two-last

It is impossible to have more than one first or last of anything, and expressions such as 'the two-first', 'the three-last' should be avoided.

Confusing words

waist	waste	deduce	deduct
write	right	negligent	negligible
riot	rite	official	officious
popular	populous	impressive	impressionable
insolvent	insoluble	ostensible	ostentatious

Quiz

A rebus uses pictures, numbers and letters of the alphabet to make words and sentences. What is the meaning of the following rebus?

```
      have to      paid
I                because
      work         I am
```

Spellings

The words most commonly misspelled are highlighted.

paganism	peaceable	physique
pageant	peasant	picnicking
pamphlet	peculiar	piety
pantomime	penance	plague
parachute	**penicillin**	**planning**
paraffin	peninsula	**pleasant**
parallel	penniless	pleasurable
paralleled	perceive	pneumatic
parallelogram	perennial	pneumonia
paralyse	perilous	poisonous
paralysis	**permanent**	porcelain
paraphrase	**permissible**	portrait
parchment	**perseverance**	**possess**
pardonable	persistence	**possesses**
parliament	persuasion	postpone
particular	pessimist	**potential**
particularly	pheasant	precaution
pastime	philosophy	precede
patience	**physical**	**preceding**

217

predecessor
preference
preferred
prejudice
preliminary
prestige
prevalent
privilege
procedure

professional
professor
programme
prominent
pronunciation
prophecy (n)
prophesy (v)
proprietor
prosecute

prospective
provident
provocation
psychology
punctual
pursue
puzzle
pylon
pyramid

WRITING 9:
REPORTS, REPORTS, REPORTS

Introduction

A report is an objective and orderly presentation of factual information drawn up to meet a specific need. It may be: a record of work completed; an account of an accident at work; the results of a specific investigation which would include conclusions and may include recommendations based on findings.

We are concerned here with written reports, but they may also be oral. Indeed, very often a report will be written, but the author may often be requested to present it orally at a meeting.

There are three main types of reports:

(1) routine reports

(2) special reports

(3) long reports.

Routine reports

Routine reports are written at regular intervals and are brief, using a simple format. Some routine reports may just involve completing a report form provided.

Fig. 1 – Routine report on form provided

Routine Insurance Company Ltd
Accident Form

Name of Person Involved in Accident: _____
Address: _____
Age: _____ Number of Years in your Employment: _____
Date of Accident: _____ Time of Accident: _____
Location of Accident: _____ (Attach map if necessary)
Circumstances of Accident: _____
_____
_____

Witnesses to Accident: _____
_____
_____

Injuries Received: _____
_____

Name of Doctor Called: _____
Signed: _____
(to be signed by Manager of Department where accident occurred)
Return completed form to:
Routine Insurance Company
21 Patrick Street
Cork

A typical routine report is the weekly summary of work completed by a department. This may be done in the form of a memo. If so, it is then called a memo report.

Fig. 2 – Routine report

To: James Connolly
From: Conor Ashe

Subject: Report of Sales Department
for week of
17 July 199? to 24 July 199?

1. Sales

The total sales recorded for the week were £15,600. This is a 15% increase on the figure for the same week last year. Confirmation of a large order from Video Equipment was received on Tuesday 22.

2. Notice of Intention to Leave

Our Sales Representative for the Western Region, Gerard O'Connor, is leaving to take up employment with Ballycrogue Company Ltd in Nenagh, Co. Tipperary. His last day with the firm will be 27 August 199?

3. Complaint

Annacarty Manufacturing Company has complained that its order of 5 June (Order No. 1756043) has still not been delivered. Reply has been sent explaining the problem with the new machine and promising delivery in two weeks.

Signed: _____   Date: 24 July 199?

      Conor Ashe

ACTIVITY 1

1. You have been in charge of the student shop at your college for the past week. Prepare a routine report on the week's activities.

2. The public telephone in your factory has been damaged and the contents of the cash box stolen. Prepare a report for the managing director.

3. At your college one of the students has been injured while playing for the official college team. Prepare a report of the accident which will be sent to the insurance company using a standard accident form as in the example at the beginning of the chapter.

4. You are assistant to the personnel officer. Your boss has been sick for the past week. He will return on Monday. Prepare a report for him on the week's work. Invent the details you need.

5. A video recorder is missing from your department. Prepare a report on the circumstances of its disappearance.

Special reports

Special reports are called for, from time to time, to respond to particular situations in a firm. The person requiring the special report states, in writing usually, the terms of reference, i.e. the exact purpose of the report. The terms of reference should be clear, precise and free from ambiguity.

A special report may be drawn up under the following headings:

(a) *Terms of reference*: Here is stated precisely the subject and limits of your report. If you are expected to make recommendations, the terms of reference will state this.

(b) *Method of procedure*: Under this heading you indicate in detail the steps taken to collect the necessary information. The worth of a report can be measured against the relevance, significance and comprehensiveness of the steps taken. Where the method of procedure is careless, findings will be suspect.

(c) *Findings*: Here all items discovered relevant to the terms of reference are noted. Great care should be taken to ascertain the facts.

The special report should contain conclusions and may contain recommendations.

(d) *Conclusions*: Conclusions should be numbered and arranged in descending order of importance. They must be based on the findings. One person looking at findings may arrive at different conclusions from another person looking at the same findings.

(e) *Recommendations*: Recommendations should be numbered and arranged in descending order of importance. To be of any benefit they must be capable of implementation. Different people working from the same findings and conclusions may make different recommendations.

All reports should be written in objective style, e.g. 'It was discovered that . . .'

All reports should be signed and dated.

Fig. 3 – Special report (formal)

Report on Parking Facilities

at

Mullingar Business College

1. Terms of Reference

'To investigate the adequacy of the parking facilities at the College and to make any necessary recommendations.'

2. Method of Procedure

2.1 The car parks in the College were visited on three occasions each day at different times over a period of three weeks.

2.2 Staff and student registers were consulted to ascertain the number and type of vehicles requiring parking facilities.

2.3 Over a three-week period a register was maintained to record the number of visitors who required parking.

2.4 Caretaker who is responsible for removing cars improperly parked was interviewed.

3. Findings

3.1 Present Position

3.1.1 There are four separate car parks in the College containing, in all, 500 parking spaces.

3.1.2 Two hundred staff members and three hundred and fifty students have a vehicle to park each day.

3.1.3 Car park near back gate is never completely filled.

3.1.4 Car park near front door is always the most crowded.

3.2 Difficulties with Present Situation

3.2.1 There are no facilities for bicycles and auto-cycles.

3.2.2 Some spaces are not properly utilised as just one auto-cycle may be parked in it.

3.2.3 Parking on double yellow lines is frequent.

3.2.4 Usually it is the same cars which are parked on double yellow lines.

3.2.5 There is usually no parking space available for visitors' cars.

4. Conclusions

4.1 The number of parking spaces available is inadequate.

4.2 Most people wish to park near the front door so the rear car park is under-utilised.

4.3 Some people are parking incorrectly even when spaces are available.

5. Recommendations

5.1 Provide separate parking facilities for bicycles and auto-cycles.

5.2 Reserve ten parking spaces in front car park for visitors.

5.3 Owners of cars repeatedly parked incorrectly should be written to by the Principal.

Emma McGrane: _____   Date: 10 October 199?
        (Chief Clerk)

Special reports need not always conform to the layout in Fig. 3. Special reports which are not so formal as the type just considered may have any layout that suits the topic being investigated. A common layout for the less formal special report follows.

Fig. 4 – Special report (informal)

Report on Care of Grounds

at

Rathduff Manufacturing Company

1. The Problem

1.1 Concern was expressed at the Board of Directors' last meeting on 25 July 199? on the general untidiness and lack of care of the grounds. The Managing Director has asked me to carry out a report on the extent of the problem and to suggest means by which it can be solved.

2. Discussion of the Problem

2.1 Present State of Grounds

The grounds to be maintained consists of four acres, of which one acre is covered by paths, driveways and shrubs, while the remaining three acres is in lawn.

2.2 Maintenance of Grounds

The difficult time for maintenance is during spring and summer when growth is strong. Cutting of grass, weeding and tending to shrubbery are the main tasks. At present, a caretaker spends two days a week during spring and summer tending the grounds, and one day a week during the rest of the year. This person has no special training in such work and the equipment available to him is old.

3. **Conclusions**

3.1 It is necessary for a person to spend more time tending the grounds, but this is not possible because of internal duties for the caretaker.

3.2 During spring and summer it is necessary to have one man working on the grounds full-time.

3.3 New equipment needs to be purchased, especially a good lawnmower.

3.4 It may be possible to contract out maintenance of the grounds.

3.5 A further and more detailed report would need to be carried out on which is the more cost-effective way of getting the work done, i.e. putting the work out to contract or replacing old equipment and assigning more of our manpower to the task.

Signed: _____   Date: 1 August 199?

       James Doyle

       (Chargehand)

ACTIVITY 2

1. The general manager of your place of employment is concerned about security of the premises. She has asked you to draw up a report on the subject and to make recommendations.

2. Visitors have commented on the untidy appearance of your factory. The managing director has asked you to investigate the matter and make recommendations.

3. The librarian wants a report on the extent to which the library facilities have been used by your class group.

4. You are asked to investigate the sports facilities for girls at your college and to make recommendations.

5. The students' union has asked you to investigate the canteen in your college and to make recommendations for its improvement.

6. During the summer, while the college is closed, local children are allowed to use the tennis courts. The nets on all three courts and the wire fencing around the courts have been damaged. Prepare a report for the principal on the extent of the damage.

7. The managing director of your company is concerned about the lack of punctuality. He has asked you to determine the extent of the problem, discover its cause and make recommendations.

8. The tea break in your factory is to last ten minutes. However, employees seem to be absent from their machines for between twelve and sixteen minutes. Employees who were asked about extending the tea break mentioned such reasons as overcrowding, tea not ready on time and milk running short. You are asked to draw up a report on the problem of the extended tea break and to make recommendations.

Long reports

A firm reviewing its normal procedures and strategies may occasionally need a detailed, in-depth exploration of itself and its markets. As well as studying itself, the firm may wish to know how similar firms are progressing. In this type of report it may be necessary to give background information and to detail the present state of research in the area before dealing specifically with the firm itself. A long report may have the following layout:

(a) *Title page*: This will contain (i) the title of the report, (ii) author's name, (iii) name of department authorising the report, (iv) date report was presented, and (v) may state whether report is confidential or not.

(b) *Circulation list*: If the report is intended for a small number of readers, a list of these will appear on the title page. If the circulation is longer, it will appear on a separate page.

(c) *Acknowledgments*: The author will, on this page, thank the individuals and organisations who helped in the compilation of the report.

(d) *Table of contents*: This will include the major headings of the report in the order in which they appear. Sub-headings may also be given. Too much detail here may be confusing and intimidating to the reader. Word processing programs on a computer will do a table of contents for you.

(e) *Introduction*: This section will explain why the present study is being undertaken and give some background information.

(f) *Terms of reference*: Here the precise statement of the problem being investigated is given. This should appear in quotation marks.

(g) *Summary of conclusions*: In this very brief section the main conclusions should be stated. This will accommodate the reader who is interested in the study but does not need, or has not time, to read the whole report.

(h) *Method of procedure*: This section details the various means used to collect, analyse and interpret the findings.

(i) *Findings*: Here the findings are presented. This will be the longest section in the report. Sub-headings should be used to facilitate understanding.

(j) *Conclusions*: The conclusions, based on the findings, should be presented in descending order of importance. Every effort should be made to avoid prejudice in reaching conclusions.

(k) *Recommendations*: Recommendations are proposals for future actions. These should be presented in descending order of importance. Avoid prejudice and personal interest. Recommendations should be capable of implementation.

(l) *Appendices*: The appendices present tables, graphs, charts, drawings, photographs and other relevant materials omitted elsewhere in the report. The writer will have to make a decision as to whether he should use appendices. Appendices should be used to present relevant information which, if included in the main body of the text, would deflect the reader from the main thrust of the report.

(m) *Bibliography*: This is a list of books, pamphlets, articles, both published and unpublished, which are relevant to the report.

(n) *Index*: The index is an alphabetical list of names, subjects, etc., mentioned in the report. It is more detailed than the table of contents. It helps the reader find specific data quickly by indicating the page and/or paragraph number of every reference to the name or subject listed in the index. For example, if Michael Argyle is mentioned four times in the report, the index will show an entry similar to the following:

Argyle, Michael, 2.3, 4.6, 10.1, 10.8

Word processing programs on a computer will do an index for you.

Fig. 5 – Title page

Work Study Institute
Carlow

A Report
on
Absenteeism in Three Manufacturing Industries
in
Carlow
by
Patricia O'Kelly
(Head of Research Department)
for
South-East Chambers of Commerce
15 April 199?

Fig. 6 – Sample table of contents

Table of Contents

Circulation List	(i)
Acknowledgments	(ii)
Introduction	1
Terms of Reference	8
Summary of Conclusions	9
Method of Procedure	11
Findings	14
Factory A	15
Factory B	22
Factory C	30
Comparison	41
Conclusions	53
Recommendations	60
Appendices	65
Appendix 1	65
Appendix 2	66
Appendix 3	67
Bibliography	68
Index	72

Fig. 7 – Sample bibliography

> Bibliography
>
> **Books**
>
> Boyle, Martin, *Absenteeism – Its Causes*. Dublin: New Book Publishers, 1988
>
> Boyle, Martin, *Absenteeism – Another Look*. Dublin: Old Gate Publishers, 1989
>
> **Articles**
>
> Allen, Michael, 'Alcoholism and Absenteeism', *Irish Work Study Weekly*, July 1987, pp. 12-18

Planning the long report

The most difficult part of drawing up a report is its initial planning and organising. This is time-consuming but very necessary, and should not be rushed.

Fig. 8 – Procedure for drawing up a long report

> **1. Planning**
>   Clarify terms of reference
>   Prepare an outline plan of work
>   Decide on method of procedure
>   List people and organisations that may have to be contacted
>   Establish a timetable for the work.
>
> **2. Research**
>   Do background research
>   Obtain information from relevant people and organisations
>   Evaluate data obtained
>   Organise data
>   Decide layout.
>
> **3. Writing**
>   Write first draft
>   Give to colleagues for comments
>   Write second draft
>   Type
>   Proofread
>   Retype
>   Proofread again
>   Make copies and bind.

The terms of reference

You need to be quite clear on the aims, extent and limitations of your report. So before you begin, establish precisely your terms of reference. Ideally these should be given in written form and should appear in quotation marks in your report. Insist, if necessary, on a meeting with the person who requires the report. If the terms of reference are given to you orally, they should be written down and submitted to your client for approval.

In addition to the precise terms of reference you need to know:

(a) The purpose of the report. Is it a preliminary report or is it one upon which important decisions are going to be based?

(b) The amount of detail necessary. Is it, for example, necessary to go into precise costings of various operations?

(c) For whom the report is intended. This information will enable you to decide what assumptions you can make about the prior knowledge of your readers. It will determine the language and tone you will use.

(d) Length of report. You can only gauge the approximate length.

(e) Date for completion of report. This will influence your plan of work.

Writing a report

(a) Begin with the body or the main part of the report and divide it into logical sections using headings and subheadings.

(b) Jot down in note form what will come under each heading and subheading.

(c) Write clearly, concisely and simply.

(d) Use an objective, unemotional style. Write 'It was discovered . . .' rather than 'I discovered . . .'

(e) Make sure that the conclusions you reach are valid.

(f) Use a suitable numbering system for each section, subsection and paragraph.

There are basically two systems, the letter numbering system and the decimal numbering system.

Letter numbering system	Decimal numbering system
1	1.0
A	1.1
1	1.1.1
a	1.1.1.1
(i)	1.1.1.2
(ii)	1.1.1.3
b	1.1.2
(i)	1.1.2.1
(ii)	1.1.2.2
2	1.2
a	1.2.1
(i)	1.2.1.1
(ii)	1.2.1.2
b	1.2.2
(i)	1.2.2.1
(ii)	1.2.2.2
11	2.0
A	2.1
1	2.1.1
a	2.1.1.1

Revising and proofreading

Your report may need one or two full revisions. It is a good idea to give your first draft to someone to read and then consider their suggestions in your revisions.

Always proofread. Again, it is a good idea to get a friend to proofread.

Review

1. What is the difference between a report and a memo?
2. How does a report differ from a letter?
3. What are the three main types of reports and how do you distinguish between them?
4. What is a memo report?
5. How do you distinguish between conclusions and recommendations?

6. What is meant by terms of reference?
7. Why is it important to clarify your terms of reference before beginning your report?
8. Explain what is meant by method of procedure.

Pitfalls

sewage sewerage

These two words are often confused. *Sewage* means the matter conveyed in pipes to, for example, a septic tank. *Sewerage* is the conduit or channel or pipe system to carry the sewage to the septic tank.

Confusing words

recent	resent	human	humane
dependent	dependant	uninterested	disinterested
horde	hoard	beside	besides
waive	wave	ascent	assent
plaintiff	plaintive	popular	populous

Quiz

The figurative expression 'to call a spade a spade' is sometimes modified to 'call a spade a shovel'. What, do you think, is the difference between the two phrases?

Spellings

The words most commonly misspelled are highlighted.

quadruple	quantify	questionnaire
quagmire	quantitative	queue
quaint	quantity	quicken
quake	quarrel	**quiet**
qualification	quarry	quit
qualify	quarter	quite
qualifying	quarterly	quorate
qualitative	quay	quorum
quality	queasy	quota
quandary	querulous	quotation
quantifiable	query	quote

PART 3

NON-VERBAL

SKILLS

⑱

INTERACTIVE SKILLS

Visitors

In most firms it is the telephonist/receptionist who is the first person in the organisation to meet visitors. Tact and diplomacy in such a position are vital. She must be skilful in dealing with people and be able to deal with awkward situations. She should have a thorough knowledge of the organisation's activities and know the jobs carried out by its various employees.

The person receiving visitors needs to know about all the appointments made and know which people are available each day and who will be away from the premises. Some firms keep a reception register in which are entered details of all visitors. The receptionist should have a diary with a page for each day. This will allow plenty of space for entering appointments, taking brief notes from visitors and entering reminders of various tasks to be done.

Courtesy at all times

Every visitor should be treated with courtesy and kindness. Never appear so busy that the caller feels a nuisance. If the person has an appointment, inform your boss before showing him in; if there is a delay, apologise for it and ask him to take a seat. It is not necessary to engage in conversation all the time. Once you have invited the visitor to sit down, you can continue with your work. If the visitor does not have an appointment, make discreet enquiries to find out whether your boss wishes to see him. If your boss does not wish to see him there are three courses of action open to you:

(a) find out if someone else in the firm can help him

(b) get your boss to telephone him later

(c) try to help him yourself.

You have the option of making an appointment for some future date, but your boss may not wish to see this particular caller. You can deal with this situation by asking if he would like to leave a written message which you will pass on.

If a visitor has to be kept waiting, provide him with a magazine, newspaper or your firm's prospectus or newsletter. No one should be kept waiting too long.

It is not possible to give specific guidelines on how to deal with every situation. Sometimes you will just have to use your common sense and discretion. Some situations could be handled in several different ways and it may be difficult to know which is best. Situations arise to which there are no easy answers. You just have to 'think on your feet' and deal with it as sensibly as you can. If your boss is going to a meeting and tells you she is not to be disturbed, that is not to be taken literally. If information comes through that a member of her family has been injured then, of course, you inform her.

Complaints

You cannot avoid complaints. Even with the best will in the world sometimes things will go wrong. There will always be dissatisfied customers. If an organisation is big it is difficult to ensure that everyone is dealt with fairly.

Receiving the complaint

Never be rude if the person making the complaint is abusive. Find out specific details of the complaint. The matter cannot be rectified unless you get to the bottom of the problem. By doing this you also show interest and concern. If you cannot deal with the complaint yourself, refer it to someone who can.

- Don't accept blame immediately if the position is unclear.
- Don't give the customer hope if he is obviously wrong.
- Tell him the procedure for dealing with complaints.
- Do not argue.
- Express regret at any inconvenience the person complaining may have experienced.

ACTIVITY I

1. *A visitor to your firm insists he has an appointment with your boss. You*

cannot find it in your diary. This very rarely happens as you are careful to note all appointments. What action would you take?
2. Describe in detail how to deal with callers who do not have an appointment.
3. What information should a receptionist have on hand?
4. Mention three important points that should be borne in mind when dealing with visitors.
5. A visitor who has an appointment calls to see your boss. Your boss does not want to see him. Write down the dialogue which might take place between yourself and the visitor.
6. What steps would you take to shield your boss from callers she does not want to see?
7. Your boss has made an appointment for 9.30 a.m. The visitor arrives at 9.25 but your boss will not be able to see him for fifteen minutes. How would you deal with the visitor in the meantime?
8. A visitor, well known to your firm, calls to see your boss on what he says is a confidential matter. Your boss is at an important meeting with some of her staff. What action would you take?
9. Describe in detail the steps you would take when dealing with a visitor who has an appointment.
10. Two visitors, neither of whom has an appointment, arrive to see your boss. Both say they are in a hurry and would like to see him first. How would you deal with the situation?

GROUP ACTIVITY

The following situations may be used to practise dealing with complaints. One person complains and the other person responds to the complaint. It may be helpful to record the situations on video and have discussions about how the complaint was made and how well the other person responded.

1. You are shopping in the supermarket. Only two out of eight checkouts are open. The queues at these are getting longer and longer. No attempt is being made to open extra checkouts. The manager is on the phone. You are in a hurry and can no longer put up with this. Approach the manager to complain.
2. Your daughter has applied to your local college to get a place on the Business Studies Certificate course. Two hundred points in the Leaving Certificate is the minimum required to gain a place. Your daughter, in fact, has 226 points, but the course director informs you that only six subjects are counted for making up the points. Your daughter sat seven subjects in her examination. If

you count just six subjects your daughter has only 185 points. Complain about what you see as the unfairness of this to the course director.

3. You have hired a chain-saw from a hire equipment company. The two previous occasions you hired it, the saw broke down after an hour's work and much of your day was wasted. Complain to the manager about the standard of equipment available for hire.

4. You are a member of your local Tidy Towns Committee. The committee has requested business people to ensure that their premises are freshly painted and that their grounds are tidy and well maintained. As a member of the committee you are required to visit a business person involved to express disappointment with his efforts.

5. A customer complains that your telephonist is seldom available at 9.00 a.m. and that sometimes the phone rings for long periods before being answered. Deal with the person complaining.

6. You bought some precious crystal, but when leaving the shop the bag burst and the box in which the crystal was packed fell on the tiled part of the shop. When you check the box you find that three of the eight glasses are broken. Complain to the manager and ask for replacements.

7. You are buying a continental quilt. You are quite slow in making up your mind and feel that the shop assistant is getting impatient. Finally he says, 'Look, Missus, I haven't all day to wait for you to make up your mind. Come back on Tuesday when you get the children's allowance and have another look at it.' You are offended and humiliated. Make your complaint to the manager.

Using the telephone

On the telephone, courtesy and good manners are essential. The consideration shown to a caller in person is just as important when she is at the other end of a telephone. The receptionist/telephonist is the first contact many people have with an organisation and it is vital that this first impression be positive. The telephonist/receptionist should have the following available:

(a) telephone directories as needed

(b) index book for keeping a list of numbers used frequently

(c) note book for recording telephone messages. Many firms have printed forms for this purpose.

Making a telephone call
- Ensure you have the correct code and number.
- If the call is non-routine, jot down the main points you must cover.
- Have available any documents you need.
- Speak clearly into the mouthpiece.
- Identify yourself by name of firm, department or your own name.
- Explain clearly and concisely your business.
- Always repeat numbers to ensure they have been correctly heard.
- Repeat important parts of the message.
- Spell out difficult names and words.
- Express thanks at the end of the call.

Receiving a telephone call
- Answer telephone immediately.
- Identify yourself by name of firm, department or your own name.
- Adopt a friendly tone.
- Listen carefully.
- Ensure you know caller's name and address or telephone number so that you can reply.
- If you can't find the person sought or the information requested quickly, promise to return the call as soon as possible.
- If you must put the caller through to an extension, do not just flip a switch and leave the caller not knowing what is happening. Say 'I'm putting you through now to Ms Scully.'
- If person being sought is not available, suggest a time when he will be back.
- Express thanks for calling at the end of the conversation.

Taking messages
Many firms have special printed forms for messages.

Fig. 1 – Form for taking telephone message

TELEPHONE MESSAGE

For: _____   Date: _____

From: _____   Time: _____

_____
_____
_____
_____
_____
_____

Taken by: _____

In taking telephone messages the following points should be noted:

(a) date and time of call

(b) caller's name, firm and telephone extension

(c) name of person for whom call was intended

(d) precise details of message.

Read back these points to the caller to ensure you have them correct. The message should be placed where the person it concerns will find it. It is prudent to check later that the person has, in fact, seen it.

Spelling words on the telephone

When it seems likely that some words may be confused, it is a good idea to use the official alphabetical code. It goes as follows:

A for Alfred	J for Jack	S for Samuel
B for Benjamin	K for King	T for Tommy
C for Charles	L for Lucy	U for Uncle
D for David	M for Mary	V for Victor
E for Edward	N for Nellie	W for William
F for Frederick	O for Oliver	X for X-Ray
G for George	P for Peter	Y for Yellow
H for Harry	Q for Queen	Z for Zebra
I for Isaac	R for Robert	

ACTIVITY 2

1. What do you think the caller is saying in the following exchange?

   Telephonist: 'Grange Products Limited.'

Caller:..

T: 'Putting you through.'

C: 'Ok, thank you.'

BC: 'You could always ring Dublin now and they'd know the exact fare and whether she stops in Naas and all that sort of thing.'

C: 'Ok, thank you.'

BC: 'Right.'

3. How should a receptionist deal with the following call?

Receptionist: 'Good morning, Athassel Products.'

Caller: 'Hello! I wanted to make a . . .'

R: 'Sorry, just hold on a sec please.'

(Half a minute later)

R: 'Now, we're right. You were saying.'

C: 'I wanted to make a complaint about . . .'

R: 'Oh, we don't deal with complaints here at all. You'll have to ring 062-71124. They deal with complaints – Mr Foran.'

C: 'Can you transfer me to him?'

R: 'No, I'm afraid not.'

Review

1. When dealing with people, why are first impressions very important?
2. Why is the telephonist/receptionist so important in an organisation?
3. How should you deal with a visitor who is abusive?
4. If your boss says she is not to be disturbed for the next two hours, how should you interpret that message?
5. 'Firms and organisations should welcome complaints.' Why?
6. How would you deal with a customer whose complaint is unjustified?
7. What, in your experience, are the chief errors made when answering the telephone?
8. What, in your experience, are the chief errors made when making a telephone call?
9. A person has telephoned your organisation and complains that your boss never seems to be available. She has telephoned six times in the past two weeks and she was always told he was not available. How would you deal with this complaint?

Pitfalls

rout route

Rout can be used in the sense 'put them to *rout*', i.e. to defeat them completely. It can also be used as in to '*rout* someone out of the bed'.

Route is a course taken, e.g. 'a man's delivery *route*', or 'I took the shortest *route*'.

Confusing words

dammed	damned	exercise	exorcise
done	deign	fair	fare
instant	instance	depravation	deprivation
dying	dyeing	intense	intents
either	ether	knave	nave

Quiz

What is a limerick? Write one.

Spellings

The words most commonly misspelled are highlighted.

radical	**recommend**	relaxation
rapidity	reconcile	reliable
rarity	reconciliation	**relieve**
readability	recruit	religion
readily	rectangle	reluctance
realise	refer	relying
really	referee	remainder
reasonable	**reference**	remember
rebel	**referred**	remembrance
rebelled	referring	remit
rebuke	refugee	remittance
receipt	regiment	remitting
receive	regret	removable
recent	regrettable	renounce
recitation	regular	renunciation
recite	reign	
recognise	rejoicing	

241

⑲ MEDIA ANALYSIS

On Friday, 29 July 1994 the Report of the Inquiry of the Beef Tribunal conducted by Judge Hamilton was delivered to the government. The report was studied by Taoiseach, Albert Reynolds and his advisers. Shortly before midnight the Government Press Secretary issued a statement claiming the Taoiseach had been 'totally vindicated'. To back up his claim, the Press Secretary cited a direct quotation from the report.

The quotation was 'The determination of where the national interest lay was a matter for decision for the Minister for Industry and Commerce . . . the basis for those decisions was that they were in the national interest and the determination of the requirements of the national interest in these matters is a matter for the Minister for Industry and Commerce.'

The part of the quotation omitted indicated by the three dots in fact amounted to thirty-one pages.

(Tim Ryan, *Albert Reynolds, The Longford Leader*, Dublin: Blackwater Press, 1994, p. 184)

The various news media in Ireland carried the government statement as the main item on the days following. It was a few days before journalists discovered that the quotation mentioned above was not so direct and simple.

Was this manipulation of the media? What do you think?

Why study the media?

There are basically five reasons why you should study the media.

1. *Your interest*: You may be personally interested in radio, TV, newspapers and magazines. You may want to know more about these.
2. *Media power*: Many people believe that the media have great power and influence. Most people believe they have some power. They are the main source of ideas of many people and they help shape our opinions and attitudes. They may shape how we think and act.
3. *Economic power*: The media employ thousands of people directly and many others indirectly. The income and expenditure of the media are

vast. Then there is the question of advertising and how much money is spent on it. The media need advertising to survive.

4. *Audience*: The media have a huge audience. Some media such as radio and TV come right into our kitchens and bedrooms. Few households do not have at least one radio and one TV.

5. *Information and entertainment*: People want entertainment and they want information. They get most of these from the media. Most people no longer have just RTE 1 and Network 2. The idea of preventing outside influences is no longer practical. We can tune into TV stations in Britain, France, Germany and USA. The world has become a 'global village'. Some surveys show that nearly 90 per cent of people get their news from TV and that they, for the most part, believe it. The media – TV, radio, books, newspapers and magazines – provide most people's entertainment. So if the media are the main providers of information and entertainment it makes sense to study them. We should look at what they provide and why.

ACTIVITY 1

1. Do a survey of your class to ascertain how many hours are spent each week on TV, radio, books, magazines and newspapers. Find out which medium is the most popular and on which days of the week students spend the most time on each medium.
2. Find out which programmes are the most popular with your classmates on radio and TV. Is there a difference in the programmes watched by boys and girls?
3. List the magazines, in the order of popularity, which the students in your class read.
4. Find out how often your classmates visit the public library each week and the reason for their visit.
5. How many radios and TVs do your classmates have in their homes?
6. What TV channels are received in your fellow students' homes and which ones are the most popular? Is there a difference in the channels watched by boys and girls?
7. Which newspapers do the families of your classmates buy every week? Do they buy a local newspaper? Do they buy two newspapers on Sunday?
8. What percentage of your classmates' families buy a British newspaper?
9. Do the homes of all your classmates possess a video?
10. How many videos do your classmates rent each week?

How to study the media

You cannot study the media just by watching TV, listening to the radio and reading magazines and books. You must look at various aspects of the media and not just what they put out. You should look at who runs and finances the media. Studying the media is not just about the product, it is also about who produces it and what is produced. It is also important to know how the product is produced. A TV station such as RTE does not have offices and cameras in every town in Ireland. It does have an office and equipment in Waterford. Are news stories from Waterford more likely to get on TV than from Kilkenny where RTE has no facilities?

Always watch for repetition in the media. Anything that is repeated may be significant. Are there similar ownership patterns? If you study women's magazines in a certain age band are certain topics repeated? Are certain topics never included? What is not covered may be as important as what is covered. Why are there no teenage boys' magazines like those for girls?

We will now look at some specific methods of studying the media.

1. *Content analysis*: In this method you can break down under headings the content of a programme or paper. You could, for example, find out how much of a paper is devoted to advertisements. You could also add up the number of close-up shots in a TV programme of the hero as compared to other male characters. There are usually many more shots of the hero and so we know that he is important by the amount of time he is given.

2. *Image analysis*: This technique seeks to break down the elements of a given image such as a TV picture or a picture in a magazine to find out how the meaning is put into the image. There are three elements to any image:

   (a) Where was the camera when the picture was shot? The camera takes the position of the viewer and this may be significant in the meaning we are supposed to get from the picture.

   (b) What devices are used to put the image together? What lighting is used and where is it placed? Is it in colour or black and white? Is it done in such a way that it seems to be an old photograph to give a sense of nostalgia?

   (c) The third element is the content of the image. What objects are represented in the picture? Is the person being interviewed surrounded by book shelves filled with weighty tomes? If so, what impression does this give?

3. *Tables of information*: It is possible to get the circulation figures of newspapers and of magazines. You can also find the viewing figures of the various TV programmes and the listening figures for radio programmes. In regard to newspapers you could also look at the cover cost. You could also find out how much it costs to advertise in the various media.

4. *Sources of information*: Your library will have in stock various books dealing with the media. These can be a useful source of information. You may also be able to find out how much it costs to make the various TV and radio programmes.

5. *Questionnaires*: You could draw up a questionnaire on a newspaper or TV or radio programme and get reactions to it. For example, what percentage of people in a particular age group read *The Irish Times*?

ACTIVITY 2

1. Find the average daily sales of The Irish Independent, The Irish Times *and* The Cork Examiner.

2. Take each of the above papers for one day and find out what percentage of the paper is given over to advertising.

3. The Cork Examiner *makes most of its sales in Muster. Is this reflected in its coverage of events?*

4. The Irish Times *is often seen as the 'quality' newspaper in Ireland. What is meant by this?*

5. The Irish Press *changed to a tabloid format a few years ago. Why?*

6. The Irish Times *sells mostly in Dublin and the east. Is this reflected in its coverage of events?*

7. The Irish Press *was founded by Eamon de Valera to put forward the viewpoint of the Fianna Fáil party. Was this reflected in its coverage of events?*

8. Analyse the TV schedules of RTE 1 and Network 2 and find out how much time is devoted to sport.

9. Analyse the TV scehdules of RTE 1 and Network 2 and find out how much time is devoted to programmes in the Irish language.

10. On RTE Radio 1 and FM 2 how much time is devoted to programmes for teenagers?

11. RTE Radio 1 always interrupts its programmes for the Angelus. What does this tell us?

Functions of the media

Why are the media there and what are they supposed to do? What are their functions for the individual and for society?

1. *Entertainment functions*: The media provide entertainment for their audience. The entertainment provided may be seen as healthy and pleasurable for us or it may be viewed as a means of diverting our attention from more important issues.
2. *Information functions*: The media provide necessary information about the world for their audience. It can be said that this helps us to form our view of the world, or it may be said that we are given a particular view of the world to keep us happy.
3. *Cultural functions*: The media provide material which reflects and develops our culture. It could be said that they develop mass culture at the expense of subcultures.
4. *Social functions*: The media provide examples of how relationships and interactions take place in our society. This helps us operate successfully as members of our society.
5. *Political functions*: The media provide evidence of political events, issues and activities. This enables us to understand the operation of politics in our society and to participate in political activity. But the media may also shape our opinions and may only raise certain issues.

ACTIVITY 3

Analyse the programmes on RTE 1 for one day and categorise them into the five functions above. Many of them may fall into more than one function.

The news on TV

Many more people watch 'the news' than any other programme on TV. It is broadcast several times a day and people have a strong desire to know and to see what is happening in the world. Most of us believe that it is accurate and trustworthy. This may be because we see pictures as well as hearing words. You can see what is happening and make up your own mind about it. But is the TV news neutral? Is there any distortion?

The production of TV news is very complicated. It is not like the weather that just happens. TV stations have lots of people who gather the news. But once the news is gathered someone must decide which items to put on and which to leave out. How do you decide what is important? If someone throws an egg at the Taoiseach is that important enough to make the news? Visually, it might be very strong.

There are many factors which influence the decision to include some stories and not others in television news.

1. The news takes up a specific number of minutes. This time has to be filled. When this time is filled nothing else will be considered unless it is of major importance. Sometimes a news bulletin is extended if a very big story 'breaks'.
2. The news appears at regular times every day. Events are planned in advance so producers can decide to cover certain events. But who decides which events to cover?
3. TV is a visual medium. Stories that provide good pictures are often chosen over items which do not have good visuals. A former prime minister of Britain, Mr Harold Wilson, complained that he almost had to pay people to throw eggs at him to get the cameras to cover his meetings.
4. The news is also part of the night's entertainment on TV. This affects its presentation. Sometimes humorous items are tagged on at the end to entertain the audience.

ACTIVITY 4

1. Can you remember any events that resulted in the news being extended?
2. See can you recognise the elements in the news that are there for entertainment.
3. Does the way the newsreader deals with certain items determine the way you are to interpret them? For example, does she read some items in a solemn voice and some in a cheerful tone?
4. Watch the news on TV for a day and then the following day read a newspaper. Are there many items in the newspaper which did not appear on the TV? Make a list of these items.
5. Did items appear on TV which did not appear in the newspaper? Make a list of these items also.

Advertising

Advertising is paid-for persuasive communication. It appears between programmes on TV and radio and in magazines and newspapers. It also can appear in other places such as shopping bags and billboards. It must be distinguished from *publicity* which is free communication. An example would be a writer talking about her book on *The Late Late Show*.

The purpose of advertising is to create awareness of the product or service, to assure existing customers of the quality of the product, to get a bigger share of the market and to hold on to the existing share of the market against competition.

Analysis of an advertisement

GOLDILOCKS AND THE THREE BREAKS
A family fairytale come true.

Once upon a time, Goldilocks was looking to get away for the June Bank Holiday with all the family when she came across 3 great offers for the luxurious Jurys Hotel Cork.

A BIG BREAK
3 nights dinner, b&b, children's activities, free family passes to your choice of local attractions for 2 adults and 2 children under 12 sharing, for £381 all-in.

A MEDIUM BREAK
2 nights b&b for 2 adults and 2 children under 12 sharing for just £71.50 per adult.

A SMALL BREAK
2 adults and 2 children under 12 sharing a family room for only £69 per night. (Meals extra).

She thought about the heated pool, sauna, gym and squash court, the lively bars and superb restaurants, so she called Central Reservations on **01-667 1333**. (Of course, she could have called the hotel direct on **021-27 66 22**.) And they stayed there happily ever after.

JURYS HOTEL CORK
Western Road, Cork.
NOBODY DOES IT BETTER

Note the title 'Goldilocks and the Three Breaks' which seeks to establish the notion of a holiday as a fairytale. It begins with the usual beginning of a fairytale 'Once upon a time'. The well-known story is carried through the advertisement with the three headings 'A Big Break', 'A Medium Break', and 'A Small Break'.

The pictures of the three little bears on the advertisement will draw the reader to it and help to break up the script and make it attractive to the eye. The extra facilities offered are mentioned by way of Goldilocks thinking about 'the heated swimming pool, sauna, gym and squash court . . .' The notion of Goldilocks contacting a modern hotel is mildly amusing. The fairytale theme is continued on to the very end with the phrase 'And they stayed there happily ever after.'

The different types of script also lend variety to the advertisement. The ad has bold at the top followed by italic. A different script is used for the headings within the ad and the telephone numbers are in bold which makes them stand out from the rest of the plain script.

ACTIVITY 5

Analyse the following advertisements:

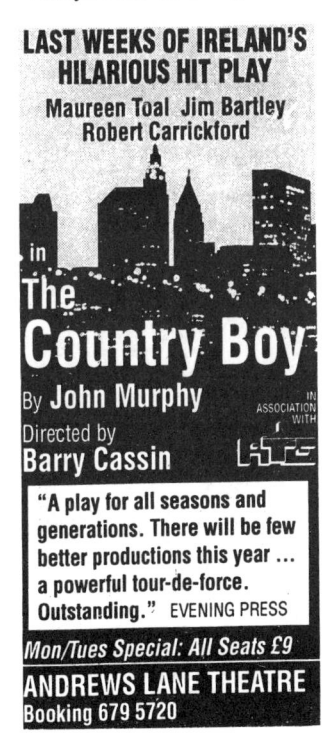

LAST WEEKS OF IRELAND'S HILARIOUS HIT PLAY

Maureen Toal Jim Bartley
Robert Carrickford

in

The Country Boy

By **John Murphy**   IN ASSOCIATION WITH

Directed by
Barry Cassin

"A play for all seasons and generations. There will be few better productions this year ... a powerful tour-de-force. Outstanding." EVENING PRESS

Mon/Tues Special: All Seats £9

ANDREWS LANE THEATRE
Booking 679 5720

NEW TO
ELEGANCE
(0504) 23772
NOW IN STOCK
Blooming Maternity Range

Because they want some time on their own as much as you do.

Our Mini Clubs make sure your kids have a holiday too. Phone 01635 565065 for a brochure.

Club Med. Because life's too short.

SPONSORSHIP THAT WORKS, EVEN ON REALLY TOUGH STAINS.

At AIB, we've always been committed to football and hurling at grass roots level. As proud sponsors of the All Ireland Club Championships, we provide support for clubs all over the country. The clubs themselves put our support to whatever use they please – whether it's contributing to new facilities, replacing old equipment or making sure the team's kit is spotless for Sunday's game.

Over the years we've also sponsored the GAA Club of the Year awards and the All Ireland Colleges and Vocational Schools competitions. In fact, AIB has provided support for every aspect of gaelic games. Now we're playing our part in supporting the GAA in the Croke Park stadium development. We offer our congratulations to everyone involved – from the grass roots up.

NOBODY SAID IT WAS GOING TO BE EASY

THE GUINNESS HURLING CHAMPIONSHIP

Small *yet* powerful.

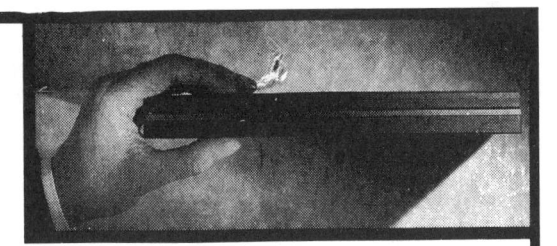

INTRODUCING DIGITAL HINOTE ULTRA

The problem is, most notebook computers aren't all that small. And the ones that are small aren't remotely powerful. Which is why the new Digital HiNote Ultra borders on the miraculous. It gives you an Intel 486 processor as fast as 75 MHz. It gives you a 340 MB hard drive and up to 24 MB RAM.

It gives you a full-sized screen, a full-sized, ergonomically sculpted keyboard, and an elegant little wedge of ˥py drive that nestles underneath, out of your way. It even gives you a 6 hour lithium ion battery. All in a package that is, amazingly, only 26 mm thick and under 2 kg in weight. So the only thing it doesn't give you is a backache.

To find out more about Digital's exciting new Notebook range, call us on **1 800 360 360** or post/fax the coupon.

YES. Please send me further details on the new Digital HiNote Ultra.

Name _____ Job Title _____

Company Name _____ Company Address _____

Telephone _____ Fax _____

Are you interested in portable PCs for: The home? ☐ Business? ☐ Or as a reseller? ☐
How many people does your company employ? Under 25 ☐ 26-99 ☐ 100 or more ☐

POST TO: **DIGITAL PC BUSINESS UNIT, PARK HOUSE, NORTH CIRCULAR ROAD, DUBLIN 7. OR FAX TO 1 868 0744.**

©Digital Equipment, 1995
The Intel Inside Logo is a trademark of Intel Corporation. All other trademarks acknowledged.

I.T. 19

digital™
PC

...pening.

...ould have done to prevent it

"Scone or scone – which do you say?" he said, assertive, now, his face flushed. It was as if he was just looking for a fight.

As ever, she rose to the bait. "Scone, as everyone knows, rhymes with gone. It's more elegant."

"Ha!" he cried, triumphant. "Bone! It rhymes with bone! – look up the phonetics in the dictionary."

"Either way!" she countered, "you can say it either way – I looked it up once." The minute she said it, she realised she might regret it.

"When?" he said, suspicious. And then, forlornly, "Who with?"

"Aha!" she said, savouring the moment of unexpected superiority. "That's for me to know and you to guess."

"I'm sorry," he said, "I got carried away. What do you want on yours?"

"Quince," she said, with a smile. "Or should that be Quince?"

The fact was, quite simply... ...dn't hear...

ANOTHER CLASSIC FROM TIPTREE.

Advertising Complaint

Häagen Daz told ad insensitive

By Michael Foley,
Media Correspondent

The ice-cream company, Häagen Daz, has been told to be more aware of public sensitivities following complaints to the Advertising Standards Authority about an advertisement with the headline 'Try Something New' above a naked man and woman.

Members of the public complained the advertisement which appeared in bus shelters, belittled women, trivialised sex and contributing to the lowering of standards. The ice-cream company responded that its consumer research indicated consumers would not be offended by the advertisement.

The authority said Häagen Daz had not established the relevance of the visual theme to the product being advertised. It did not take further action as the campaign had finished.

The authority also upheld a complaint against Bord Gais for claiming in a magazine advertisement that 'natural gas is not just the most cost effective fuel, but it also protects our world'. The complaint came from a reader in Glasgow.

The Irish Times, 22 June 1995

The closure of *The Irish Press*

In May 1995 *The Irish Press, The Sunday Press* and *The Evening Press* closed. The newspaper *The Irish Press* was founded by Eamon de Valera in 1931. Below is an article from *The Irish Times* (3 June 1995) by Fintan O'Toole detailing the history and contribution of the newspaper.

Press threatened by insistence on de Valera dynastic control

By Fintan O'Toole

If Irish Press Newspapers goes into liquidation next Tuesday, history may well judge that a great tradition died because of events, not in May 1995, but in May 1985.

Almost exactly 10 years ago, Irish Press Ltd stood at a fork in the road. One route led away from the control of the company by the de Valera family and towards the regeneration of a troubled, but still strong, group of titles. The other led backwards towards the re-enforcement of the dark side of the group's traditions, the unresolved ambivalence about whether it was a public trust or a private empire.

The latter route was taken and, after a decade's journey, that road seems to have reached its dead end.

In a very real and tangible sense, the demise of the *Irish Press* is the bitter end of de Valera's Ireland. For it represents quite literally the squandering of Eamon de Valera's legacy.

Both in the letter and in the spirit, de Valera's heirs kept a grip on the *Irish Press* that has proved to be a stranglehold.

From the very beginning the *Irish Press* was meant to be much more than a newspaper. It conceived of itself as the voice of the National Movement.

The finger on the button to start the presses rolling on the night of September 4th, 1931 was that of Margaret Pearse, sister of the 1916 martyrs Patrick and Willie, bringing the almost mystic touch of revolutionary authenticity to the enterprise. And the guiding hand behind that finger was that of the Chief himself, Eamon de Valera, soon to take his natural place as Taoiseach.

But if that first print run of 300,000 copies was the *Press*'s Garden of Eden, its primal innocence was already tainted with original sin.

The paper's original £200,000 capital came largely from money raised in 1919 in the US by Eamon de Valera as a Dail loan, and from public subscriptions in Ireland and America.

Yet the paper was effectively placed in the hands of a private de Valera dynasty, with first Major Vivion de Valera and then Dr Eamon de Valera inheriting, not simply an effective majority of the shares, held through a secretive American-based trust, but also the title of editor-in-chief.

That conversion of a public enterprise into private property was always problematic in principle, but for a long time it did not seem to matter in practice.

Like him or not, Eamon de Valera did genuinely embody the self-image and aspirations of at least a large section of the Irish people. The blurring of distinctions between public and private in the ownership of the *Irish Press* was covered over by the greater blending of public and private personae in that towering political leader.

Its closeness to the heart of a very powerful vision of Ireland made the *Irish Press*, and in time its sister Sunday and evening titles, hugely successful. So long as Irish people remained largely rural, nationalistic and egalitarian, so long as the broader Fianna Fail ethos which the papers reflected and sustained represented the core of Irish society, the Press group was the Irish media mainstream.

By the early 1960s, the three Press titles were easily, and deservedly, the most successful in their respective categories. They had just enough political radicalism to make them lively without being subversive, just enough sophistication to make them cultured without appearing elitist.

Social change, though, meant that a more complex society was emerging in Ireland, one in which that kind of balancing act was increasingly difficult.

The political instability and moral division of the 1980s was also the period of really dangerous decline for the *Irish Press* – sales dropped from 104,000 in 1981 to 64,000 in 1989.

The fragmentation of the Fianna Fail consensus was dramatised on January 27th, 1983, when the *Irish Press* published its premature two-page political obituary of Charles Haughey. The paper's special connection to a wider political and social world-view was broken.

But there was still a very real chance that the group could reinvent itself. In 1984, after threats of closure, the unions agreed to 230 redundancies and new technology.

As a necessary and obvious part of this painful process, de Valera family control seemed about to be broken. Two men outside the dynasty, Mr Donal Flinn and Mr Sean McHale, had been co-opted onto the board, the former becoming chairman. By May 1985 Mr Flinn, though a long-time friend of the de Valeras, had concluded that family control would have to be reduced if much-needed new capital was to be brought in.

Dr Eamon de Valera moved to assert control by nominating his cousin's husband, Elio Malocco, to the board. An outraged Mr Flinn resigned.

A week later Mr McHale also resigned, saying that the company was 'lacking in strong management'. Malocco, of course, proceeded to misappropriate large sums of the company's money.

That was, almost certainly, the key moment in the decline of the Press. The process of radical readjustment was stopped, and all core values were subordinated to the need to ensure that at least one corner of Irish life would be forever de Valera.

In the last decade the Press board has shown itself ready to make any change, however wrong-headed, except the most obvious one of ending dynastic control.

The *Irish Press* was made a tabloid in 1988, speeding up its decline. The alliance with Mr Ralph Ingersoll the following year was compatible in only one respect – Ingersoll was another figure at the fag-end of a family dynasty.

The even more desperate alliance with Independent Newspapers put the very titles themselves in hock to the group's traditional rival. The aura of apostolic succession was dispelled, revealing the clear lineaments of private interest.

If it were merely the end of de Valera's Ireland, though, the probable demise of the *Press* would be a bad melodrama rather than a tragedy. It is a tragedy because a newspaper is not, after all, the product of one family, with however distinguished a name, looking into its own heart or looking after its own interests.

It is a whole chorus of voices speaking to a public that is interested enough in what it hears to listen in every day. If that chorus is silenced, the public realm in Ireland will be narrower and poorer.

Review

1. Go to your public library and find other material about the Beef Tribunal such as a book by Sean Duignan and another one by Fintan O'Toole.
2. Find three examples of media manipulation which occurred in the past three months.
3. Find out the readership of your local newspaper and the audience for your local radio.
4. Find out how much it costs to advertise on your local radio.
5. Find three advertisements which you think do not give accurate descriptions of the product or service they are selling.
6. Give three advantages and three disadvantages of advertising.

Pitfalls

unique

A thing is *unique* or *not unique*. You should not say 'It is *somewhat* unique'. There are no degrees of uniqueness.

Confusing words

fir	fur	route	root
hire	higher	their	there
its	it's	too	two
main	mane	seen	scene
not	knot	steel	steal

Quiz

What famous writer can you find in this anagram?

I ask me has will a peer,
we will all make his praise.

Spellings

The words most commonly misspelled are highlighted.

repetition	resolute	rheumatic
replaceable	resolution	rhubarb
reply	responsive	rhyme
reprieve	restaurant	rhythm
repulsive	restrain	ridiculous
reputation	resume	righteous
repute	resumption	righteousness
rescue	**retrieve**	riot
rescuing	retriever	riotous
resemblance	reveal	rival
resemble	revelation	rivalling
resent	revenue	rivalry
resentful	reverent	rogue
reside	reverse	roguery
residence	revival	roguish
resign	revive	rubbish
resignation	revolution	rumour

VISUAL PRESENTATION

Introduction

There are several ways of presenting information. Your report must be presented in the clearest, most effective way possible. Just writing everything, paragraph after paragraph, is not always the best means. Readers, whether they are nine or ninety years old, respond to variety and vigour in presentation.

Charts, graphs, illustrations, diagrams, photographs, posters, symbols and signs are all forms of communication that can be used to replace or enhance the written, or indeed, spoken message. These methods of communication are called visual communication. They have several advantages over the written message. They attract attention, arouse interest, give variety, and drive home the message to the reader. Pages of statistics can be uninformative and intimidating, but put them in graphs and a person can grasp overall trends immediately. Even where these methods of communication are not absolutely necessary it can be a good idea to use some of them to give variety.

ACTIVITY 1

1. Signs are generally very easy to understand. What do the following well-known signs mean?

Taken from Rules of the Road
(Department of the Environment)

2. Find ten signs, other than road traffic signs, which would be easily understood by the public.
3. Draw a sign for your local library to indicate that people who steal books will be prosecuted.
4. Draw a sign for your school to indicate that students are to ascend the stairs on the right hand side and descend on the left.
5. Find one sign, in general use, which you think would be unclear to the general public.

Types of presentation

Information can be presented visually by way of:

(a) tables

(b) charts

(c) graphs

(d) combination of the above.

The method chosen depends on the type of information, the object of the presentation and the audience.

Tables

Tables, or tabular presentation, simplifies and sometimes summarises information. It facilitates comparison and contrast. Tables can be understood and interpreted by those who have a bent for mathematics. However, many people do not have the gift for drawing conclusions from tables of figures.

Fig. 1 – Sample table

Population: International Comparisons 1992

Country	Thousands	Per sq km	% under 15 years
Australia	17,529	2.3	22.0
Belgium	10,045	329.3	18.2
Canada	28,436	2.9	20.7
Denmark	5,170	120.0	17.0
France	57,372	104.5	20.0
Germany	64,846	260.8	15.5
Greece	10,300	78.0	19.4
Ireland	3,547	50.5	26.8
Italy	56,859	188.8	15.7
Japan	124,320	329.1	17.3
Luxembourg	390	150.0	17.7
Netherlands	15,184	372.2	18.3
Portugal	9,858	106.7	19.1
Spain	39,085	77.4	18.4
Sweden	8,674	19.3	19.0
Switzerland	6,875	166.5	16.8
UK	57,848	236.3	19.2
US	255,610	27.3	21.9

(Source: *Administration Yearbook & Diary 1995*)

Design of tables

Tables should not be too large. If possible, break a large table up into a number of smaller tables. This will help the reader. If at all possible a table should not cover more than one page and should not be stretched across two facing pages. All tables should have a title. All columns should have headings. Footnotes to tables should be included by using asterisks or some other sign. If numbers are used to indicate footnotes, they may cause confusion. Unit descriptions (points, tons, acres, etc.) should be placed above the columns as part of the headings. Do not allow the table to have a cluttered appearance. Separate the headings of columns and rows with a line if necessary, but do not use lines to separate related information. Separate related information by using extra space.

Charts

There are basically three types of charts that might be useful in the presentation of a report.

(a) *Organisation chart*: An organisation chart shows the chain of authority in a company. It shows who has responsibility for what and the relationship each member of staff has to others in the organisation.

Fig. 2 – Organisation chart

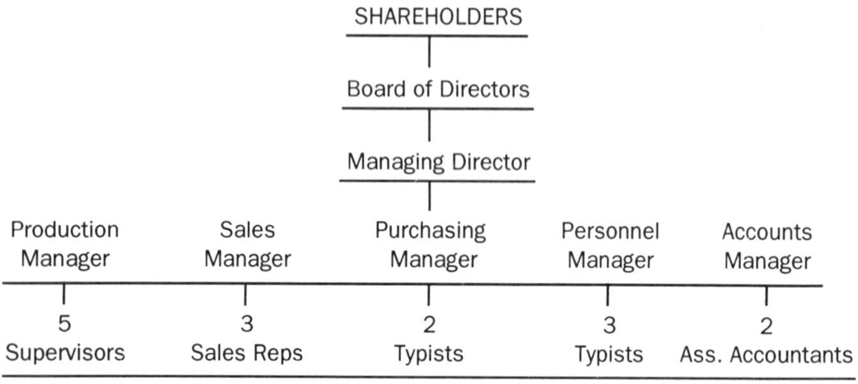

```
                       SHAREHOLDERS
                            |
                     Board of Directors
                            |
                     Managing Director
                            |
Production      Sales       Purchasing     Personnel     Accounts
Manager         Manager     Manager        Manager       Manager
    |             |             |             |             |
    5             3             2             3             2
Supervisors   Sales Reps    Typists       Typists      Ass. Accountants
```

(b) *Flow chart*: A flow chart is a diagram showing how a job can be performed by laying out, in detail, the logical sequence of actions to be performed. It must have a single starting point and single end point.

Fig. 3 – Sample flow chart showing steps to be taken for approval of new course at your college

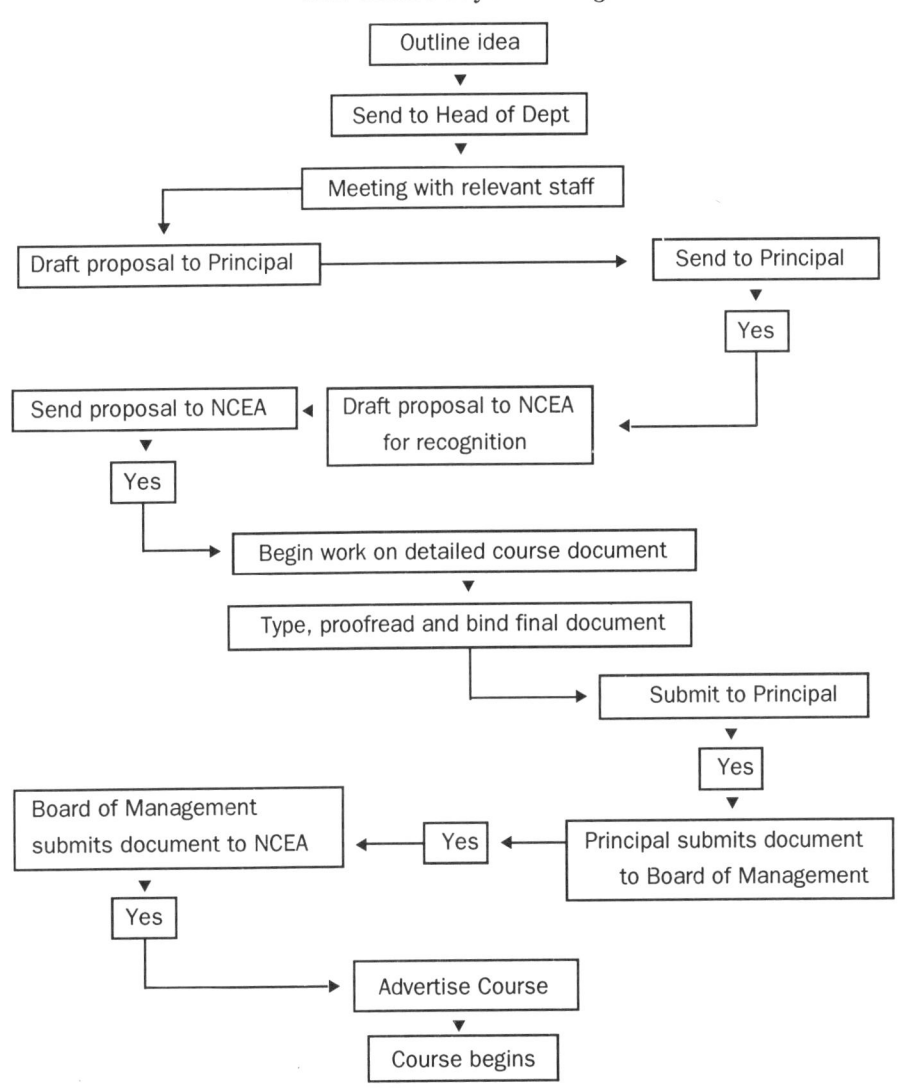

```
                    Outline idea
                         ▼
                 Send to Head of Dept
                         ▼
              Meeting with relevant staff
              │                        │
              ▼                        ▼
   Draft proposal to Principal ──→ Send to Principal
                                         ▼
                                        Yes
                                         ▼
   Send proposal to NCEA ◄── Draft proposal to NCEA
          ▼                    for recognition
         Yes
          ▼
         Begin work on detailed course document
                         ▼
         Type, proofread and bind final document
                         │
                         ▼
                   Submit to Principal
                         ▼
                        Yes
                         ▼
   Board of Management         Principal submits document
   submits document to NCEA ◄── Yes ◄── to Board of Management
          ▼
         Yes
          ▼
                   Advertise Course
                         ▼
                    Course begins
```

(c) *Algorithm*: Algorithms are like flow charts and they can help in decision-making or to simplify complex instructions. The reader is taken along a route by answering a series of questions.

Fig. 4 – Sample algorithm

Your Personal Guide to Share-Buying

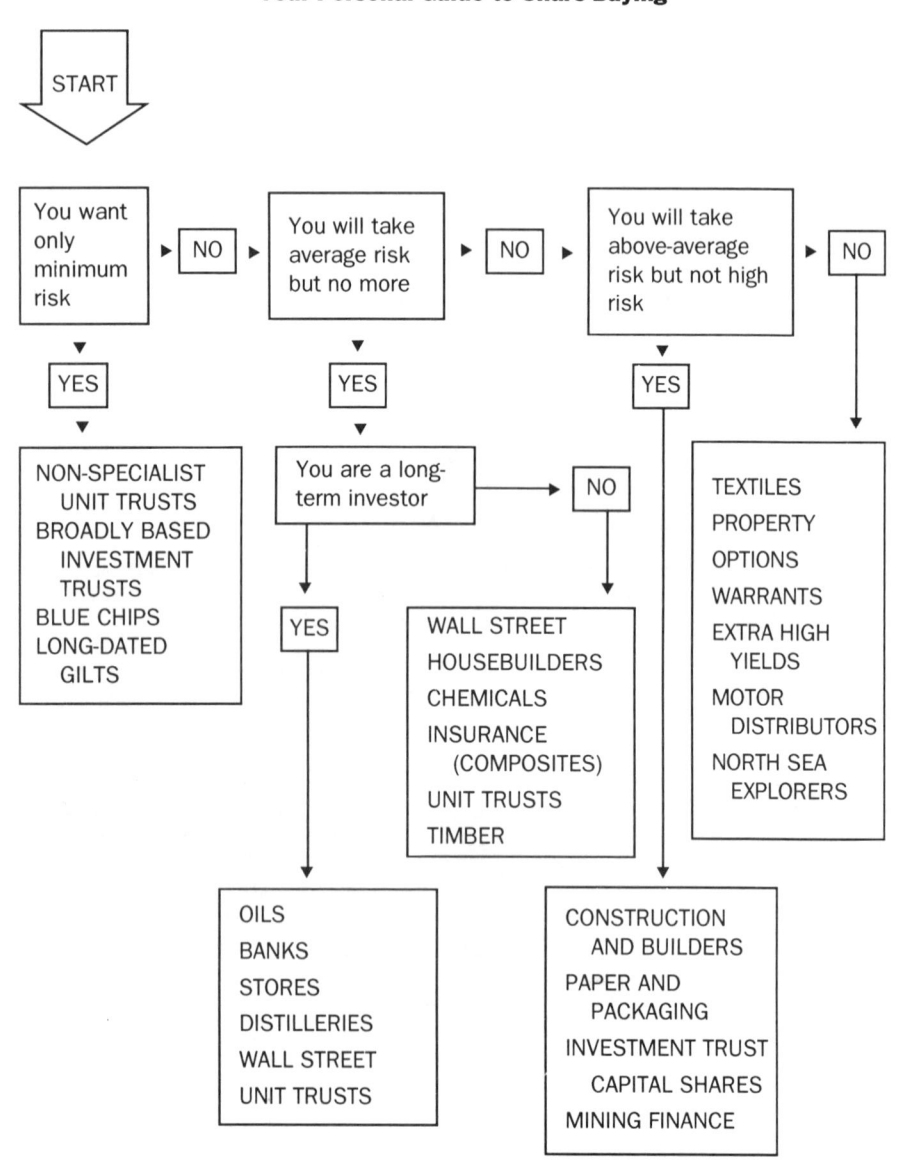

```
START
  ↓
┌─────────────┐     ┌─────────────┐     ┌─────────────┐
│ You want    │ NO  │ You will    │ NO  │ You will    │ NO →
│ only        │ →   │ take        │ →   │ take        │
│ minimum     │     │ average risk│     │ above-      │
│ risk        │     │ but no more │     │ average     │
│             │     │             │     │ risk but    │
│             │     │             │     │ not high    │
│             │     │             │     │ risk        │
└─────────────┘     └─────────────┘     └─────────────┘
  ↓ YES             ↓ YES               ↓ YES
```

- NON-SPECIALIST UNIT TRUSTS
- BROADLY BASED INVESTMENT TRUSTS
- BLUE CHIPS
- LONG-DATED GILTS

You are a long-term investor → NO →

YES ↓

- WALL STREET
- HOUSEBUILDERS
- CHEMICALS
- INSURANCE (COMPOSITES)
- UNIT TRUSTS
- TIMBER

- TEXTILES
- PROPERTY
- OPTIONS
- WARRANTS
- EXTRA HIGH YIELDS
- MOTOR DISTRIBUTORS
- NORTH SEA EXPLORERS

- OILS
- BANKS
- STORES
- DISTILLERIES
- WALL STREET
- UNIT TRUSTS

- CONSTRUCTION AND BUILDERS
- PAPER AND PACKAGING
- INVESTMENT TRUST CAPITAL SHARES
- MINING FINANCE

(Source: *Sunday Times Business News*, 11 January 1976)

Design of charts

Charts should be given plenty of space so that they look uncluttered and clear. It may sometimes be useful to use different colours. The amateur should attempt only very simple charts. If the chart is to be in any way complicated it makes sense to get a draughtsperson to execute it.

Graphs

(a) *Bar graph/chart*: These are a useful means of comparing simple magnitudes by the length of equal width bars. They can show quantity changes over a period of time and over geographic distance. For example, if it is necessary to show the profit of a company over a ten-year period, the bar chart is appropriate as comparisons can be made.

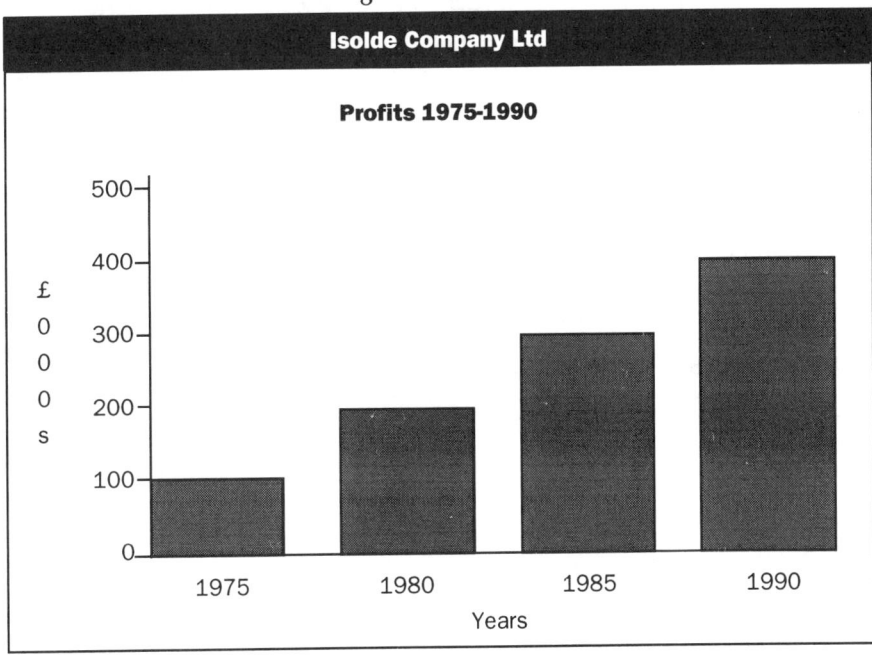

Fig. 5 – Bar chart

Isolde Company Ltd

Profits 1975-1990

(b) *Grouped bar chart*: Two or three variables can be compared in a single graph by use of grouped bars. The bars are distinguished from one another by using different fill-ins in the bars.

Fig. 6 – Grouped bar chart

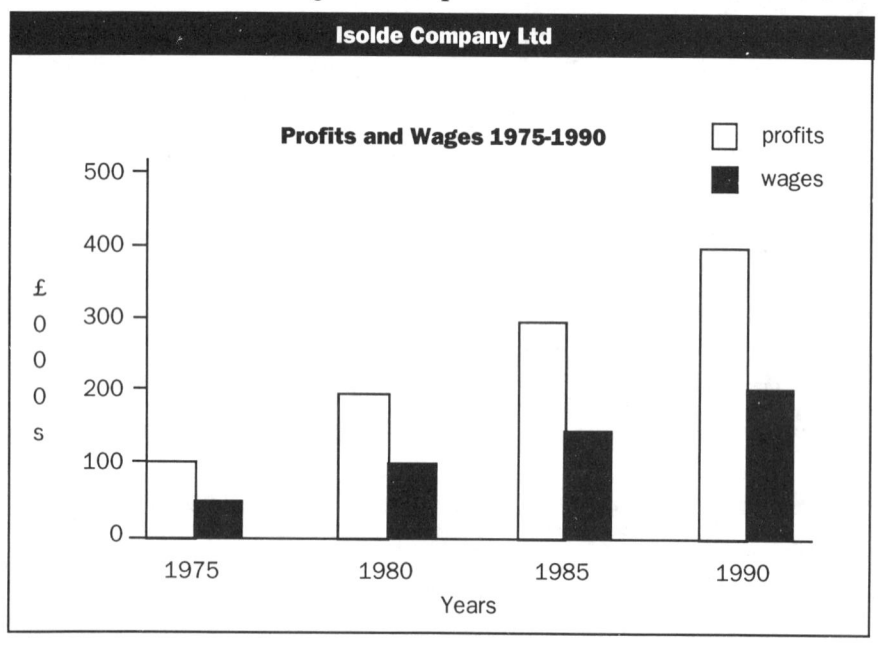

Isolde Company Ltd

Profits and Wages 1975-1990

(c) *Stacked bar chart*: Stacked bar charts may be used to display the same information as you would put on a grouped bar chart, but you wish to display it in a different way.

Fig. 7 – Stacked bar chart

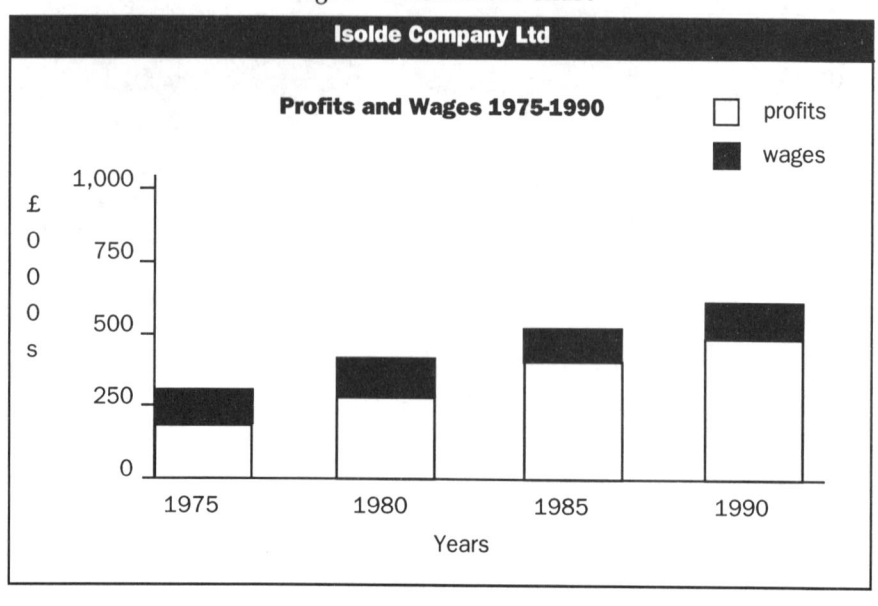

Isolde Company Ltd

Profits and Wages 1975-1990

(d) *Horizontal bar chart*: The graphs we have shown so far are vertical graphs. But it is also possible to have horizontal graphs. Whether to design a graph vertically or horizontally is a matter of choice. It depends on which format will help clarity and look well.

Fig. 8 – Horizontal bar chart

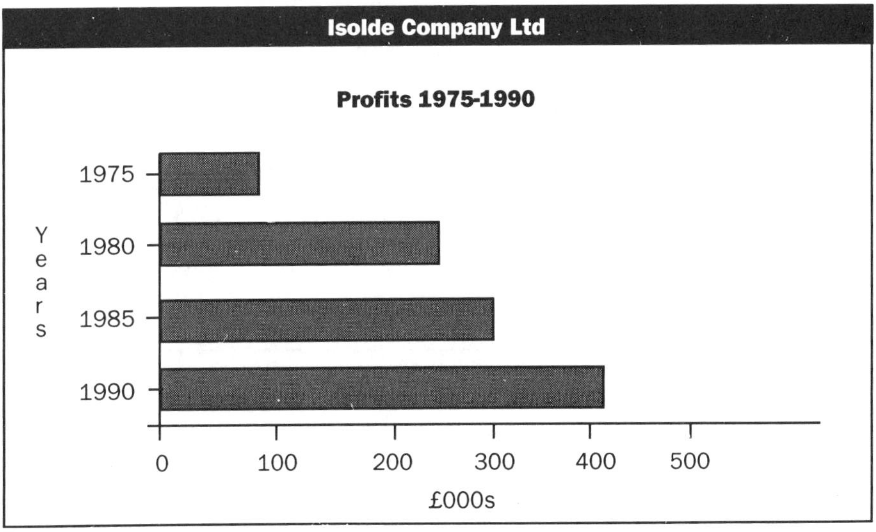

Isolde Company Ltd

Profits 1975-1990

Years	£000s
1975	~75
1980	~250
1985	~300
1990	~425

Design of graphs

Computers will now draw graphs in several different ways and you can choose whichever presentation best suits your purposes.

(a) *Histogram*: A histogram shows the frequency of occurrence of the subject being studied. For example, the speeds in shorthand for a class of forty students are shown here, first as a table and then as a histogram.

Words per minute	No. of students
60	4
70	6
80	10
90	12
100	5
110	3

Fig. 9 – Histogram

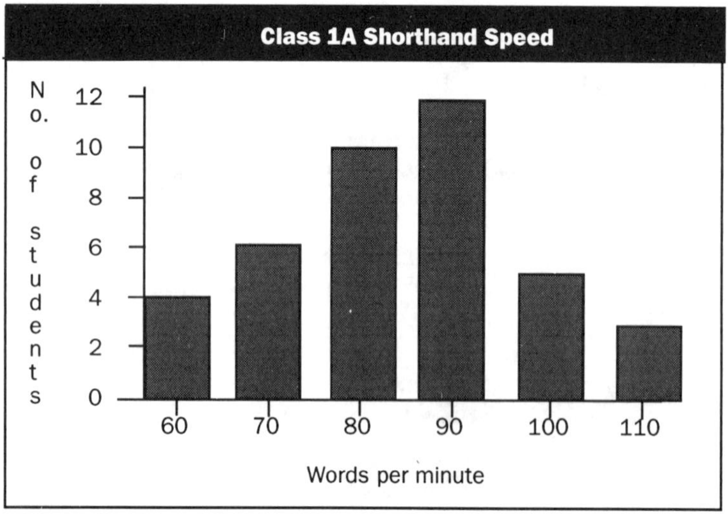
Class 1A Shorthand Speed
No. of students
12
10
8
6
4
2
0
60
70
80
90
100
110
Words per minute

(b) *Pie chart*: The pie chart, sometimes called a pie graph, uses a circumference of a circle as its scale and the component parts of the chart are shown as segments of this circle. The 360 degree circle, therefore, represents 100 per cent. This type of chart is useful to show how a whole is composed. It can lose its effectiveness when too many segments are employed. Pie charts are not useful to show comparisons unless the comparisons are very obvious.

Fig. 10 – Pie chart

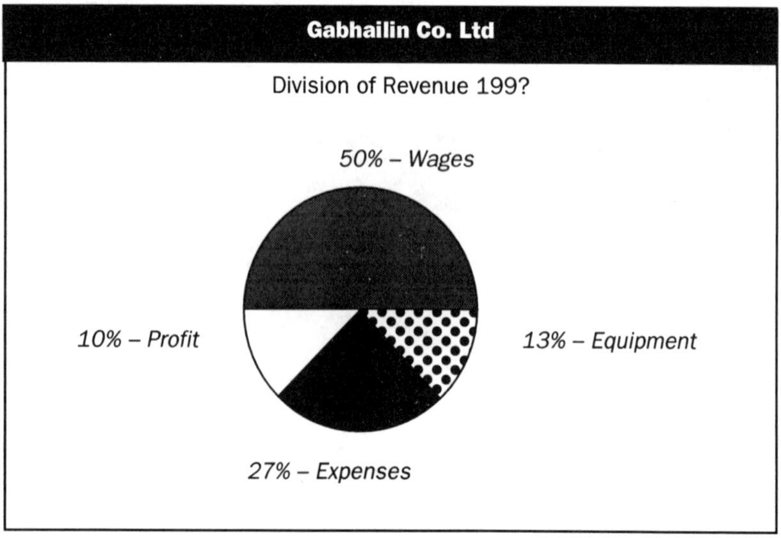
Gabhailin Co. Ltd
Division of Revenue 199?
50% – Wages
10% – Profit
13% – Equipment
27% – Expenses

(c) *Line graph*: Line graphs are useful for showing rising or falling trends. A line graph plots a series of quantities measured on the vertical scale against a period of time measured on the horizontal scale.

Fig. 11 – Line graph

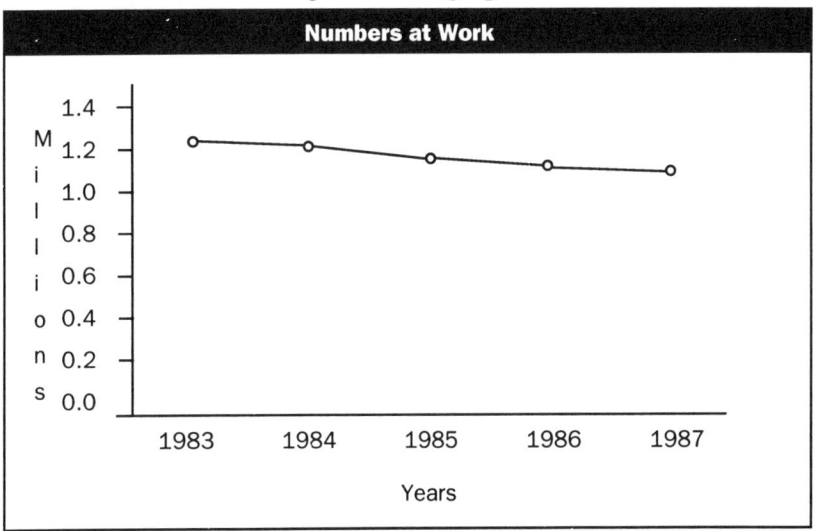

```
                    Numbers at Work
     1.4
M    1.2  o─────────o─────────o─────────o─────────o
i    1.0
l    0.8
l    0.6
i    0.4
o    0.2
n
s    0.0
         1983      1984      1985      1986      1987
                           Years
```

(d) *Z chart*: Z charts can show three types of information. Let us take the example of a shop renting videos over a period of one week. The owner may need to know the following:

(a) the number of videos borrowed each day of the week

(b) the cumulative total borrowed as the week progresses

(c) the moving weekly total. This can be found by adding the totals for the preceding seven days. For example:

	Daily total	Moving total
Monday	3	
Tuesday	4	
Wednesday	5	
Thursday	6	
Friday	5	
Saturday	7	
Sunday	9	39
Monday	2	38
Tuesday	3	37

No. of Videos Rented Week 24-29 July 199?

Monday	250
Tuesday	300
Wednesday	350
Thursday (half day)	180
Friday	400
Saturday	460

Fig. 12 – Z chart

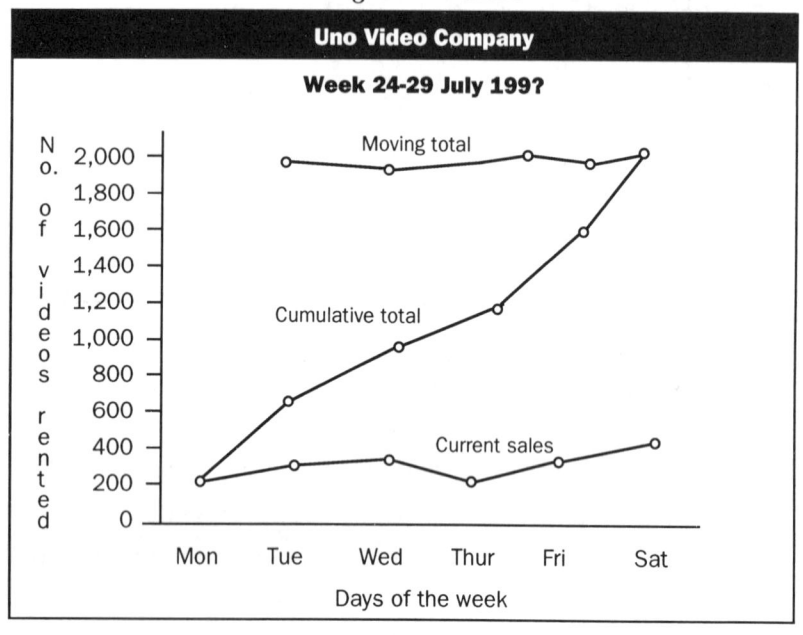

Uno Video Company
Week 24-29 July 199?

As can be seen from Fig. 12 a Z chart resembles a Z and hence its name.

(e) *Pictogram*: A pictogram is a picture, or series of pictures, which conveys information very simply. Pictograms add warmth and humour to what otherwise might be a cold presentation of statistics. They will not convey information in a very precise manner but will give fairly accurate trends.

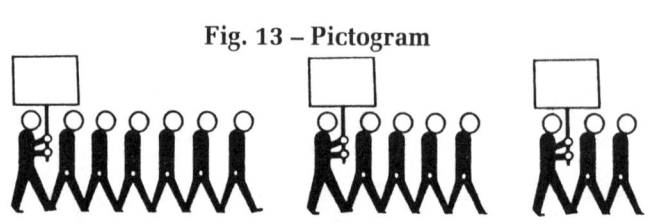

Fig. 13 – Pictogram

General guidelines on illustrations

(a) All illustrations should be numbered so that they can be referred to easily, but they should appear in the most appropriate place.

(b) They should make an immediate impact. They should not be included as a form of padding.

(c) All drawings must be to scale, and when a number of drawings refer to the same figures they should be to the same scale.

(d) Illustrations should have a balanced look and should be pleasing to the eye.

(e) Do not clutter any one illustration with too much information. If a graph or drawing has too many lines the reader may have difficulty in distinguishing what is essential to your argument.

(f) It should be possible to understand each illustration without reference to the text.

(g) All symbols used should be sufficiently explained.

ACTIVITY 2

1. Find the growth in student numbers in your college for the past ten years and present it on a suitable graph.

2. Draw a graph for the following figures:

    Rathclogheen Insurance Co.
    % Breakdown of Assets

	1985	199?
Mortgages	20.2	39.7
Buildings	12.5	30.6
Stocks	20.6	14.3
Land	40.5	10.2
Others	6.2	5.2
	100.0	100.0

3. Illustrate the following table:

    Number of Student in Education in Country X

	1965	1970	1975
Primary School	400,000	420,000	450,000
Secondary School	300,000	350,000	375,000
Third Level	18,000	24,000	26,000

4. You are treasurer of the students' union. Use a graphic aid to illustrate how last year's income was spent.

5. Use an organisation chart to illustrate the line of authority in your college.

6. Draw a suitable graph to compare the growth in your college of student numbers in each department.

7. Put the following information on a suitable graph:

Ireland: Births, Marriages and Deaths 1986-1992*

	Births	Marriages	Deaths
1986	17.4	5.2	9.5
1987	16.5	5.2	8.9
1988	15.3	5.1	8.9
1989	14.7	5.1	8.8
1990	15.1	5.0	9.1
1991	15.0	4.8	8.9
1992	14.5	4.6	8.7

*Rates per 1,000 estimated population

8. Present the following information on a graph:

Changes in the population of the Republic of Ireland, 1926-1991

1926-1936	−3,572
1936-1946	−13,313
1946-1951	+5,486
1951-1956	−62,329
1956-1961	−79,923
1961-1966	+65,661
1966-1971	+94,246
1971-1979	+389,969
1979-1981	+75,188
1981-1986	+97,238
1986-1991	−14,924

9. Present the following on a pictogram:

Labour force and number at work 1992

Agriculture	153,000
Industry	318,000

Services   668,000

Unemployed   221,000

10. How would you present the following information?

Current Budget Deficit 1980-1994

	£m	% of GNP
1980	547	6.1
1981	802	7.4
1982	988	7.9
1983	960	7.1
1984	1,039	7.0
1985	1,284	8.1
1986	1,395	8.2
1987	1,180	6.4
1988	767	3.8
1989	263	1.2
1990	152	0.6
1991	300	1.2
1992	446	1.7
1993	379	1.4
1994	269	0.9

11. Draw a graph showing how you spend your day.

12. Draw a graph showing how you spend your money each week.

13. The following table gives the numbers of full-time students which the Department of Education projects will be enrolled in first, second and third level education in Ireland from the years 1988/89 to 1999/2000. Present it on a suitable graph.

Number of Full-Time Students Enrolled by Level (000s)

	First Level	Second Level	Third Level
1988/89	568.3	341.8	62.8
1989/90	562.2	342.9	65.1
1990/91	553.0	342.5	67.4
1991/92	542.2	342.3	69.0
1992/93	528.8	343.2	69.8

1993/94	512.3	344.9	70.0
1994/95	496.0	345.1	70.1
1995/96	479.6	344.0	70.6
1996/97	465.9	339.2	71.1
1997/98	453.9	332.2	71.6
1998/99	443.1	329.9	72.0
1999/2000	433.0	315.1	72.0

These figures were issued by the Department of Education in 1988/89. Some of the projected figures were not quite accurate. Find the actual figures for the years 1990-1996 and draw a graph comparing them with the figures above. Both sets of figures must be on the same graph.

Review

1. Why use graphs in a report?
2. What is a Z chart?
3. When would you use a pie chart rather than a bar chart?
4. Should one ever use tables in a report?
5. Why might you use a horizontal bar chart rather than a vertical bar chart?
6. What is a pictogram?
7. Should one place graphs and charts in the body of a report or in the appendices? Why?
8. What is a flow chart?
9. What are the uses of an algorithm?

Pitfalls

taller tallest

When comparisons are made sometimes the incorrect word is used. For example:

John is the *tallest* of the two (incorrect).

John is the *taller* of the two (correct).

Confusing words

symbol	cymbal	boy	buoy
eminent	imminent	revere	reverie
villain	villein	tour	tower
hue	hew	straight	strait
prise	prize	augur	auger

Quiz

What is a metagram? It is a word that can be turned into a number of other words by changing its initial letter.

Make six different words out of *kink* by changing its initial letter.

Spellings

The words most commonly misspelled are highlighted.

safeguard	sensibility	situation
safety	sensible	skeleton
salutation	sensitive	skilful
sandwich	sensitivity	skill
satisfaction	**sentence**	skirmish
satisfactory	**separate**	slaughter
satisfy	**separately**	sociable
Saturday	sergeant	socialism
saucepan	seriously	specimen
saucer	serviceable	spectacle
scarcely	settlement	spectator
scarcity	severe	sphere
scene	**severely**	spoonful
scenery	severity	stationary (not moving)
schedule	shining	stationery (notepaper)
scheme	shoulder	**statutory**
scientific	shrewd	stealth
scissors	shriek	stomach
sculptor	shrubbery	straight
sculpture	sign	strength
seasonable	signature	struggle
secret	signed	stubborn
secretary	**similar**	student
seize	**sincerely**	studious
seizure	sincerity	stupidity
	singular	

275

PART 4

NEW INFORMATION TECHNOLOGY

NEW TECHNOLOGY

Secretaries under threat as computers take letters

Christopher McKevitt

'There are people who will certainly feel the skill they have is becoming redundant. But we see it's the keyboard that's becoming redundant. In fact the keyboard's days are numbered.'

That was the rather ominous note from William Burns of IBM Ireland who spent last week introducing the latest company toy to selected target groups around the city.

It's called the VoiceType dictation system and it's likely to present a major threat to anyone who types for a living because this system allows users to dictate straight into their computers without needing to put a finger near a keyboard. It all costs just over £1,000 including VAT.

Operators are initiated into the system by speaking 150 sentences which cover all of the phonemes in the English language, thus allowing the system to learn the user's voice pattern.

The more the operator uses the system, the more the system learns the nuances of the speaker's turn of phrase. According to Burns, it even learns how to interpret homonyms and once computer and operator get used to each other the accuracy rate runs at around 95%.

The news is not good for the hundreds of people, mainly women, who make their living from typing. IBM's system is considerably cheaper than the £2 per page that a typing service will charge or indeed the £7.15 an hour which is around the minimum a temping agency will charge.

'Do you mean to tell me I'm out of a job,' said Christine Fitzpatrick, who was named 'Secretary of the Year' last year and who works for Patrick Campbell, of the Campbell Bewley Group. And while she does spend anything between two and eight hours a day typing, she's pretty sure a computer would be unable to replace her or any of her colleagues in the industry.

'I do much more than typing. I arrange meetings, I have to deal with a lot of Patrick Campbell's correspondence if he's out of the office and he's usually out two or three days a week.'

And, IBM take note, Fitzpatrick works up to 12 hours a day, which is not at all unusual for secretaries who hold similar positions.

STATS

Secretary

Cost: £12,000-£25,000 per year

Pros: Will usually work late if requested. Can field unwanted calls, arranges meetings, answers the phone (unless replaced by voice mail or answering machine). Can correct typos. Is unlikely to break down. Can take much of the responsibility for general correspondence.

Cons: Takes holidays, days off and Christmas bonuses.

The Sunday Tribune, 18 June 1995

IBM VoiceType Dictation

Cost: £881-£970 per month

Pros: Doesn't need to eat, sleep or drink. No requirement for tea break. Doesn't take holidays. No need for luncheon vouchers.

Cons: Useless for a drink after work. Has no conversational ability. Is unlikely to organise the Christmas party. But that could be a cost saving.

Introduction

'Paperless office'

'Electronic office'

'Microchip threatens traditional office'

'No more typewriters'

The old traditional office with just a manual typewriter and a filing cabinet is no more. Even quite small concerns have now invested in some of the new office technology. Over the last twenty years the office has seen revolutionary changes. Firms have invested in the new technology because it is economical and efficient. It has led to major increases in productivity for office workers.

The invention of the microchip meant that computers could be much smaller and cheaper than previously. This put computers within the reach of small businesses and meant that technological advances did not just benefit large companies.

These developments have led to changes in the training and education of office staff. The traditional skills, such as the ones featured in this book, are still the most vital, but others are also necessary. The old typing and shorthand courses are gone forever. Now every modern secretary and clerical worker must be able to use a range of office equipment which would have bewildered the office staff of twenty years ago.

Office equipment

Cellular telephones
These are cordless or wireless telephones which operate within a network of cells (hence the word 'cellular'). A call is picked up as radio waves by a telephone exchange and then relayed over the national telephone network.

OHP
An OHP is an overhead projector and is used at seminars and classes to enhance presentations and to enlarge drawings and graphics. The information is put on transparent plastic sheets and is then projected on to a large white screen. The transparencies can be produced on computer. The software package *Powerpoint* is particularly useful for this type of work.

OCR scanner
OCR stands for optical character recognition. This equipment can convert incoming letters on paper into electronic files stored on the computer.

Telephone answering systems
These are machines which record messages on cassette tape. They are particularly useful when the public need to be informed of routine information such as a change of telephone number. They are also used when a telephone is unmanned.

Electronic diary
An electronic diary does the same job as a desk diary. There are several software packages available. They usually display a calendar with a page for each day. The day can be divided into suitable units, for example half-hour or hour slots. Appointments are entered into the diary in the usual way and the equipment can ring a bell as a reminder of an upcoming appointment. Jobs can be given priority through colour coding. If the electronic diary on your computer is connected to other computers in a local area network (LAN) you can check when the other people are available for a meeting. Generally a password is needed for this.

Microfiche reader
A microfiche reader looks somewhat like a television with the facility to insert a card of film containing information so that it can be read on the screen. Storing information on microfiche is now quite common and a large quantity of information can be stored on each card.

Collators

Collators are machines which hold stacks of pages of a report which need to be bound in numeric order so as to provide sets of individual documents. Many advanced copying machines will now perform this function.

CABX

This is the name for the type of switchboard used in modern offices. CABX stands for computerised automatic branch exchange. Typical features of a CABX system are:

- provides a printout of calls made

- plays music while putting a caller on hold

- automatic re-dial

- break-in facility, that is the ability to interrupt a conversation in case of urgency

- conference, that is linking several extension users so that they can converse with each other

- abbreviated dialling, that is some numbers commonly used can be given a short code in two or three numbers.

Radiopaging

Mobile staff can stay in touch with the office by using mobile telephones. A less expensive form of contacting mobile staff is radiopagers. These are small devices which are sometimes called bleepers. They can pick up a radio signal which causes them to emit a bleeping sound. Such a signal tells the person to call the office. The modern type of bleeper has a panel which can accept short messages such as *'Call 0503-33333'*.

Fax

The fax machine is rapidly replacing the telex. Whereas with a telex you must type the message on the telex machine and then it is reproduced on the receiver's machine, a fax transmits *copies* of documents to a receiver who has a compatible fax.

A fax is connected to the public telephone system. You simply turn on your fax, and dial your receiver's machine. Her fax must also be connected to the telephone. You insert your document into your fax and it is reproduced on your receiver's machine. The cost is the same as the cost of a telephone call of the same duration.

Fig. 1 – Sample fax message

01/02 9? 19:20   050 99999   Joe Bloggs

Joe Bloggs
Box 485
Anywhere, 5555
Victoria, Australia
Phone: (050) 88888
Fax: (050) 99999

FACSIMILE

Fax No. Int.
Nat.

COMPANY: *Carlow Technical College*

ATTENTION: *Director*   **FAX NO.**

FROM: *Joe Bloggs*   **REF:**

DATE: *1-2-9?*   **NO. OF PAGES:** *1*

I am at present doing a study of education in various countries of the world and contacting many colleges.

It would be greatly appreciated if you could forward any information available - e.g. school magazine, students and teachers information booklet etc. outlining details of your college.

If unable to assist an address where this request could be forwarded would help.

Thanks in anticipation,
Regards from Victoria

RECEIVED FROM *Joe Bloggs*

The advantages of the fax are:

(a) It will transmit pictures, graphs, charts, drawings and diagrams as well as text.

(b) It is quick.

(c) Document does not have to be retyped as with a telex.

(d) Once original document is correct, the reproduction made by the fax will be correct.

(e) The machines are cheap.

A fax will give you a printout confirming that your document has been received at the other end.

Telex

Telex machines have been available much longer than fax. These can be bought or rented from the telephone company. Telex reaches two million users worldwide in over 190 destinations, covering five continents twenty-four hours each day. The message is typed on the keyboard of the telex machine and almost immediately reproduced on the machine of the receiver.

Today's telex machines are much more high-tech than the old machines which often produced badly presented messages with poor printer quality. Modern telex offers a range of computer based facilities to make life easier for telex users. These are time-savers designed to transfer the repetitive work from the telex user to the exchange.

Fig. 2 – Sample telex

13029? 12.59

* 99999 ANT EI

888888 OTHER G

REF: 0855 9?-02-13 13:10

ATTN: MRS L. BOW

REF: INSURANCE CLAIMS

FURTHER TO OUR TELEX DATED 8.1.9? WHICH LISTED ALL OUTSTANDING CLAIMS FOR 199? WE ARE NOW INFORMED BY YOURSELVES THAT ITEMS UP UNTIL 31.11.9? ARE CANCELLED.

WE HAVE NO NOTIFICATION OF ANY REJECTS ARISING FROM THESE CLAIMS AND HAVE NOW INFORMED OUR INSURANCE THAT NO FURTHER ACTION IS NECESSARY.

PLEASE ADVISE ON THE REMAINING CLAIMS FROM 199? IN ORDER TO UPDATE ALL PARTIES CONCERNED.

REGARDS

JOE BLOGGS

A. N. OTHER & CO. LTD.,

DUBLIN.

* 99999 ANT EI

888888 OTHER G.

13-02-9? 13:12

Cost: There is no charge for connection of the telex. However, you must pay a rental charge for the line each quarter and for the telex itself. There are then charges for international calls, national calls and operator-assisted calls. In general it can be said that, at the moment, telex is more expensive than fax.

Extra facilities:

(a) Broadcast telex allows you to send the same text simultaneously to up to ten different telex numbers.

(b) Terminals: modern telex terminals will set up the call, and send and clear the message automatically. You can also have a VDU on your terminal, with full word processing facilities and high-speed printer. You can even carry on word processing work while your terminal is receiving a message.

(c) Easicall: this is a store and forward facility that sends routine messages at off-peak times and keeps re-trying busy numbers.

The great advantage of telex is that a document sent by telex can be proved in a court of law to have been sent on a specific date and at a specific time. This is not true of a fax message.

Telephone services

Phoneplus

Phoneplus is a service offered by Telecom Éireann and other telephone companies. It gives you the following services:

(a) If you are away from your office you can key in another local number where you can be reached and your calls will be automatically transferred.

(b) While you are on the phone, it can signal that someone else is trying to get through. You can then push a button to hold your first call and converse in private with your second caller.

(c) You can use your phone as an alarm clock. Key in the time at which you want to be reminded to do something and the phone will ring accordingly.

Freefone

This service enables businesses to provide customers with a convenient method of responding to their media advertisements. With Freefone, customers may call the advertiser free-of-charge.

Telecard

A Telecard enables customers to transfer to their business or home account charges for calls made from other telephones.

Audio Conference Calls

This service enables up to ten customers to be connected to each other at one time. A mixture of national and international connections can be facilitated.

Eircell

Eircell is a mobile telephone network. It allows you the freedom to stay in touch with the office while on the move. Calls can be made nationally or internationally once the phone is located within the service coverage area.

ACTIVITY I

1. What are the advantages of a telephone answering machine?
2. What are the advantages of storing information on microfiche over the traditional method?
3. Describe two electronic diaries which are currently on the market.
4. List three advantages of electronic diaries over handwritten diaries.
5. What advantages does a fax have over a telex?
6. What one major advantage does a telex have over the fax?
7. What are the advantages of having a CABX switchboard from the point of view of the receptionist?
8. List the various facilities which modern photocopiers incorporate.
9. Photocopiers can be expensive to buy and if used by many people are liable to break down. Investigate whether your college should buy a photocopier or lease one.

Review

1. What is meant by the 'paperless office'?
2. What is a fax machine?
3. What is a telex?
4. Mention three special telephone services?

Pitfalls

theist atheist agnostic

A *theist* is a person who believes in a god. An *atheist* is a person who believes there is no god. An *agnostic* is a person who doesn't know whether a god exists or not.

Confusing words

seam	seem	tale	tail
seas	sees	team	teem
shear	sheer	timber	timbre
sole	soul	yews	ewes
vein	vain	wrap	rap

Quiz

Can you punctuate this so that it makes sense? The word 'had' appears eleven times, consecutively.

'Michael where Valerie had had had had had had had had had had had more effect with the examiners.'

Spellings

The words most commonly misspelled are highlighted.

stylish	submitted	substitute
subdue	subscribe	subtle
subduing	subscription	**subtlety**
submission	subsequent	subtraction

suburb	suitable	surround
suburban	sultry	surveying
succeed	**summary**	survival
success	superintend	survivor
successful	superiority	suspicion
successfully	**supersede**	suspicious
succession	**suppression**	sustain
successive	supremacy	syllable
successor	surgeon	sympathetic
succour	surplus	sympathy
sufficient	**surprise**	symptom
suicide	**surprising**	**synonym**
suitability	surrender	**synonymous**

㉒

COMPUTER LITERACY

THE BIGGEST BREAKTHROUGH IN INFORMATION TECHNOLOGY SINCE THE QUILL

| Computers |

Background

A number of attempts were made in the eighteenth and nineteenth centuries to construct a mechanical adding machine. Charles Babbage is generally credited with the term 'father of computers'. He was interested in making a machine that would count automatically.

In the 1940s and 1950s the modern electronic computer evolved. The first computers were very heavy, bulky and took up the space of large rooms. They were not very dependable because they were constantly breaking down. However, they were a significant milestone on the road to the modern computer as they carried out calculations at great speed. In 1946 the first modern electronically powered computer was demonstrated in Pennsylvania, USA. It was called the ENIAC – Electronic Numerical Indicator and Calculator. In 1949 the first computer with stored memory was invented in Cambridge, England. It was called the EDSAC.

Since then the move has been towards making computers smaller. This trend was helped by the invention of the transistor by Brittain and Barden in 1947. The forerunner of the word processor was IBM's Selectric Typewriter in 1964. This was a typewriter with a memory. Then in 1971 Intel Corporation (USA) produced the first commercially applicable microprocessor.

The desktop microcomputer you see in most offices today is smaller and much more powerful than its predecessors. It can store enormous amounts of information and locate any one piece in seconds.

Elements of a computer

(a) *The keyboard*: All computers or word processors have a keyboard for putting information into the computer. This keyboard is much the same as on a typewriter except that it has more keys. It is the usual 'QWERTY' keyboard plus the functional keys and the numeric pad. The functional keys are used to give commands to the central processing unit (see below) which will then perform the various operations of deleting, inserting or moving text.

(b) *The central processing unit (CPU)*: This is the 'brains' and memory of the computer. It holds the program which enables the computer to carry out its various functions. It takes in the information from the keyboard and processes it in the way you want.

(c) *The visual display unit (VDU)*: This part of the computer looks like a television and displays the text or numbers keyed in on the keyboard. A cursor indicates the point on the screen where the next letter or number will appear.

(d) *The printer*: A printer is connected to a computer to give you a 'hard' or written copy of documents you have stored in your computer. It can print text at great speed and it can give you draft or letter quality. The quality of your printed copy will depend on the quality of your printer.

There are basically four types of printers:

(i) *The dot matrix* – text is produced by means of needles punching dots through the ribbon on the printer onto the paper to form letters or numbers.

(ii) *The daisy wheel* – this is very much like a typewriter's keys. A printing head like the spokes of a wheel rotates very quickly and delivers the correct letter or number by hitting the ribbon onto the paper.

(iii) *Laser printer* – the text or numbers are etched onto the paper. It works very much like a photocopier.

(iv) *Ink-jet printer* – ink is drawn from a cartridge into a series of tubes. The ink is then ejected onto the page.

Computer terminology

- Analogue – conveys meaning by symbols rather than numbers.
- Digital – conveys meaning by numbers.
- Bit – short for binary digit. It is one single pulse in the computer.
- Byte – eight bits make a byte which is equivalent to a single character or number.
- Chip – term used for the microelectronic circuit etched onto a silicon chip or microprocessor.
- CPU – central processing unit. The part of the computer that does the remembering, editing, sorting, etc.
- Input – data put into the computer. Hence an input device is any means of putting information into the computer such as a keyboard.
- Kilobyte – 1,024 bytes of information are often referred to by the letter k, e.g. 256k.
- Megabytes – 1 million bytes of information, e.g. 30mb.
- Memory – this refers to how much information the computer can work on at any one time. To deal with information the computer must take it from the disk or input device and hold it in the memory. A computer may have, for example, 640k of memory.
- RAM – random access memory. This memory stores information which has been created by the user.
- ROM – read only memory. This memory enables computers to carry out various calculations and functions.
- Operating system – this is a set of instructions which has been installed on the computer to allow it carry out its various functions. A

popular operating system is MS-DOS. MS stand for Microsoft, the company which created the system, and DOS means disk operating system.

- Output – data which comes out of the computer. Hence a printer is an output device.
- Program – a set of instructions which tells the computer how to carry out various tasks. There are different programs for word processing, spreadsheets, database, etc.
- Hardware – items such as the CPU, VDU, keyboard and printer.
- Software – items such as the operating system and the programs.
- Mouse – a small device used for pointing to commands or icons.
- Icon – a small picture or graphic on the computer screen. An example is the Pegasus logo on p. 297.
- Floppy disks – items upon which information is stored by the user. Floppy disks are inserted into the disk drive in the computer. At the end of the session the disk can be taken out and stored in a safe place. Floppy disks come in two sizes, 5.25 and 3.5 inch. Some floppy disks are referred to as high density or double-sided. This simply means that they store more information than a single-sided disk.
- Hard disk – some computers come with a built-in disk. You do not have to insert a floppy disk in order to begin working. The hard disk, sometimes called a fixed disk, will also hold the operating system and the programs.
- Diskcopy – to copy the data held on one disk to another.
- Format – to prepare a disk so that it will accept data from a computer.
- Boot-up – to switch on the computer and install its operating system and program.
- User-friendly – a term used to describe computers, operating systems and programs that are simple and easy to use.
- Back-up copy – a copy of a program, disk or file which is held as a precaution in case the original is damaged or erased. It is good practice to always have a back-up copy of everything.
- Cursor – the rectangular light which shows on the VDU where the next keystroke will be located.
- Scroll – to move the screen up and down.
- Cell – a space for receiving information on the screen.
- On-line – an item connected to a computer, e.g. a printer.

- CPS – characters per second. Printers are usually measured by the speed at which they print.
- Computer languages – means of writing instructions or programs for computers. Two well-known languages are BASIC (Beginner's All-purpose Symbolic Instruction Code) and COBOL (Common Business Oriented Language).

Computer applications

Computers have taken much of the drudgery out of office work. They enable you to write, display, edit and store text and numbers electronically. Computers have word processing, spreadsheet, database and graphic facilities.

Word processing

The modern secretary will probably use the computer mainly for word processing. With word processing it is possible to do letters, reports, memos, minutes and, indeed, all the traditional office documents.

Fig. 1 – How computer screen looks when word processing is in progress on WANG computer using the program Microsoft Word

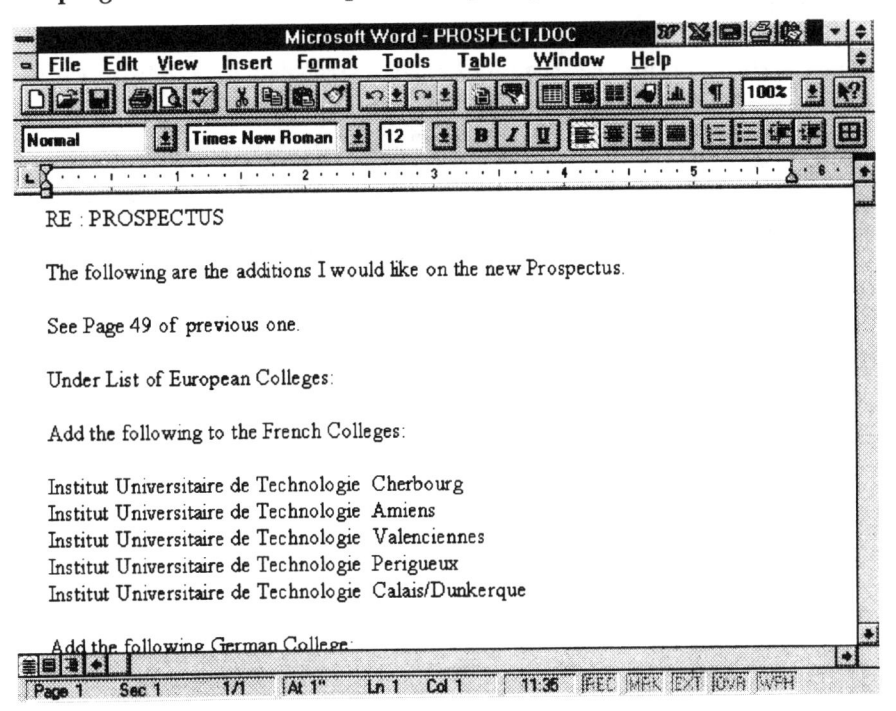

RE : PROSPECTUS

The following are the additions I would like on the new Prospectus.

See Page 49 of previous one.

Under List of European Colleges:

Add the following to the French Colleges:

Institut Universitaire de Technologie Cherbourg
Institut Universitaire de Technologie Amiens
Institut Universitaire de Technologie Valenciennes
Institut Universitaire de Technologie Perigueux
Institut Universitaire de Technologie Calais/Dunkerque

Add the following German College:

The computer allows you to do the following:

(a) enter text by using a keyboard

(b) delete text

(c) replace text

(d) correct errors

(e) indent text

(f) centre text

(g) copy text

(h) change margins

(i) check spelling

(j) choose type styles

(k) send the same letter to several people with individual information on each, such as 'Dear Mr Ryan'. This is called mail-merge.

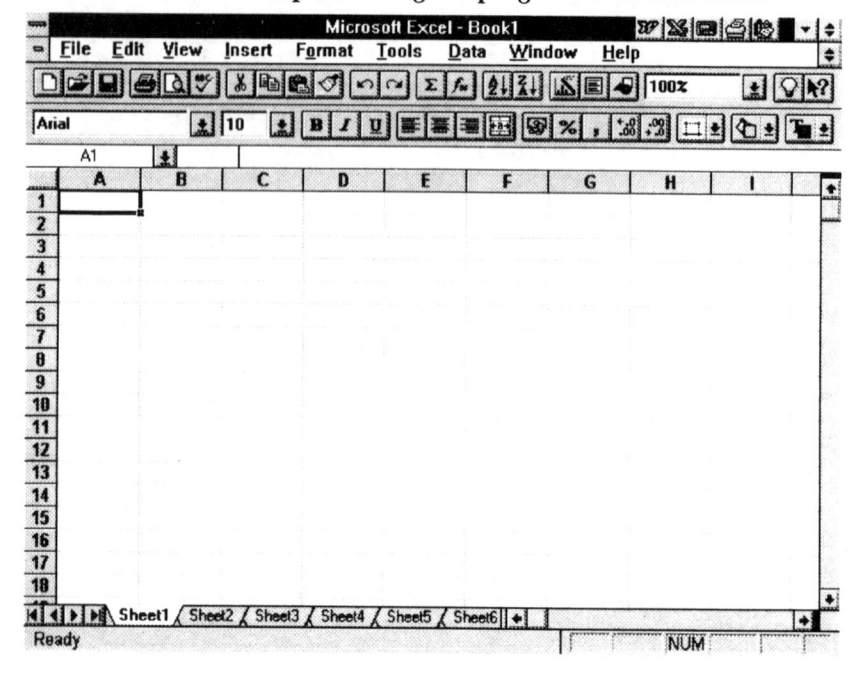

Spreadsheet

Your computer can also organise, find and calculate numeric information. On spreadsheets you can analyse figures, calculate totals and averages and make projections.

Fig. 2 – How computer screen looks when spreadsheet is in progress on WANG computer using the program Microsoft Excel

Fig. 3 – Sample spreadsheet

No.	Payment Date	Beginning Balance	Interest	Principal	Ending Balance	Cumulative Interest
1	26/06/95	6,000.00	55.00	100.07	5,899.93	55.00
2	26/07/95	5,899.93	54.08	100.99	5,798.94	109.08
3	26/08/95	5,798.94	53.16	101.92	5,697.02	162.24
4	26/09/95	5,697.02	52.22	102.85	5,594.17	214.46
5	26/10/95	5,594.17	51.28	103.79	5,490.38	265.74
6	26/11/95	5,490.38	50.33	104.74	5,385.63	316.07
7	26/12/95	5,385.63	49.37	105.70	5,279.93	365.44
8	26/01/96	5,279.93	48.40	106.67	5,173.25	413.84
9	26/02/96	5,173.25	47.42	107.65	5,065.60	461.26
10	26/03/96	5,065.60	46.43	108.64	4,956.96	507.69
11	26/04/96	4,956.96	45.44	109.63	4,847.33	553.13
12	26/05/96	4,847.33	44.43	110.64	4,736.69	597.57
13	26/06/96	4,736.69	43.42	111.65	4,625.04	640.99
14	26/07/96	4,625.04	42.40	112.68	4,512.36	683.38
15	26/08/96	4,512.36	41.36	113.71	4,398.65	724.75
16	26/09/96	4,398.65	40.32	114.75	4,283.90	765.07
17	26/10/96	4,283.90	39.27	115.80	4,168.09	804.34
18	26/11/96	4,168.09	38.21	116.87	4,051.23	842.54
19	26/12/96	4,051.23	37.14	117.94	3,933.29	879.68
20	26/01/97	3,933.29	36.06	119.02	3,814.27	915.74
21	26/02/97	3,814.27	34.96	120.11	3,694.16	950.70
22	26/03/97	3,694.16	33.86	121.21	3,572.95	984.56
23	26/04/97	3,572.95	32.75	122.32	3,450.63	1,017.31
24	26/05/97	3,450.63	31.63	123.44	3,327.19	1,048.95

On your spreadsheet you can:

(a) draft yearly budgets

(b) project loan payments

(c) compute interest payments

(d) calculate wages.

The various facilities such as inserting, deleting and copying are available on the spreadsheet also. If you change a number on the spreadsheet the computer will automatically recalculate all the figures affected by the change.

Database

A database is a bank for storing information. Your phone book is a database. A computer database can store, organise and retrieve information.

Fig. 4 – How computer screen looks when database is in process on a WANG computer using Microsoft Access

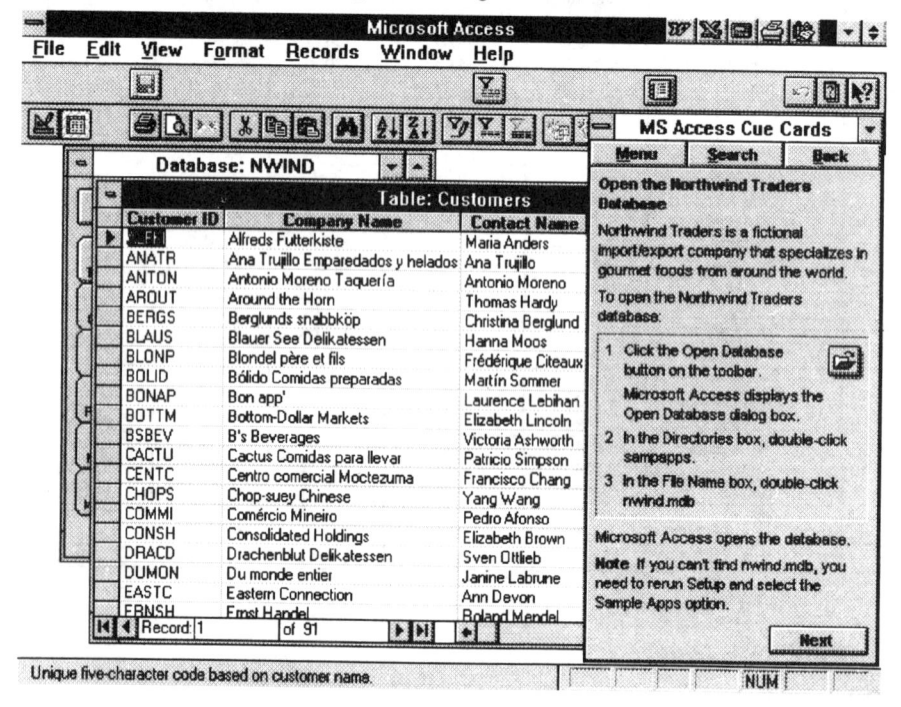

In the old days this type of information was stored on cards in a drawer. Now it can be stored in the computer.

Once the forms or cards are stored in the computer you can manipulate them in a variety of ways:

(a) search for a particular form

(b) search for a group of forms that have something in common

(c) search for forms alphabetically or by number

(d) get a printout of a selection of forms.

Graphics

Your computer can also create bar charts, pie charts and line graphs. You can graph the numbers you type in or you can extract numbers from a spreadsheet and show them on a graph. This facility is particularly useful when writing reports.

Communication by computer

Computers can communicate with other computers. You can connect your computer to another computer with a special cable or the connection can be over the telephone lines.

You can then exchange files with another computer or look up information on the other computer. You can keep in touch with people using an electronic mail service or you can communicate with people using computers in your own organisation.

A company which has its computers networked (joined together) can send memos, reports, letters and other messages from one computer to another.

The advantages of this system of transferring messages are:

(1) it is fast and reliable;

(2) replies can be sent quickly;

(3) messages can be sent at times convenient to everyone;

(4) receiver need not be at his computer to accept message;

(5) special codes can be used so that messages can be read only by authorised personnel;

(6) messages can be sent from anywhere once a computer and telephone are available.

The Internet

Internet's relentless march

THE relentless gallop of Internet, the global information network that encourages otherwise sane people to spend countless hours at their computer screens, takes another leap forward this week.

Pipping others to the post, softwriters claim to have developed the wherewithal to allow Internet users have conversations over the network exactly as if they were using a telephone. The upgraded version of the Vocaltec's Internet Phone eliminates the need for each party to wait until the other has stopped talking before responding.

Tribune Reporter

'We thought we would launch this product only in about six months' time. But there was a lot of pressure from clients,' according to a spokesman for the Israeli-based company. The new software will be launched on June 5.

The software, which in communications parlance is full duplex instead of half, will eliminate pauses similar to those experienced in conversations over citizen's band radios.

The company's original Internet Phone, launched in February, allowed users to dial into their local Internet provider and talk all over the world for about the same price as a local phone call. Users needed only the software, a microphone and a sound card, a piece of computer hardware that generates audio sound. But the limitation of allowing only one user to speak at a time created a delay as users waited for each other to finish talking.

With rapid fire 'conversation' now available on the Internet, it seems only a matter of time before software is developed allowing for simultaneous multi-person computer talk a bit like telephone chat lines.

The Sunday Tribune, 4 June 1995

The Internet is the global information network which can send information all over the world through computers which are connected to one another. It is the world's largest network and it connects thousands of networks worldwide. There are a number of networks in Ireland. Two major ones are the HEAnet and the RTCnet.

Fig. 5 – RTCnet

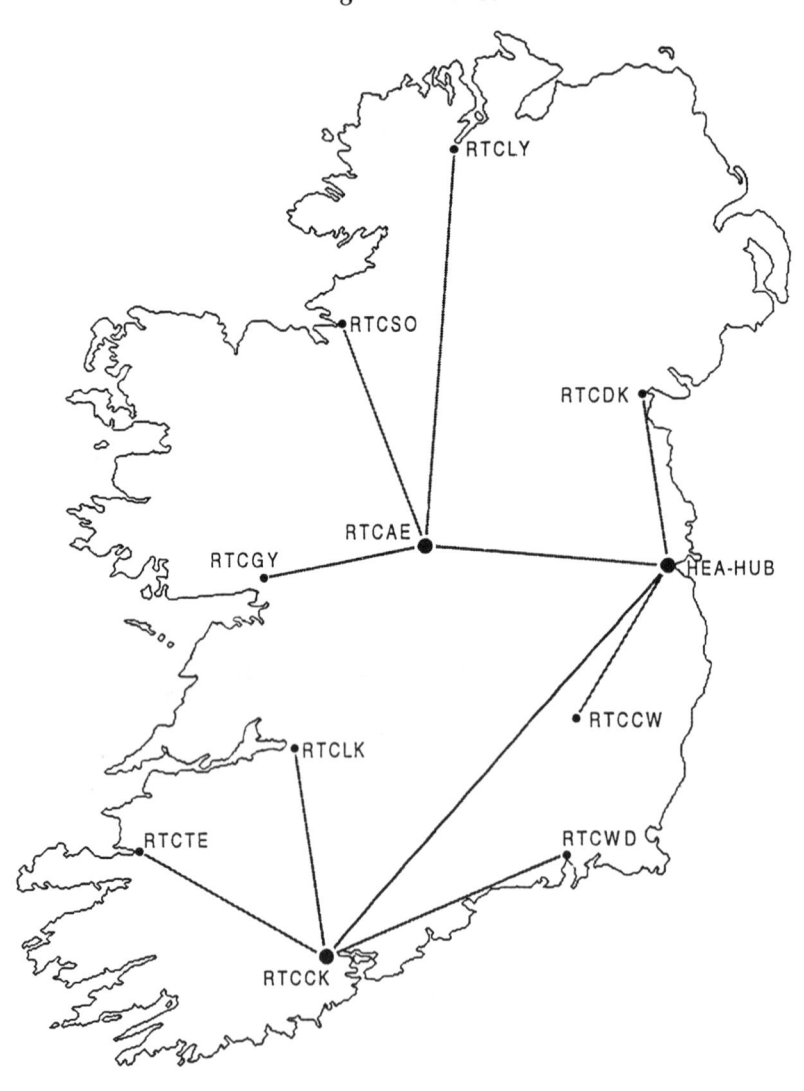

A network such as the RTCnet can have the following tools:
- Electronic mail
- Telnet
- FTP and Archie
- Gopher
- World-Wide Web.

Electronic mail

Fig. 6 – The Pegasus logo

A popular electronic mail system is *Pegasus Mail*. It will enable you to communicate with computer users in your own place of work or you can communicate through the Internet to anywhere in the world. Each user is provided with a mailbox where messages are stored. The same message can be sent to several different people and you can get confirmation that the receiver actually read your message. Some messages can be marked as urgent. You can also attach any computer files you wish to your message.

Telnet

Fig. 7 – Telnet

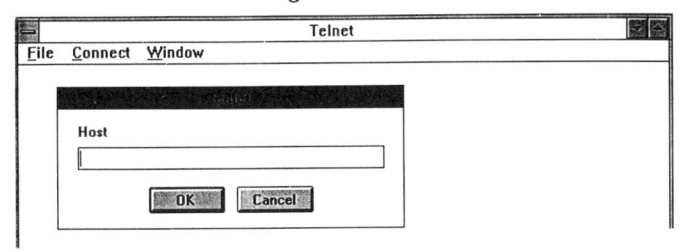

Telnet is an application that allows you to connect or log-in to other computers either at your place of work or at sites anywhere else. Through the RTCnet, for example, a user at Carlow RTC can connect to the computer in the library at UCD to check if a particular book is available. Other on-line database services are available such as X500 directory service which allows you to search for a person or organisation within a specified part of the world.

FTP and Archie

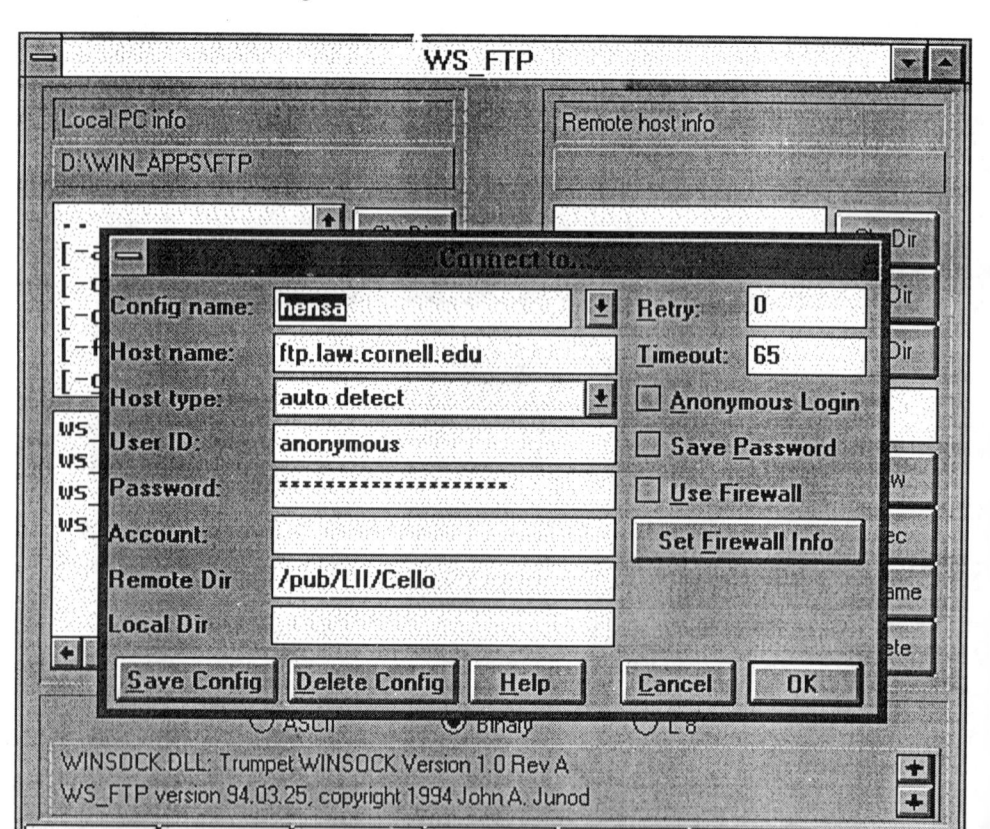

Fig. 8 – The WinSock RTP main menu

FTP stands for File Transfer Protocol. It is a standard protocol for transferring files of any kind from one computer to another. The FTP protocol defines how one computer is to receive information from another and assemble it into a file. There are vast numbers of FTP sites around the world that allow you to connect to and copy over files from them to your own computer.

The major use of FTP is to access the enormous amount of information stored at the FTP sites world-wide. Journals, reference materials and information on any number of subjects, as well as software and computer information are all available from FTP sites. To use FTP you need to know the address of an FTP site. A directory service called Archie can provide this information.

Archie is a database of many of the various FTP sites throughout the world. It provides a quick and easy method of locating files relevant to a particular topic.

Gopher

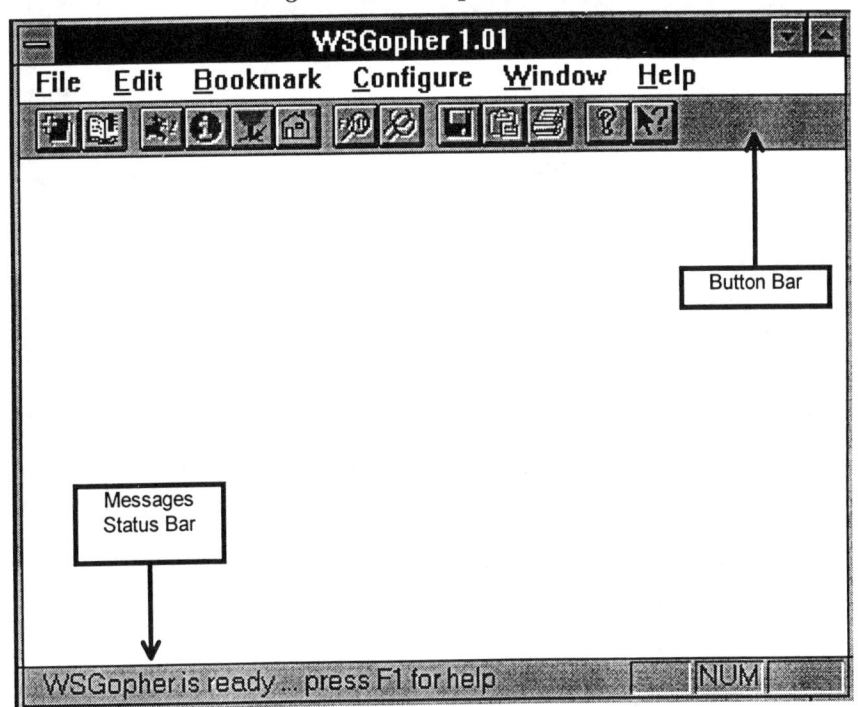

Fig. 9 – Main Gopher window

Gopher is a tool for gathering information in a network of computers. It is sometimes used as a means of browsing through computers to see what information is available. Others use it daily to gather information for various projects. Gopher originated in the University of Minnesota in the US. It is based on the concept of directories, just like the directories on your computer. Everything on a Gopher directory is on the network, rather than on your local disk drive.

The World-Wide Web and Mosaic

Fig. 10 – NCSA Mosaic for MS Windows

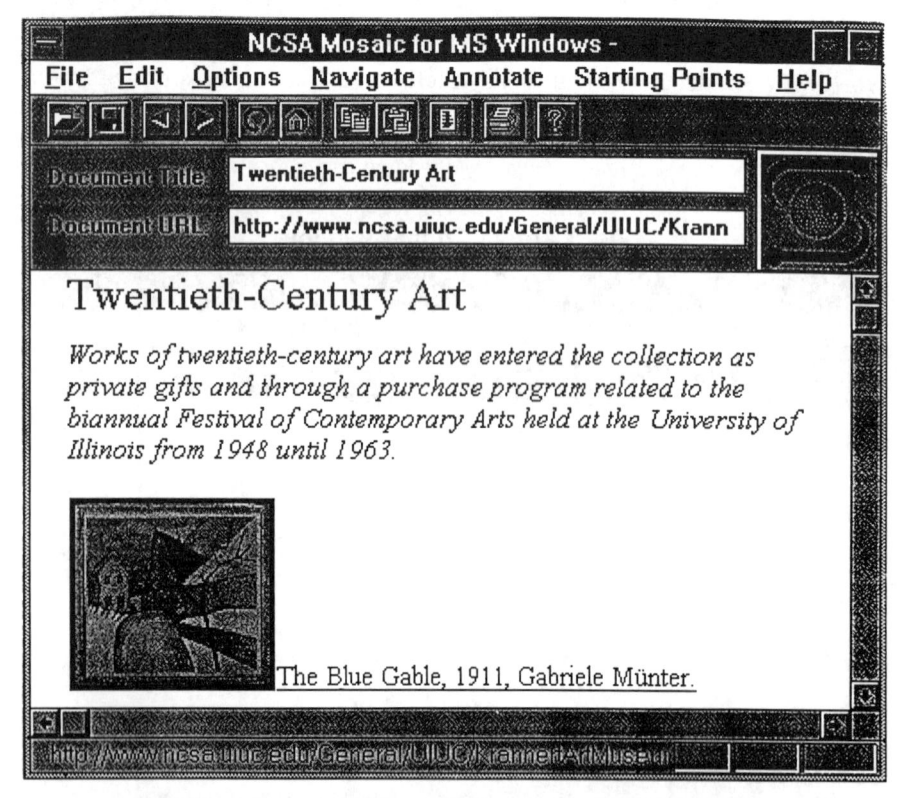

The World-Wide Web is a means of providing international access to various sites of information around the world. The Web can be accessed by using NCSA (National Centre of Supercomputing Agency) Mosaic. By using NCSA Mosaic you can send requests for documents to various sites. If the documents are available they will be sent to you. An example would be if you wanted a copy of 'The Downing Street Joint Declaration'. This was available on the Web from Trinity College, Dublin. The World-Wide Web is currently composed of thousands of these transactions taking place throughout the world, creating a web of information.

By using Mosaic you can explore the Web. If you type in **http://slarti.ucd.ie/rtc-ug/rtc-ug.html** on Mosaic this tells it to establish a connection to a file at slarti, ucd.ie, which is a machine located in UCD, and retrieve a file entitled rtc-ug.html. When Mosaic has located the file it is displayed on your monitor.

ACTIVITY 1

1. What are the advantages of word processing on a computer over working on the traditional typewriter?
2. Who invented the computer?
3. Write a 200-word history of the computer from its invention to the present day.
4. Early computers were very large while modern computers are small. Why?
5. Find out how many computer companies are located in Ireland.
6. What does the term 'computer literate' mean?
7. Computers are sometimes accused of creating unemployment. Why?
8. Investigate the various computers on the market and suggest the one which would be most suitable for use in your home. Give reasons for your selection.
9. Write a letter on the computer; set the left margin at 12 and the right margin at 70. The letter is to have the final paragraph in italics.
10. Design a spreadsheet to keep account of the results of your typing assignments during the year.
11. Design a spreadsheet to keep account of the results of your class and include all subjects being taken this year.
12. Design a database form which your college might use to store information on its students.
13. What are the advantages of electronic mail?
14. What is the World-Wide Web?
15. What is Archie?

Review

1. What does ENIAC stand for?
2. Explain the difference between an ink-jet printer and a laser printer.
3. How many bytes are there in 500k?
4. What does MS-DOS stand for?
5. Name one other operating system.
6. How much information can a floppy disk hold?
7. Why should you always make a back-up copy of your files?
8. What sort of information can you find on the Internet?
9. What are the disadvantages of e-mail?
10. What is a modem?

Pitfalls

sincerely

Be careful of the spelling of the word 'sincerely', as in 'Yours sincerely'. Many people incorrectly omit the second 'e'.

Confusing words

first	firstly	credence	credibility
historic	historical	diverge	divergent
abrogate	arrogate	oral	verbal
appraise	apprise		

Quiz

Should one say the *first two* or the *two first*? Which is correct? Are both correct?

Spellings

The words most commonly misspelled are highlighted.

tactics	testimony	trafficking
talented	theatre	tragedy
tapestry	theatrical	traitor
tarpaulin	thief	**transfer**
taunt	thieves	**transference**
tease	thirsty	**transferred**
technical	thirteen	transient
technique	thirty	traveller
technological	thistle	treachery
tedious	thorough	treasurer
telegram	thought	tremendous
telegraph	thwart	tributary
telephone	tiresome	tricycle
temperance	tomato	trivial
temperate	tomatoes	triviality
temporary	toothache	truncheon
temptation	torrential	tuition
tendency	torture	**twelfth**
testament	towards	tyrannous
testimonial	traffic	tyrant

PART 5

FINDING EMPLOYMENT

㉓

GET THAT JOB

Introduction

When you have obtained your qualification, or indeed, before that, you must start looking at the job market. You must put the same energy into looking for a job as you would into studying for your examinations.

Before you leave your college you should have drawn up a good curriculum vitae. Make several copies of it. You should also get references from some of your lecturers. Also, ask them if you may use their names as referees. Many colleges conduct mock interviews and these can be of great assistance in giving you the experience of the interview situation. You must pursue every avenue that might provide a job. Apply for every job that seems suitable to you. You should even write to companies who have not advertised to find out when they will be recruiting. They may ask you to apply later or they may keep your application on file. Keep a scrapbook with all the details of the jobs for which you have applied.

A selection of job ads

P.A. IN P.R. COMPANY, based off Merrion Square. You will need superb organisational and W.P. skills to work with a very senior Accounts Executive. Tel. 6604591 or Fax 6618489. Griffin Personnel, 11 Hume St., D.2.

ATLAS TEMP urgently require a bright enthusiastic Secretary to operate Wang w.p. system. Excellent typing skills required. Top rates paid. For immediate interview please telephone 6776477.

TELE SALES PERSON for Dun Laoghaire publishing company. Some experience necessary. W.P. essential. Ph. 2809476 2.30-5 p.m.

YOUNG PERSON (18-20) for research office. Dun Laoghaire. Good telephone manner, W.P. ability. Some office experience an advantage. Ph. 2809557 mornings.

AT SHEEHAN O'NEILL – Secretary, min. 2 yrs. W.P. exp. and excellent d/t for D.2, D.4 and Southside. Perm and Temp. Tel: 6610448.

AT HALLMARK PERSONNEL – Accounts Assistant required to work with Financial Controller, prestigious company, D.2 (23-28), exp. in purchases essential. Excellent salary and prospects. Contact Peg at 6765589 for immediate interview.

BOOKKEEPER required, good knowledge of Wang accounts system preferred, but not essential; attractive salary and good working conditions. Apply with C.V. and references to Simpson & Co., Solicitors, 68 Lr. Leeson Street, Dublin 2.

EXPERIENCED BOOKKEEPER REQUIRED. Must have full knowledge of computerised and manual systems. Apply with C.V. to: Brian Redmond, Neolith Ltd., Davitt Road, Dublin 12.

LONDON
Senior Secretary
Junior Secretary

One post is for a friendly and well-organised secretary (ref G/OG/430b) to provide administrative support to two senior lecturers in the Medical School Department of Obstetrics & Gynaecology on our Guy's Campus. You would have a varied role, including organising meetings, co-ordinating the departmental library and assisting with the preparation of legal and research reports. You needn't have medical secretarial training, but WP skills and the ability to cope with unfamiliar terminology are necessary.

The other post is for a junior secretary (ref G/OG/510), working alongside the above. This post is suitable for a college-leaver with typing skills, flexibility and enthusiasm.

The salary range for the secretary post is £9,083-£12,066 and for the junior secretary £6,554-£8,000 per annum. Both salaries are inclusive, and will depend on age, qualifications and experience. In addition we offer generous holidays, a low-interest season-ticket loan, a subsidised canteen and on-site sports facilities, including swimming pool. We may also be able to offer accommodation for up to three months.

Further information from Mr M G Chapman on 01-955-4387. To apply, send your CV (2 copies) to The Personnel Officer, United Medical & Dental Schools, St Thomas's Campus, Lambeth Palace Road, London SE1 7EH, before 16 March quoting the relevant reference number.

Or, alternatively . . .

We are NOT looking for another Scarlett O'Hara, so why do we feel like David O. Selznick did?

Because we, too, are in search of a STAR, just as old SELZNICK was. And just as he did for so long, we have SO FAR searched in vain. A self-driven, modest but personable, star-in-waiting. Age bracket 30/40 best. A HE or a SHE, but a winner, who will play a key part in keeping us the NUMERO UNO in our business.

A hard-working, educated, intelligent achiever; good with people, cool under pressure, with quiet determination and a tolerance for occasional anti-social hours. And SYMPATICO is a must. BASIC design sense also. Sales experience not necessary, and perhaps a disadvantage.

So what's the job? DONT GUESS – PHONE! It took years to cast Scarlett – we don't have the patience of Selznick. If you think you can fill the bill, phone us and we'll take it from there. C.V.'s and references WILL come later. Oh yes, and the MONEY? About £30,000.

Phone: 8426308/8428158/After 6.30: 2823405

Sliderobes

Designer Storage Space

Montrose and Santry

Sources of information on jobs

(a) *FÁS (Foras Áiseanna Saothair)*

FÁS is the training and employment authority in Ireland. It has a network of over seventy offices throughout the country. It provides practical advice, information and training aimed at helping the unemployed find employment and employers recruit suitable employees.

What can FÁS do for jobseekers?

(i) Provide you with information about training and development courses.

(ii) Assist you in finding suitable vacancies.

(iii) Give you information and advice about starting your own business as well as informing you about available grants.

(iv) Give you a detailed occupational guidance and counselling service.

FÁS provides an information service and a range of schemes to assist you identify and pursue job opportunities.

(i) An up-to-date list of job vacancies from a wide range of industrial and commercial sectors is available in all FÁS Employment Service Offices.

(ii) Details of your skills and experience are matched with these job vacancies.

(iii) You will be provided with assistance in selecting a career path.

(iv) Facilities are available for you to make an appointment with a potential employer.

(b) *Daily newspapers*

Read the newspapers every day for details of jobs advertised. Usually there is one day each week when most of the jobs are advertised.

(c) *Local newspapers*

These are a good source for jobs available in the newspapers' circulation area.

(d) *Employment agencies*

Small towns may not have an employment agency, but large ones will. These are private businesses whose task it is to locate suitable employees for client companies. You go to the agency, register with them by giving details of your qualifications and experience, and state the type of job you would prefer. You may have to pay a fee to the agency or your employer may pay when you go to work for him. Many companies depend on employment agencies for providing temporary staff.

(e) *College employment officers*

Your school or college may have a careers officer or employment officer or perhaps the principal may carry out this function. It is likely that local employers contact your college when they want staff.

(f) *Community notice boards*

Community notice boards located perhaps in supermarkets or advice centres may also occasionally have details of jobs available in the community.

(g) *Personnel departments of large companies*

It may be worth writing to the personnel departments of large companies to find out when they will be recruiting and what qualifications they require for various positions.

(h) *Friends in employment*

Friends who are already in employment may know when vacancies are occurring at the places where they work.

(i) *Teletext*

Teletext on RTE has a page devoted to information on jobs available.

Analysis of job ad

Placing advertisements for jobs in newspapers is expensive so companies will not use unnecessary words. Therefore, the ad should be read closely to ascertain the type of person the company has in mind.

> **A SENIOR SECRETARY.** Excellent dictaphone exp. and WP skills. Financial institution. Busy environment, salary c 11k. Phone Patricia 6614452 at The Recruitment Business.

The above ad is looking for a 'Senior Secretary' so a person straight out of a secretarial course will not be appointed. The person appointed must have experience of working on a dictaphone and must also be able to do word processing. It is likely that the person sought will have a number of years' experience. The job is in a financial institution so it involves working in banking, insurance, a building society or some similar type of company. It is apparently a busy office. The salary is 'c 11k'. The 'c' stands for the Latin word *circa* meaning *around*, and 11k means £11,000.

So we now have a picture of the type of person this company has in mind. You must analyse all job ads in this way and draw up a profile of the type of person required. If you feel that you are that type of person, then move on to the next stage.

Attractive package of dynamic job ads

SOME of the most fascinating reading in newspapers is to be found not on the news pages, but on those patchwork pages of recruitment ads. With the supposed liftoff of the economy over the past two years, recruitment advertising in newspapers has rocketed, giving a substantial boost to the coffers of the national newspapers, particularly the Sundays. And it has given the readers lots of extra pages of challenging reading.

The recruitment ad is an art form in its own right, with several advertising agencies either specialising in it or basing a substantial part of their business on job ads. Although given Ireland's cyclical employment patterns it is hardly the strongest foundation on which to build a business.

Like all art forms, the job ad uses its own language – some would say jargon – which is usually impenetrable to the outsider. Recruitment advertisers would say that job ads have to be targeted, so if you don't understand the ad it is not targeted at you. But what if it is aimed at you and you still don't understand what they are saying?

For example, what exactly is a self-starter? It sounds like a car part, but whatever it is employers want lots of them. Then there is the expression 'graduate calibre'. What does this mean? Either someone is a graduate or is not a graduate. Apparently the phrase is used to tempt older managers, who may feel insecure about not having any formal qualifications. It is certainly more classy than saying 'University of Life alumni welcome'.

'Graduate calibre' may become a problem, however, when it comes to the not inconsiderable matter of pay, or 'remuneration package'. Most ads state 'salary commensurate with qualifications'. If you don't have any but are of graduate calibre, where does that leave you?

Companies also like to use their recruitment ads as 'corporate advertising', to tell the world how great they are. This is why every company that has ever published a job ad is invariably 'dynamic and forward-looking', a 'major player' and 'one of the leading companies in its field'. This is particularly true of monopolies.

(Sean Whelan, *The Sunday Tribune*, 11 February 1990)

ACTIVITY 1

1. Choose a job advertised in the newspaper and write a paragraph (150 words) on it outlining the type of person the firm is seeking.

2. Visit your local FÁS office and register for employment. After your interview with the officer, evaluate your performance. Did you present yourself well? Did you provide all the necessary information?

Making an application

Your application is your first introduction to a prospective employer. It is important that you should make a good impression. The purpose of your application is to obtain an interview.

Application form

If the firm supplies an application form, complete it very carefully and thoroughly. Get it typed if possible. Always keep a copy of it. Include all relevant information, and accentuate the positive rather than the negative. Where application forms require the names of two referees, be careful to select people who know you well.

Fig. 1 – Application Form

Position applied for: <u>Computer Operator</u>

Application for Employment

Name <u>   Hanley   Josephine   </u>
         (Surname)   (First Names)   (Maiden Name if applicable)

Permanent Address   <u>23 Brookville Lawns,   </u>
<u>   Rathfarnham, Dublin 16   </u>

Temporary Address <u>—   </u>

<u>   </u> Dates at this Address <u>—</u>

Telephone Number: Home <u>01-4972133</u>   Business <u>01-4934576</u>
                                                   (if convenient)

Nationality <u> Irish   </u> Sex <u> Female </u> Date of Birth <u>29.2.19??</u> Age <u>23</u>

Marital Status <u>Single   </u> Children's Ages <u>—   </u>

Physical Disabilities <u>   None   </u>

Major Illnesses or Accidents (last 3 years) <u>None   </u>

Are you willing to relocate? If so, state areas of preference: <u>Yes. Galway</u>

Do you hold a Current Driving Licence? <u> Yes   </u>

Have you had any major car accidents in the last 3 years? <u> No   </u>

Have you been convicted of a driving offence in the last 5 years? <u> No </u>

How did you hear about this opening? <u> The Irish Times   </u>

Have you applied for employment
with this company before? <u>   No   </u> If so, when? <u>   </u>

Name any relatives or friends employed by this company <u> None   </u>

How much notice is required by your present employer? <u> 1 month   </u>

Please give the name of one Referee, preferably
one who is able to recommend you for this position:

Name <u> Ms Joan Flynn   </u> Company <u>   Asphalt Paving Company   </u>

Address <u>   Merrion Rd., Ballsbridge, Dublin 4   </u>

If this is your present Manager and you do not want the reference taken until you have accepted a position please tick here [√]

EDUCATIONAL RECORD

Type of School or College	Name of School/College	Location	Dates From To	Courses Taken	Subjects Studied	Results	
Primary	Laurence O'Toole	Rathfarnham	19??-??				
Community School	Rathfarnham Community	Rathfarnham	19??-??	Junior Certificate	Irish	H	Q
					English	B	
					Maths	B	
					French		B
					Commerce	B	
					Science	A	
					Music	B	
							B
				Leaving Certificate	Irish	H	Q
					English		C
					Maths	B	
					French	C	
					Biology		C
					Music	B	
						B	
Secretarial College	Merrion Secretarial College	Ballsbridge	19??-??	Secretarial Certificate	Shorthand	110wpm	
					Typing	40wpm	
					Computers	B	
					French	B	
					Office Procedure	B	
					Communication	B	

Name and Address of Employer/Military Service (present employer first with full address)	Position/Rank	Job Content
Asphalt Paving Co., Merrion Road, Ballsbridge, Dublin 4	Computer Operator	Putting data into computer. Sending and processing data from computer. Typing letters and reports and some reception duties. Also in charge of petty cash.

Reason for any time between employment periods _____

Outline current activities and responsibilities
in present position and/or relevant experience   I am responsible for putting data into the computer and extracting relevant information. I am also in charge of data base of customer information. I do some typing of letters and reports and also do some reception duties. I am also responsible for the petty cash. I have worked on a number of different computers, IBM, Amstrad and Apple Mac.

Give details of any specialised training, professional
qualifications and membership of professional institutions   My company has sent me on a number of specialised courses on computers. The programs I have experience of are ABILITY, Microsoft Word, DBase II, Hypercard and Excel.

Give any other reasons making you suitable for this position   My secretarial course trained me on computers and I have four years' experience of being a computer operator. I am very interested in the whole computer area and look forward to working more with them.

Hobbies and outside-work interests   Cycling, Basketball, Reading, Drama and Music.

What do you expect to achieve in the position for which you are applying?
I look forward to working on computers and I would hope that a large, well-known firm such as yours would provide me with the opportunity for further training and development in this area.

Immediate Supervisor	Dates		Gross Annual Salary		Reason for Leaving
	From	To	Starting	Ending	
Ms Joan Flynn	June 19??	Present	£8,002	£10,000	Still working with company
					but would like to work with
					a large computer firm.

Breakdown of present salary (Basic + other allowances)   £10,000, no allowances
Minimum Expected Salary   £10,000
Do you have a company car/allowance?   No
Languages spoken   Irish—Leaving Certificate Ordinary Level
                     French—Leaving Certificate Ordinary Level

I confirm that the information on this form is correct to the best of my knowledge and belief and I understand that any offer of employment arising out of this application may be withdrawn if the information is incorrect.

Signed   *Josephine Hanley*   Date   14/3/??

If an application form is provided adopt the following procedure:

(a) Photocopy form and complete a rough draft first.
(b) Get a friend to check it for accuracy.
(c) Type form if possible.
(d) If it is to be completed in own handwriting, use a good pen, preferably black but never red or green.
(e) Write legibly.
(f) If at all possible do not leave sections blank.
(g) Do not crowd the information too closely together. If you have information which does not fit on the form it can be put in a covering letter.

Covering letter

You may have to write a covering letter with an application form to give further details of your qualifications and experience. If so, clip the letter to the application form. If no application form is provided, submit a curriculum vitae with a covering letter. The covering letter should:

(a) be brief
(b) state title of job and where you saw the advertisement
(c) emphasise the qualities and qualifications you have that are particularly suited to the job
(d) state that curriculum vitae is enclosed
(e) point out that you are available for interview at company's convenience.

In preparing your covering letter:

(a) Write a rough draft first.
(b) Get someone who is competent to check it.
(c) Type on good quality paper. Some job advertisements will specify that the application must be in your own handwriting. If so write slowly and clearly and use a good pen.
(d) Always proofread.

Example

> **SECRETARY TO PERSONNEL MANAGER**
> **REQUIRED** for medium sized grain Company. Some experience of personnel work necessary. Attractive salary and conditions. Send CV to Personnel Manager, Ballindoney Grain Company, Dromline, Co. Tipperary.

Fig. 2 – Covering letter

45 Friar Street,
Clonmel,
Co. Tipperary.

22 October 199?

Personnel Manager,
Ballindoney Grain Company,
Dromline,
Co. Tipperary.

Dear Sir,

I wish to apply for the position of Secretary to the Personnel Manager with your firm which was advertised in *The Irish Times* of 20 October 199?

Since completing the National Certificate in Secretarial Studies this year I have been employed by Marko Engineering Company in the personnel department. I am responsible for maintaining employees' files and also write minutes of meetings between the personnel manager and the unions. A high degree of accuracy in recording discussions and complete confidentiality are very important to my position.

I studied computers during my secretarial course. I worked on Amstrad, IBM and Apple computers. I have experience of using the following programs: Ability, DBase II, Wordstar, Lotus and SuperCalc.

I am aware of the work carried out by your company. Since I have some experience of working in a personnel department, I feel that I am familiar with the duties involved in the post advertised.

I enclose details of my education, qualifications and experience. I am available for interview at your convenience.

Yours faithfully,

Claire Scully

Curriculum vitae

A curriculum vitae generally gives four types of information:

(a) personal – name, age, address, telephone number;

(b) education – schools attended, examinations passed;

(c) work experience – jobs, including part-time, holiday work and work experience programmes;

(d) other information – hobbies, travel, special awards, community activities and names of referees.

A curriculum vitae should be neat, tidy, well laid out and checked for errors.

Fig. 3 – Curriculum Vitae

NAME: Claire Scully
DATE OF BIRTH: 19 February 19??
ADDRESS: 45 Friar Street, Clonmel, Co. Tipperary
TELEPHONE NO: 052-34812

EDUCATION:
19??-19??   Clonmel National School
19??-19??   The Convent Secondary School, Thomastown, Co. Tipperary
19??-19??   Carlow RTC, Kilkenny Road, Carlow

EXAMINATIONS:

19??   19??
Junior Certificate   Leaving Certificate

Subject	Level	Grade
Irish	O	C
English	H	C
Economics	H	B
Accounts	H	B
Business Org.	H	C
Biology	O	D
History	O	D

Third Level 19??
National Certificate in Secretarial Studies
　　　Typing 45 wpm
　　　Shorthand 110 wpm
　　　Communications
　　　Accounts
　　　Office Practice
　　　French
　　　Computer Applications
　　　Personnel
　　　Marketing

WORK EXPERIENCE:	
19?? – present	Marko Engineering Company 27 Side Street Dublin 2.
	Worked in Personnel Department as Assistant to the Personnel Manager.
INTERESTS:	Debating, Drama, Hockey, Travelling.
	I was on the team that won the Scor Competition for debating in Co. Tipperary in 19??. I also won the best actress award at the Waterford Drama Festival last year.
REFEREES:	Mr Lorcan Bergin Personnel Manager Marko Engineering Company 27 Side Street Dublin 2
	Mr Kevin Connolly A.C.A. Business Studies Department Carlow RTC Kilkenny Road Carlow

ACTIVITY 2

Apply for the following positions.

1. *Social Trust Fund Ltd, 27 Cox Street, Dublin requires an experienced Clerk/Typist, preferably aged 19-24. Experience of word processing desirable. Reply in writing to the Manager.*

2. *A very good secretary, 23/25, with excellent shorthand and dictaphone typing is required for senior partner in busy firm. Ability to use the spreadsheet Lotus an advantage.*

3. *Book-keeper required for accountant's office. Applicants should have at least two years' experience and be adaptable; typing is not essential but would be an advantage. Applications in writing only to Carol Brady, Dylan Brennan & Co., 81 Newgate Square, Dublin 6.*

4. *Office Manager required. Ability to use the computer package Finax a definite advantage. Apply giving details of experience, qualifications etc., to J. Mahon & Son Ltd, Main Street, Kilree, Co. Kildare.*

5. *Secretarial post available in Merrion Square. Experience P.B.X. switchboard desirable. Box 477 (Irish Times).*

6. Junior Audio Assistant required by solicitors, south side. Write giving details of education, experience and salary expected.

7. Secretary required. Experienced person required immediately by major company in Dublin 2 area. Good shorthand, typing and administrative ability essential. Excellent conditions and salary. Box 380 (Irish Independent).

8. A Book-keeper/Typist required for general office duties in midland town. Familiarity with Wordstar essential. Excellent wages to suitable applicant. Ability to get on with people essential. Box 110 (Irish Press).

9. Receptionist/Telephonist required for south-side Dublin hospital. Age not exceeding 25 years. Accurate typing and word processing skills essential. Good manner. Box 7190 (Irish Times).

10. Find a position offered in today's newspaper and apply for it.

Scrapbook

You should have a scrapbook to keep track of your job applications. Cut out the ad from the newspaper and paste it into the scrapbook. You should keep the following information on each job for which you apply.

Fig. 4 – Scrapbook for job applications

Date application sent: _____

Reply received: Yes _____ No _____ Date _____

Interview: Yes _____ No _____ Date of Interview: _____

                  Place: _____

                  Time: _____

List of Questions Asked: _____

_____

_____

_____

Comments on Interview Performance: _____

Positive points: _____

Negative points: _____

Special comments: _____

Job Obtained: Yes _____ No _____

Now for the interview

Before the interview

(a) You have now been called for an interview so take out your scrapbook and study the job advertisement again. Reread your curriculum vitae/application form and covering letter. You must be totally familiar with them.

(b) Find out as much as you can about the company. If possible speak to someone who works there or in a similar company.

(c) Keep up to date with topical events. Read a good daily newspaper and perhaps a general business journal such as *Business and Finance* or *Irish Business*.

(d) Prepare any documents you need to take with you, e.g. references, projects, reports.

(e) Review your work experience and be prepared to give an interesting and balanced account of it.

(f) You may be questioned on your future plans. What are your ambitions? Where do you see yourself in five years?

(g) Think up possible questions that might be asked, write them down and mentally formulate your answers.

(h) Give someone the job advertisement and your curriculum vitae plus covering letter and get them to put you through a 'mock' interview.

(i) You will probably be provided with a chance at the interview to ask questions of your own. You could ask about training, promotion opportunities, responsibilities in the job etc.

(j) Make your travel arrangements carefully to ensure you arrive in good time.

Questions at interviews

Questions at interviews generally cover a number of areas.

(a) *Family background*

Have you always lived in the same place?

If you moved about, which place did you like best? Why?

Would you mind leaving home now?

What are the advantages/disadvantages of being from an urban/rural background? Advantages of being from a small/large family?

(b) *Education and training*
What subjects did you like/dislike? Why?
How did you get along with your teachers?
Are you happy with your examination results?
Why did you stay on or leave school?
Why did you go or not go to college?
Why did you go to a particular college?
Why did you choose a certain course?
What did you think of the course?
Have you carried out any projects?
What did you get out of your time in college?
What did you dislike about it?
Do you speak any foreign language?

(c) *Work experience*
Describe your last job.
What was your boss like?
What type of boss do you like to work for?
What were your colleagues like in the last job?
What skills were needed for the job?
What personal qualities were needed?
Were you good at the job?
In what ways could you improve the job?
What was the most difficult aspect of it?
What problems did you encounter?
What did you learn from the job?
Why do you want to leave?

(d) *Motivation*
Why do you want this job?
Which aspect of it appeals to you most?
Are you willing to work overtime?
Would you mind travelling?
Would you mind moving to another part of the country?
Do you mind irregular hours?
How do you see your career developing over the next few years?

(e) *Interests*

What are your hobbies?

How much time do you devote to them?

Have you had any success?

Do you join clubs?

Do you hold any positions in social organisations?

Do you read?

What do you read?

Newspapers?

Favourite book/writer.

Films?

(f) *General*

What is your best achievement?

What are your three best qualities?

What qualities do you have that you would prefer not to have?

How would you deal with a difficult boss?

What would you do if you disliked some of the people with whom you worked?

There may also be several questions on situations that may arise in the job.

At the interview

(a) Dress appropriately.

(b) Be on time. Arrive about a quarter of an hour before time of interview.

(c) You will be nervous but so will all the other candidates and the interviewers will allow for it.

(d) If the members of the interview board offer to shake hands, do so. Sit when offered a chair.

(e) Try to remember the name of the interviewers as they are being introduced and use their names as you answer their questions, e.g. 'Well, Mr Smith, it has been my experience . . .'

(f) Be friendly and smile naturally.

(g) Give good rounded answers – not just 'yes' and 'no'.

(h) Do not use slang and answer clearly.

(i) Be positive, but answer honestly. If the interview board discovers mistakes you have made in the past, admit them. It shows maturity and honesty to admit errors.

(j) Do not argue, but maintain your point of view.

(k) If you are given a hard interview be glad. It means you are being considered seriously for the job.

(l) Try to convey enthusiasm as the interviewers will be trying to judge your motivation for the job.

(m) At the end thank the interview board.

After the interview

Whether or not you get the position you should assess your performance.

Make a list of the questions you were asked. This is good preparation for your next interview.

Was your preparation sufficient? Were there any questions you handled particularly well? Particularly badly? Did the interview follow the course you expected? Were there any questions which completely surprised you? Did you present yourself in the best possible light? Were there any favourable points about yourself that you did not emphasise?

Fill in the evaluation section in your scrapbook (see Fig. 4).

ACTIVITY 3

1. Imagine an interviewer asks you to tell him about your life up to the present. Record your answer on a tape recorder. Listen critically to the recording. Assess your own performance.
2. What do you consider to be your positive qualities?
3. What is the purpose of the interviewer's question 'Why did you apply for this job?'
4. Why do interviewers want to know about your hobbies?
5. Choose a job advertisement in a newspaper and outline how you would prepare for the interview.
6. What types of questions might you ask an interviewer?
7. How would you, as an interviewer, react to a candidate who asked only the following questions: How much do you pay? How long are the holidays?

GROUP ACTIVITY

Each member of the class should choose a job advertisement from a newspaper and write a letter of application for it. Members of the class should interview each other as part of the preparation. An interviewer should then be chosen who will interview each student for the job for which he/she has applied. FÁS may help in this matter. If your school or college has a closed circuit television system, record the interviews. Later, play back the interviews, discuss the performances and have each student complete the evaluation part of the scrapbook.

Review

1. Why should job advertisements be read carefully?
2. Visit your local FÁS office and find out how many jobs are available locally to suit your qualifications.
3. Explain to your friend who is leaving school the various sources of information on job opportunities.
4. Advise your friend on why it is important to keep a scrapbook when job hunting.
5. What is the difference between an application form and a curriculum vitae?
6. Use your dictionary to find out the meaning of curriculum vitae.
7. What is a covering letter?
8. If called for an interview, explain the preparation you would engage in before the interview.
9. What type of questions should you, the interviewee, ask at an interview?
10. Give examples of three questions which are usually asked at interviews.

Pitfalls

amoral immoral

Amoral means 'totally unconcerned' or 'outside morals'.

Immoral means 'not conforming to' or 'opposed to a certain type of morality'.

Confusing words

peace	piece	pealing	peeling
personal	personnel	plum	plumb
rain	rein	read	reed
relic	relict	rote	wrote
scene	seen	sealing	ceiling

Quiz

Finish the following 'Knock, knock' joke:

Knock, knock

Who's there?

Ammonia

_____ (2 words)

_____ (8 words)

Spellings

The words most commonly misspelled are highlighted.

umbrella	vacancy	visibility
umpire	vagrant	volcano
unconscious	valiant	volcanoes
uncouth	valour	volume
underrate	valuable	vulgarity
undoubtedly	**vapour**	
ungrateful	vegetable	warily
unique	vehement	wary
university	vehicle	wealthier
unnecessary	**vengeance**	wealthy
until	ventilate	wearily
urgency	verification	weariness
usage	veteran	**weather**
usefulness	**vicious**	**Wednesday**
usual	victorious	whether
usually	vigorous	wield
utensil	**villain**	**wilful**
utterance	violence	wizard
	virtuous	wondrous

wool	**xylem**	**yolk**
woollen	xylophone	
woolly		zany
wrangle	**yacht**	zealot
wreckage	yachtsman	**zealous**
wrestle	yahoo	zebra
wrestler	yardage	zenith
wretched	yardstick	zero
write	yawn	zigzag
	yearn	zinc
xenophobe	yield	zodiac
xenophobia	yoghurt	zombie
Xerox	yogi	zoology
X-ray	**yoke**